THE WEST INDIAN
LAWYER
- KEITH SOBION -

JUSTIN SOBION

BALBOA.PRESS

A DIVISION OF HAY HOUSE

Balboa Press books may be ordered through booksellers or by contacting:

Balboa Press
A Division of Hay House
1663 Liberty Drive
Bloomington, IN 47403
www.balboapress.com
844-682-1282

Because of the dynamic nature of the Internet, any web addresses or links contained in this book may have changed since publication and may no longer be valid. The views expressed in this work are solely those of the author and do not necessarily reflect the views of the publisher, and the publisher hereby disclaims any responsibility for them.

The author of this book does not dispense medical advice or prescribe the use of any technique as a form of treatment for physical, emotional, or medical problems without the advice of a physician, either directly or indirectly. The intent of the author is only to offer information of a general nature to help you in your quest for emotional and spiritual well-being. In the event you use any of the information in this book for yourself, which is your constitutional right, the author and the publisher assume no responsibility for your actions.

Originally published in 2019 by the Council of Legal Education c/o The Norman Manley Law School, Research Publications and Legal Education Unit, Kingston, Jamaica.

Cover and back designed by 10 Caribbean Marketing Ltd.

The artwork on the cover is based on an original photograph originating from the archives of the Judiciary of the Republic of Trinidad and Tobago.

This book was also made possible through the kind assistance of the Keith Stanford Sobion Foundation.

@kssfoundation
Email: kssfoundationtt@gmail.com

The Keith Stanford
Sobion Foundation

Scripture quotations are from the Holy Bible, King James Version (Authorized Version). First published in 1611. Quoted from the KJV Classic Reference Bible, Copyright © 1983 by The Zondervan Corporation.

Print information available on the last page.

ISBN: 978-1-9822-5614-2 (sc)
ISBN: 978-1-9822-5615-9 (e)

Balboa Press rev. date: 10/28/2020

"A powerfully moving tribute of a Son to his Father and, incorporating a rare combination of emotional and academic intelligence."

Reginald Armour SC, Chairman, Council of Legal Education

"The several roles of Keith Sobion as a Lawyer, Father, Husband, Politician, Institution Builder and the list goes on, are captured in this book so lovingly written by his son Justin. The Norman Manley Law School (NMLS) was pleased to be involved in the publication of this work, which highlights one of its former Principal, a "dyed-in-the-wool" regionalist, who sought to inculcate and refresh the mandate of the school to provide global education. A must read by all those who seek to lead."

O. A. Carol Aina, Principal of the Norman Manley Law School, Jamaica

"The acutely detailed and fascinating recount of Trinidad and Tobago's history through the enthralling memoirs of an unforgettable Caribbean man, will make you fall in love with the Sobion family all over again."

Ria Rambally, Presenter and Executive Producer, CNC3

"*The West Indian Lawyer* is a son's tribute to his father who made an indelible mark on the Caribbean. This is the perfect non-fiction Caribbean read, and it was truly Caribbean because Keith Sobion was born in Trinidad, lived in Barbados and Jamaica, and widely travelled throughout the region."

Cindy Allman, creator of #ReadCaribbean initiative

To my grandparents Otto Sobion and Lucina Connor
who never read a page of this book but through their
whispers and testimonies have become authors of it.

And to my dear friend Kaya
(3rd April 1997 – 9th May 2004).

Yes a chapter has ended;
But, my son, the book is far from being completed –

Le Papa, Keith

"Help me, dear Father, to understand the mystery of eternal life. Someday I shall understand. Until then I am content to know that my beloved is with Thee, safe in thy everlasting arms." — extract of a poem written by Helen S. Carpenter which was presented to me by my grandmother Lucina Connor after my father passed away.

CONTENTS

FOREWORD

When Keith Sobion died in a Kingston hospital on St Valentine's Day, 2008, he was still only 56 years old. But yet, as this tender, loving and at times painfully honest memoir amply demonstrates, he had by then already lived a full life by any measure. A much-loved member of a closely-knit family, Keith was in his time a brilliant scholar, outstanding legal practitioner and law tutor, social activist, Member of Parliament, Cabinet Minister and, for the last 12 years of his life, a hugely successful law school administrator. At different stages of his life, he also had the good fortune to call three Caribbean islands home and to travel extensively throughout the region. So, by that means, as well as by inclination, he fully qualified for the label, 'Caribbean Man', a role he greatly enjoyed.

The sheer breadth of his engagements and interests naturally brought Keith into contact with many persons from all walks of life and his special gifts of friendship and caring ensured that virtually all his connections were warm and lasting. In the writing of this book, Justin has been able to tap directly into many of these sources. It may well be as a result of this that the finished product conveys such a startling sense of contemporaneity, belying the fact that we lost Keith well over 10 years ago.

To read the book is to relive many of the transforming events of his – and our – times. In his native Trinidad and Tobago, these included the 'Black Power Revolution' of 1970; Abu Bakr and the Muslimeen in 1991 (including Keith's happily abortive late night mission to seek the ear of the leader with a view to persuading him to end the armed insurrection); Keith's election to Parliament on a People's

National Movement (PNM) ticket in 1991 (after, to some, something of a turnaround, or straightening-up in his political direction); the 'power' years, as a member of the 1991 Manning Cabinet, Attorney-General and Minister of Legal Affairs at the precocious age of 40; and the still notorious hanging of the convicted murderer, Glen Ashby in the early hours of 14 July 1994, even as proceedings were underway simultaneously in Port of Spain and London in a vain effort to stay the execution. As the book explains, this last event would stir national, regional and international outrage, much of it directed at Keith, causing him much angst and self-searching virtually to the end of his life.

And then, as the nature of politics often, if not inevitably, dictates, the 'power' years ended almost abruptly with the unexpected calling of national elections in November 1995. This was followed by Keith's loss of his parliamentary seat, a change of government and the end of all of that.

As disappointing and disruptive a series of events as this no doubt was for Keith and the Sobion family, it was in truth, for them and the wider region, a blessed release. That release freed Keith to make himself available for appointment in 1996 as the first West Indian trained Principal of the Norman Manley Law School in Jamaica. It also exposed the rest of the family to a different slice of Caribbean life, the impacts of which are obviously still in play in the lives and careers of his three sons.

The outpouring of shock, dismay and grief which greeted Keith's unexpected passing in early 2008 demonstrated, Keith's tremendous success as Principal of the Norman Manley Law School. Fair, generous and even-handed in his dealings with everyone, he quickly garnered the respect and affection of colleagues, other staff members, students and the practicing legal profession. More generally, he played a pivotal role as a key member of the Council of Legal Education, in whom successive Chairmen would quickly come to place implicit confidence, and provided the intellectual impetus for many of the developmental initiatives undertaken by Council during his tenure.

Beyond Council, but obviously related, Keith was also a tireless advocate for the establishment of the Caribbean Court of Justice (CCJ), crisscrossing the region several times in the quest to gain as quickly as possible, complete acceptance for the CCJ. Like many others, he considered the inauguration of the CCJ in Port of Spain in 2005 to be a triumph for the region, the culmination of many, many years of agitation and exhortation. But despite those heady days of 2005, I have no doubt that in the current dispensation, with only two additions in 14 years to the number of states which have signed on to the CCJ's appellate jurisdiction, Keith would be the first to recognise that the CCJ project is still a work in progress.

This lovely book is about all of this and much, much more. For, at its core, it is really a family story. It is a story about Otto Sobion and his wife Clerine, Keith's parents, and the wider Sobion and Frontin families of Mayaro. It is also the story of Keith's wife Judith, also Mayaro born, their three boys, Jules, Justin and Darien, and the life they made together. It is a story of a devoted father, who showed deep interest in and enjoyed all of his children; and who one day jumped on a plane from Jamaica to Barbados to help his son, a struggling law student at the Cave Hill Campus of the University of the West Indies, to unravel the mysteries of Family Law shortly before exams.

Above all, it is a son's account of his father's life, a deeply personal story about a man of great strengths and, like all of us, some weaknesses; a man who, despite going so soon, remains large in memory.

Dennis Morrison

Kingston, Jamaica

15 August 2019

"It is strange this feeling I'm feeling,
But Jah Love, We will always believe in,
Though you may think my faith is in vain,
'Till Shiloh we chant Rastafari's name."

Buju Banton

PREFACE

Ethiopia, November, 2007

On the 21st November 2007 as faith would have it, I found myself in the ancient city of Addis Ababa, the capital of Ethiopia. I say faith, because as a Rastafarian, I longed for my feet to one day touch the soil of the horn of Africa – I just did not know exactly when. I was to spend exactly twelve days in Ethiopia: as that was the length of time which my limited budget would have afforded.

On reflection, my actual twelve days sojourn in Ethiopia was also resoundingly significant. As Ethiopia is predominantly a Christian country, the twelve days symbolised the twelve apostles of Christ or even the twelve Tribes of Israel, the offspring of the holy patriarch Jacob.

During this time, I was a postgraduate law student at the University of Cape Town and my financial resources were extremely limited. I was therefore very thankful when my Uncle and godfather, Kenny Frontin, wired money to my bank account in South Africa to purchase my return airfare from Cape Town to Johannesburg and then finally to Addis Ababa.

After spending a few days in Addis Ababa – literally translated as "New Flower", my two Ethiopian friends Tariku Tsegaye and Mihret, made arrangements for me to travel further north to the lakeside town of Bahir Dar.

I was amazed by the electrifying atmosphere of Bahir Dar. The city was teeming with busybodies, churchgoers and children on the streets. It was particularly a pleasant surprise to see the swarm of children who would come up to me and hold on to my hand as they yelled "Rastaman" "Bob Marley" and "Haile Selassie". Such actions clearly indicated that these children identified the locks on my head with two international icons. It was as if they knew beforehand of my culture, my background or the reason why I had come to Ethiopia in the first place. Some children latched on to me simply to make friends or maybe hoping that I would buy them some food, sweets, or a book for school. The lake, the monasteries, the church bells, made me immediately fall in love with Bahir Dar.

At Bahir Dar, I stayed at the Ethio-Star Hotel. From my hotel room about three stories up, I had a breath-taking view of the Lake Tana, the source of the Blue Nile. It was here I was able to make friends with the hotel's porter, a young boy called Ademe. At the time I met Ademe, he was 20 years old and due to his circumstances was working hard, with a very modest salary, to take care of his family. I became immediately impressed with Ademe, because he was young, determined and very intelligent for his age. Even though his mother-tongue is Amharic, he had a decent command of English. To Ademe, I was more than a tourist with a flashing Kodak camera, but someone from the Caribbean seeking that inner knowledge of Ethiopia *'the land where the gods loved to be.'* It is therefore not surprising that up to today, Ademe and I are still friends and that we still keep in contact by telephone and email.

After spending a few nights in Bahir Dar, I decided to travel in a slightly north-easterly direction to the holy town of Lalibela. In order to do so, I had to catch an early morning bus at the station which was located a short distance away from the Ethio-Star. I had agreed the night before with Ademe, for him to meet me by the hotel to guide me to the bus station. That morning, Ademe was on time, and he was adamant that he would carry my luggage all the way to the station. So, there we were, walking on the streets of Bahir Dar in the wee hours of the cold morning.

The air was fresh and crisp due to the climatic conditions caused by the village's proximity to Lake Tana. Even though the sun had not yet risen, the city was bustling with people. Present that morning were men, women and children wrapped in white swaddling clothes heading to the Orthodox Church. The distinct sound of Christian hymns sung in Amharic echoed over the Church's loudspeaker and like a magnet, it drew the masses to their place of worship. There were street vendors everywhere getting ready to open their businesses. These vendors were selling trinkets from Ethiopian religious relics such as *meskels* (hand-held Ethiopian crosses), pictures of Jesus Christ, his mother Mary and a wide assortment of local hand-knitted scarves. Yet, there we were, amid this hustle and bustle; me, with my hands swinging and Ademe transporting my suitcase firmly over his head.

Bahir Dar's bus station was a big open dirt yard with about two dozen *country style* buses parked inside. After Ademe made the necessary inquiries, he identified the bus that was going to

Lalibela. He then conversed with a gentleman on the bus in Amharic and the next thing I knew, I was invited to sit in the front of the bus right next to the driver. Apparently Ademe had told the gentleman, that I was visiting Ethiopia for the first time and that he was to make sure that I arrived at my destination 'safe and sound'. The gentleman then spoke to the driver and that was how I had been granted such a privileged position on the bus.

As soon as I assumed my designated seat, my suitcase was taken from Ademe and hurled at the top of the bus together with the luggage of other passengers. The luggage on top of our transport included other suitcases and crocus bags filled with rice, coffee, wheat and fruits. Once the luggage was properly fastened with rope we set off on our destination. The gentleman, who turned out to be my 'guardian' for the entire bus trip, then sat down directly behind me and the bus driver. As the ignition of the bus tumbled, I thanked Ademe for all his assistance. Over the roar of the bus' engine, I told Ademe that I would see him in Bahir Dar within the next few days.

When the bus drove out the dirt-yard, I suddenly felt a strange feeling. As Amharic words buzzed around the bus, I realised that out of the thirty or so passengers, I was the only foreigner. What was even more disturbing was that no one on the entire bus could speak English. For the remainder of my trip, the only mode of communication between me and my guardian took the form of gesticulations and body language.

Within a matter of minutes, the bus was travelling on the main road to Bahir Dar. The sun was now emerging, painting the skyline with various hues of oranges and blues. My guardian turned to me and his eyes and facial expression gave me some reassurance – *"Don't worry, everything will be alright."*

One thing was certain – the journey through the Ethiopian plains and highlands was very picturesque. The eyes are truly windows to the world and oh what a sight to behold! Looking on through the window of the bus, I felt like I had been swallowed up back into the Biblical times. In the countryside, the land looked like it would never end as it stretched almost way beyond where the eyes could ever see.

Along the journey, there were farmers tending to their crops, children at the side of the dusty road attentively enjoying a game of "foosball" and women decked off with white shawls flung across their shoulders. I also caught a glimpse of boys, who armed with sticks, were leading their sheep to an unknown destination across the lush green undulating fields. There were also smiling faces everywhere. So much so, that I formed the impression that notwithstanding the poverty, Ethiopians are a very happy and contented people.

The bus continued, with its wheels rolling up steep hills and descending valleys. Random stops were made along the way to pick up persons who stood up on the roadside waiting. On one occasion, the driver picked up a lanky gentleman handling a long shot gun just as slim as him. To my astonishment, the man casually placed his weapon on the dashboard of the bus and quietly took his place on an available seat at the back of the bus. My guardian, perhaps reading my thoughts, gave me a look which I understood to mean that what I had witnessed was quite normal. I was later told by locals that the man was likely a farmer or a shepherd.

After driving for many hours, the bus finally slowed down and came to a sudden halt. My guardian looked at me and put all his five fingers together on one hand and tenderly touched his lips numerous times. We were stopping for food or maybe a drink. I considered it an ideal opportunity for a 'pit stop', as I was famished. I hastily descended the bus and ordered the local dish of *injera* and lentils and some Ethiopian tea. Half an hour later, we were back on the road and I continued to take in the scenery along the way.

As the sun started to set, the bus stopped in another large vacant dirt-yard. I turned to my guardian once again, with the look which he had grown accustomed to – *Where are we?* – and, *What do we do now?* I was met with a surprised face and it seemed as if my guardian too, did not know why the driver had stopped. *'Are we in Lalibela?'* I wondered to myself.

I immediately posed the same question to my guardian in one word - *"Lalibela?"* He shook his head side to side with a rather confused look; then he muttered something in Amharic which of course I could not understand. Passengers started to descend from the bus and unload the luggage that was on top. Villagers came from out of nowhere to assist with this process. I was in total awe. I had no working cell phone. I couldn't speak Amharic. For some reason however, I knew we were not in Lalibela.

Dusk was now kicking in. I screamed within my head: *'Where the hell am I?'* My guardian spoke to the driver and afterwards he intentionally closed his eyes, making signals that it was time to sleep. He then pointed to what looked like a bar which had flaking exterior paint and which was annexed to a guesthouse across the road. It was in this guesthouse where we were to spend the night.

It was at this bar that I met an Ethiopian teacher by the name of Yimer Adamu. I was pretty much relieved to know that he could speak English. After consulting with my guardian, Yimer explained to me that the bus driver had to rest and that we would spend the night in town. We would then continue our journey to Lalibela, early in the morning. The name of the town was *Nefas Meewcha*, otherwise known as *Gayint* by the locals. *Nefas Meewcha* was about 135 kilometres away from Lalibela.

On a straight and well-paved road, such a distance would take one or two hours by car. But, given the mountainous terrain and the narrow and winding roads, I would later discover that there was another day's journey ahead, before reaching our final destination.

After 'chit-chatting' with Yimer and enjoying my *injera* and lentils, I decided to retire early to my room. I had had a very rough yet exciting day. It was one filled with adventure and curiosity. It was time to call it a night.

In my small, poorly lit room, I started to think. I thought about how I was so many miles away from my family in Jamaica and Trinidad. I thought about what my brothers or parents were doing at that very moment. It was a very weird and eerie feeling to be lying down on that cold single bed. I was thinking to myself: *"Wow – I'm so many thousands of miles away in a remote part of Ethiopia."* As I had absolutely no telephone contact, I thought mainly of my father. He was always known in the family for being the one who would call to find out where you are or to monitor your movements. If he had called, he would have surely asked, in his make-shift Jamaican patois: *"Kiddo, where yuh dey?"* And I would have replied, competing with his patois, *"Bwoy I doh even know"*. Then he would probably laugh and make a joke about it. So, the feeling was very surreal. It was a nostalgic, isolated type of feeling.

While thinking about all this, I immediately penned a poem about my father called *"Like my fadda."* It was a poem describing him as my role model. I still have it to this day.[1] Little did I know that less than three months later, I would be reciting that same poem in the form of a eulogy at my father's funeral.

Suffice to say, I made it to Lalibela and back to Bahir Dar. I had lost all contact with my guardian. I often try to remember his name, but time has gotten the better of me. I just remember his short and wiry frame, his chocolate brown skin and kinky hair on the crown of his head. Most of all, I remember his act of kindness, his hospitality. It is these gentle acts that I consider to be more important and which will leave an indelible print on one's mind. I find some pleasure, some solace in believing that he is somewhere in Ethiopia helping someone else right now. His kindness was more than his name.

Back at Bahir Dar I met with Ademe and told him about my adventure. Later, I also met with my friend Mihret at a rooftop restaurant overlooking the Lake Tana. As I began to tell him about my trip to Lalibela, he cut me short. He said that my father had been in continuous contact with him by mobile phone, regarding my whereabouts. Mihret had told my father that all was well and that I was happily exploring the countryside of Lalibela.

When this fact was revealed to my father, he couldn't help but repeatedly thank him. Mihret quoted my father as saying: *"Thank you…thank you so much for taking care of my son".* It turned out that Mihret was not the only one my father made contact with. Apparently my father had a similar conversation with my other Ethiopian friend Tariku Tsegaye. Minutes later, after

---

[1] Poem listed in Annex I.

more *injera,* a lentils and chick peas dish, I borrowed Mihret's mobile phone and telephoned my father, just to give him the reassurance that all was indeed well with me in Ethiopia.

On 5th December 2007 I was back in Cape Town from Ethiopia. With my coursework completed, I had exactly one week to pack up my belongings, vacate my cosy post-grad flat and fly back home to Trinidad. Anticipating my return to Trinidad, my father wrote me an email on the 12th December 2007. In that email he said he was anxious to hear about my stories of Cape Town and the time spent in Ethiopia. He also promised to be in Trinidad when I returned. Dad fulfilled his promise in the email, as he was there at Piarco Airport waiting for me two days later. By writing these *Memoirs,* it is my aim to give the reader a true account of my father; what he stood for and the close relationship that he had with his family.

This account will not only focus on his 'public persona', but also on some aspects of his private life – through the eyes of his sons. Where I was not present, the information recorded was handed down to me by the loved ones who came before, who were present to tell the tale. At the end of the day, my aim is to depict the man, my father – the ever-glowing paternal figure who contributed to the individual who I am today.

This is my story.

Chapter 1

My family roots

A visit from my grandfather

Towards the end of 2005, my grandfather, Otto Sobion paid me a visit at the law firm J.D. Sellier and Co., where at the time I was working as an Associate Attorney at law. Located at the top of Abercromby Street in Port of Spain, *Sellier*, as it is commonly known, is a prominent law firm in Trinidad. It was this very firm that my father once roamed with a legal brief in hand, also starting off as an Associate Attorney, then later being elevated to a Partner.

Although I had no prior knowledge that my grandfather was going to drop by that morning, I was not at all surprised. This was because my grandfather was known to attend weekday lunchtime mass at the 'Living Waters Chapel', on upper Frederick Street. So, it was not unusual for my grandfather to make a minor detour at *Sellier*, on his way to the 'Living Waters Chapel' to check up on me, one of his grandsons.

Once the receptionist informed me that my grandfather was downstairs, I immediately descended, two steps at a time, to the ground floor. My grandfather, Otto Sobion, was affectionately known by his family as "Dad Otto". It was my older brother Jules, the first grandchild, who first started calling my grandfather 'Dad Otto', when he was a toddler. Since then, the name has become a household name, so that even my father and all his siblings referred to my grandfather as *Dad Otto*. There were however instances when my father would simply refer to Dad Otto as '*the Old Man.*'

That morning Dad Otto was sitting down waiting for me in the reception area. When I gazed at him, I saw the twinkle in his eyes. At the time of this visit Dad Otto was about 82 years old. His memory was not that sharp and there was talk floating around the family that he was experiencing the initial stages of Alzheimer's disease.

Dad Otto, who usually appeared collective and very soft-spoken, didn't seem to have much to say. In fact, I found myself being the one initiating and setting the pace of our conversation. Suffice to say, these meetings at *Sellier* were never planned or calculated in my grandfather's head. He just showed up at my office when he wanted to – at his whim and fancy. His decision to visit me may have just been at the spur of the moment while taking his daily morning stroll from City Gate to Living Waters.

After speaking generally about his health and my clients, the topic abruptly switched to family. I asked my grandfather several questions about his own parents and siblings. As I started to ask questions I could see Dad Otto's forehead cringe, as he stared into space, pondering on past distant memories. When the information started to flow, I quickly took out a pen and piece of yellow paper from my note pad and jotted down all that he said. This yellow paper, which has since turned light brown due to its age, contains some valuable snippets of the history of the Sobion family. It is this fragile piece of paper which holds cherished details of where I came from.

Where did the name 'Sobion' come from?

My grandfather was born Otto Berton Sobion on 26th September 1923 in a house in Radix Village, Mayaro. Although Dad Otto was born on the 26th September 1923, his birth certificate declares that his birth was registered on 8th October 1923, almost two weeks after his actual birth. There was nothing unusual about this fact, as in those days the places where the births were registered and recorded were usually miles away from the place of birth itself. Thus, the fact that Dad Otto was a 'home birth', together with the lack of motor vehicular transport, meant that the late registration of his birth was quite a common phenomenon. Otto's mother was Dora Domingue, and she was listed on his birth paper as being a "domestic worker", although in reality, she was a 'housewife'. Dora lived a simple life, rearing chickens and ducks on her beachfront property in Mayaro.

Stanford Sobion – Otto's father, was a schoolteacher. Stanford and Dora never married, and Dora raised her son as a single mother in Mayaro. The relationship between Stanford and Dora, also produced another son called Clyde, who was my grandfather's younger brother. Clyde died when he was a baby.

My grandfather's grandfather was Aman Sobion. Not much is known about Aman, although our oldest family member, Harold Frontin, knew that Aman Sobion did exist. But it goes even further; the name Sobion was an English corruption of the original name *"Sovignon"*. My paternal family tree traces all the way back to *Alphonse Sovignon* who was the grandfather of Aman.

Alphonse came to the West Indies from the Kingdom of Dahomey (modern day Benin) with French families. Other families with direct lineage to *Alphonse Sovignon* are the 'Archers', the 'Chandlers' and the 'Richardsons'. My family tree is consistent with modern literature. In the book *Heroes of Mayaro* written by Harricharan Narine, the name *Sovignon* is spelt like *Savignon*. In that book, Narine traces back the line of *Alphonse Sovignon* to more than two hundred years ago when the first French Settlers came from Martinique to Mayaro with their slaves.

For the sake of the palate and the further corruption of the name, *Alphonse Sauvignon* is a French wine originating from Loire, France. In 2015, my wife's grandfather, who is French and always drinks *un verre de vin rouge* with his meals, explained to me that *"Sauvignon"* is a variety of a plant which produces grapes. From that day onwards, every time I see a bottle of wine bearing the name *Sauvignon* I can't help but think of my own family name.

Another French friend of mine, upon seeing my last name brought to my attention that *Saubion* is the name of a commune in the southwest of France. *Saubion,* the commune, is also pronounced similarly to Sobion. So, whether it is *Sauvignon, Savignon, Sovignon, Saubion or Sobion;* they all seem to have French origins; the latter being the recognised spelling of my family name.

Nowadays one could see the name *Sobion* being spelt with an 'a' or an 'e' – like *Sobian* or *Sobien*. This is incorrect and my father would always be quick to point this out whenever the newspapers misspelt his name. When this occurred, he would politely remind the reporter that his name is *Sobion,* with the 'n' silent and pronounced using three syllables as *'So-bee-yor'*.

Stanford and Dora

When my grandfather was about four years old, Stanford moved to Maracaibo, Venezuela where he established the Stanford Commercial Institute, a school, teaching English. Maracaibo, the second largest city after Caracas, is an oil-rich region booming with industrial activity. In these circumstances, Stanford took it upon himself to teach English to Spanish-speaking expats and the local population within the community. Due to the time spent in Venezuela, Stanford became bilingual and adopted Spanish as his second language. Today, my family still has cherished photos of Dad Otto and his wife Clerine visiting Stanford in Venezuela. Stanford clearly had a positive impact within my family because both my father and my older brother Jules, carry his name as a middle name.

Turning to Dora Domingue my father's grandmother; I still have visions of my great-grandmother. Dora was known by all in the family as *'Tanty Dora, 'Tanty'*, being *creole* for 'Aunty'. This name was first adopted by her own son Dad Otto. It was only later in my life that I understood that Tanty Dora was a teenager when she gave birth to Dad Otto. I also learnt that Dad Otto was raised by Tanty Dora's older sister, 'Tanty Carmen', at her humble abode on the Guayaguayare Main Road. As Tanty Carmen played a major role in the rearing of Dad Otto as a child, I wonder if this was the reason why he called his own mother by the title *Tanty*.

From the moment Dad Otto mentioned Tanty Dora's name to me at *Sellier*, my mind travelled back to the early 1980s, to the home I grew up in at Dorrington Gardens, Diego Martin. As a toddler, Tanty Dora used to live with us in Dorrington Gardens. As a member of the household, she was one of the individuals who was directly responsible for my brothers' and my own upbringing. Tanty Dora was dark-skinned with brawny arms and legs which gave her a very robust frame for her age. At home, she would be the first to rise in the morning to prepare us a cup of 'Milo'. I would never forget her singsong refrain while handing me a cup of Milo – '*Jus – Tea, Tea?*'

Then there were the times when Tanty Dora would scold us when we sang calypso songs during the Lenten season. She would tell us that Lent was a period of fasting and reflection and that since Carnival was over, we should abstain from those worldly pleasures. This was a rural tradition; something which is most likely forgotten in this present generation or even never heard of. This was the custom in which Dad Otto, my father and his siblings had grown up. It was an oral tradition which was handed down from generation to generation – one which I now feel a sense of duty to pass on.

When Tanty Dora died, I was about ten years old. I had a heavy heart seeing her coffin lowered six feet under at the Radix Cemetery in Mayaro. Older relatives sprinkled rum in her grave and I wondered why, because Tanty Dora was not really a drinker. Then I was told the significance behind the gesture – the sprinkling of rum was to give life to the spirit to travel to the new realm. After the funeral, we proceeded to our relatives' home at Radix Village on the Guayaguayare Main Road. For all my life, I knew this home as being the home of Stephanie Joseph, also known as *Bubbles*. But *Bubbles* did not live there alone; she was just one member of the extended family who lived in the household.

At *Bubbles*, the atmosphere was lively. Food and drinks were in abundance. Family members were present, some I knew, some I met for the very first time. Everyone was talking and remembering good times. As a young one present, Tanty Dora's funeral seemed to be more of a celebration rather than a time of mourning.

The Frontins

Just like the *Sobions*, I tried to ascertain the root of the *Frontins*. While undergoing research for these *Memoirs*, I found the name Sextus Julius Frontinus – a Roman Senator in the year 1 AD. Later down in history, I came across a Pedro Max Fernando Frontin, a Brazilian, who was the Chief Commander of his country's Naval Division during World War I, on the side of the Triple Entente – made up of the Russian Empire, France and the United Kingdom of Great Britain and Ireland.[2] Regarding the Roman Senator, more than two thousand years have elapsed, thus making it difficult to draw a connection between the present-day Frontins. Admiral Frontin, though more recent in terms of history, also proved challenging to reasonably conclude that he was a distant relative. My father never referred to the Roman Senator or the Brazilian Frontin. He did however mention that the Frontins descended from the Népoui tribe and like the *Sobions,* came to Mayaro from Martinique. If my spelling and pronunciation are correct, Népoui is a village in New Caledonia, a French territory in the South Pacific. But I have known my father to have had a very wild imagination. This was the same man who told us that he once witnessed it snowing in Mayaro. Whether the Népoui family lineage is accurate is also subject to much debate within

---

[2] I came across a Wikipedia page and other internet sources in the name Pedro Max Fernando Frontin.

my family. Another story, often cited with more authority within my family, is that the Frontins were originally three brothers who left France for Martinique and eventually settled in Mayaro, Trinidad during World War I.

While researching I also came across, via social media, some Frontins living in Lagos, Nigeria. One Frontin from Africa explained to me that his grandfather was a Chief from a small village called *Imoru* in Nigeria. The history from this village was that these Frontins in *Imoru* originally migrated from the Benin Empire and spread over Nigeria, Ghana, Sierra Leone and Liberia. Some were sold into slavery and brought into bondage in the West Indies. I was told that the name *Frontin* has been in existence for over two hundred years in Africa and the title of 'Chief' is handed down to the first born in the family.[3]

My father's mother was born Clerine Frontin on 7th November 1923 in a house at Grand Lagoon, Mayaro. *Granny Clerine*, as we called her, was less than two months Dad Otto's junior. Her father was Edwin Cornelius Frontin and her mother Emelda Williemena Frontin. Emelda was formerly a Richardson hence the family connection among the Frontins, the Richardsons and eventually the Sobions. By marrying my grandfather, my grandmother Clerine Frontin became a Sobion.

A great deal of information on the Frontin family was passed on to me by Harold Frontin, the older brother of my father's mother Clerine. Uncle Harold, my great uncle, was a former teacher in Mayaro, who taught the renowned local author

---

[3] According to this source, the last Chief in the Imoru village was Adebayo Adegbe Frontin who passed away sometime in 2001.

Michael Anthony. At 91 years at the time, Uncle Harold was the last living member of that generation of the family. While writing these *Memoirs*, I had several chats with him about our family's history. His memory was sharp like an elephant as he took me down many trips to memory lane. The destination was always Mayaro, not the Mayaro as I knew it – but rather a vintage Mayaro in the early 20th century.

"Clerine was the youngest of all the siblings..." Uncle Harold's voice echoed over the phone line thereby stirring me out of my reverie. He continued by explaining the order of seniority among the siblings which was – Austin, Hubert, Conrad (Uncle Harold referred to Conrad as 'the mathematician'), Beryl, Harold, Clerine and Claris. There was also another brother called Matthew. He was the youngest of all and he died at childbirth. Clerine and Claris were twin sisters. Claris also died at a tender age.

Keith's mother, Clerine Sobion née Frontin in Mayaro in the 1940s.

The story goes, that when Claris was a few weeks old, a white foreigner visited Mayaro and held her in her arms while commenting on the child's beauty. Less than twenty-four hours later, Claris became severely ill and died. The talk in the village at the time was that the unidentified woman placed a spell called *mal yeux* on Claris and that was the cause of death. A more contemporary medical explanation might have been that the foreigner's hands were dirty when she played with Claris. I distinctly remember my father telling us this story of his aunt Claris and her short lifespan on earth. In concluding this story, he would always add that a twin skips a generation and that there is a likelihood that someone in our generation would give birth to a twin. Whether such a statement is medically proven or not is another story. At the time of writing, no one in our generation is yet to be blessed with the birth of a twin. I for myself simply took this story for what it was – a part of our family history – and managed to quietly store it deep in my heart not knowing that one day I would have to gather up the courage and place it in writing.

Uncle Harold then referred to a piece of land which formed part of *St. Margaret estate* in Grand Lagoon, Mayaro. All those lands were once owned by my father's great grandmother, Marie Ann Frontin (also called Ma Gabrielle – the name *'Gabrielle'* being the first name of her husband, Gabrielle Frontin). That was where Harold and his siblings grew up.

On that estate Ma Gabrielle grew coconut trees, coffee, cocoa and various assortments of tropical fruits. As Uncle Harold said – *"You name it we had it."* Ma Gabrielle ran that estate on her own. The thing is, Ma Gabrielle could not have spoken one word of English. She spoke *patois* or broken French. So, when she wanted the young ones to buy something for her in the shop she used to give her instructions in *patois*. When Ma Gabrielle died, my father's grandparents Edwin and Emelda Frontin took over the estate. Subsequently, Edwin Frontin lost the estate after entering into a bad deal with a wealthy family.

A bad deal. My level of concentration paused for a fraction of a second when I heard those three tragic words. Again, this story rang a bell. At that moment, the conversation with Uncle Harold became like pieces of a puzzle which came together to form a perfect picture. It was as if everything started to make sense. At that point, my memory again switched gears to conversations which I had with my father about his grandfather Edwin Frontin, also called *Pa*. My father said he could not understand why *Pa* always looked so sad and dejected. How *Pa* would always keep to himself. My father said, sometimes he would try to speak to *Pa* and that *Pa* would just sit there and give him a blank stare.

It was only after many years, that my father was able to find out the cause of *Pa's* depression. According to him, *Pa* signed over the estate in Grand Lagoon as collateral to a wealthy family in Mayaro to pay off some bad debts. *Pa* defaulted on the loan. *Pa* lost the land. It was simple as that. *Pa* thought he was duped and never to be forgiven by his family. He felt like a traitor, a recluse, one who had betrayed his immediate family and by extension his future generation. After that, *Pa* became senile. The issue of *Pa's* early senility was also confirmed by his wife Emelda.

Despite this land issue, Edwin and Emelda Frontin were a notable couple in Mayaro. One account even referred to them as the *Mayaro elite*. The Frontins were high up in the hierarchy of the Mayaro church and the first two pews were reserved for the family for Sunday mass. Emelda was also one of the persons who prepared the altar for Sunday and weekday mass (this duty was later taken over by Tanty Carmen who raised Dad Otto).

My father often spoke of his grandmother Emelda. He once boasted to one of his friends in Moruga, that his grandmother baked the best bread he had ever tasted, in her outdoor dirt oven. I would always remember how delighted my father was when he found an old black and white picture of his grandparents standing in a churchyard in Mayaro. He immediately had it framed and hung it up on the wall right by the entrance of our home in Kingston. He would not hesitate to explain this picture to all his guests and it inevitably became a conversation piece.

As a little boy, visiting my paternal grandparents, I remember Emelda. What I particularly remembered her for, was her stark stare made remarkable by the blue-grey colour of her eyes. These same blue-grey eyes came back to life every time I saw the coloured, yet old, picture of her in my family's photo album.

The story about *Pa* and "the bad deal" could perhaps explain how the name '*Frontin Road*' in Mayaro originated. The conjecture proffered is that when the present owners were researching the Deed and they found out that the original owner was a *Frontin*, they decided to pay tribute to the name.

My grandparents meet

The next obvious question to Uncle Harold was – "So how did Granny Clerine and Dad Otto meet?" In the 1930s, Mayaro was a small community where everyone knew everybody and treated all like family. Motorcars were quite rare and Harold and his siblings used to walk to school and to church. Every day, he and his siblings would walk three miles back and forth to school. As Clerine and Otto came from Mayaro, this environment was conducive for both to meet. Clerine and Otto met at church – a church bazaar in Mayaro to be accurate. Uncle Harold remembered the day when Otto wanted to get married to his sister Clerine.

Uncle Harold paused briefly to contain his gentle chuckle as he revealed to me how the union commenced.

"You see in those days, if a man wanted to get married, the man had to write a letter to the lady's parents asking for permission for their daughter's hand in marriage. One day, I saw Otto running down the road fully decked in a three-piece suit with the letter tucked away under his arm. Even though the sun was hot like hell, he still was very proud to have that opportunity to show off his suit. Anyway....I don't know what happened next, maybe he was running so fast or maybe he was nervous, but just before he reached the gate to our home, he tripped and fell and both he and the letter ended up flat on the road. That did not deter him however. He quickly got up and brushed off the dirt off his suit, picked up the letter and delivered it to my parents. I guess the rest is history."

On reflection, I am happy that I spoke to both Dad Otto and Uncle Harold about our family history. We are often reminded that we must appreciate our elders especially since they hold valuable and sacred family knowledge in trust for the younger generation. Yet, we sometimes fail to pay heed to this reminder, with the result that this knowledge is lost and gaps are left in our history with no one left to plug them in.

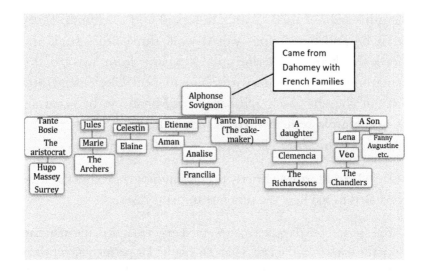

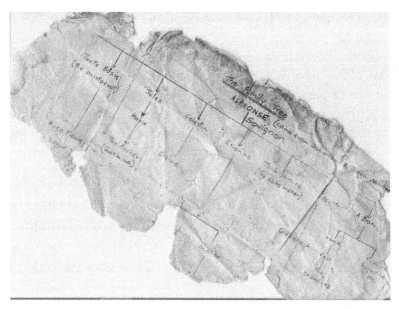

Part of the old Sobion family tree (below) with an improvised version created (on top). The family tree notes one Alphonse Sovignon (at the head) who came from Dahomey (modern day Benin) with French families. Keith and his siblings were the 6th generation from Alphonse Sovignon coming through the lineage of Aman.

My Mayaro mother

My mother, Judith Anne Marie Sobion was the daughter of a union between Lucina Connor and Knolly Massy. She was born in a house on Peter Hill, Mayaro (the midwife was a lady only known by the name 'Ma Turin'). My mother's 'navel-string' was buried on Peter Hill and it was there she grew up under the care of her great grandmother, Clemencia Connor. The Connors were, and still are, a household name in Mayaro. To prove this, there is a Park situated within walking distance from Peter Hill named after Edric Connor – the cousin of Lucina Connor.

My mother was schooled at Mayaro Government School and only moved to town for the first time at eleven years of age. I say all this to illustrate that my mother is probably *'more Mayaro'* than my father as she spent her formative years growing up in the country. Like most West Indian families, *the Connors* did not originally come from Trinidad. The mother of Clemencia Connor came from Anguilla – a charming English speaking island tucked away in the northern Caribbean.

Based on my family history, I cannot deny my heritage. Equally, I cannot deny that the region where I was born is very unique and somewhat complicated. Some claim that the Caribbean was named after the indigenous Caribs who originally inhabited this region. We are identified as "West Indians" after Columbus accidentally stumbled upon these Caribs while sailing west with an intention to arrive at the *East Indies*. Despite this nomenclature, over the years our contribution as "West Indians" to the Caribbean region has been very deep and profound. Even though my ancestors did not come from one country, my genes flow through every blue water and particle of sand of these islands. Yet, I am fully aware that my journey did not start in this region. It began on the continent of Africa. It is a heritage of which I am extremely proud!

Chapter 2

Country boy in the City

The blue seas and clear lagoons

The flat, smooth and pearly-white stone hopped, skipped and jumped about half a dozen times over the azure colour sea before sinking, hitting hard the sand beneath. On the shoreline are my father, my brothers and myself. My father is teaching us the art of "skipping" rocks over the surface of the ocean. We are on Mayaro beach in the late 1980s.

With his words of advice, he illustrated one more time the technique. *"Sploosh, Sploosh, Splooooooosh…….."* That was the sound that the stone made each time it made contact with the whitecaps before descending to the sand beneath. Frantically, my brothers and I combed the shoreline looking for those perfect smooth stones. When we did find one that fit the description, we imitated the technique used by my father. At first we were terribly unsuccessful, as the stones hit the ocean with a loud *"thud!"* before being completely swallowed up by the sea. As my father would say - the technique of the throw was all in the wrists. This is the same beach where my father and his own siblings first practised "skipping" stones in the ocean many years before. My father was in his element, the 'city boy', coming back to grips with the country.

In the 1980s, Mayaro beach was much more different than it is now. An old family friend once told me that many years ago, the sky looked bluer than it is today. However, I could use that same analogy with the colour of the sea before me. When

I was about eight years old, I found that the colour of the sea at Mayaro was bluer than it is today. There were times when my parents would take us for walks on the beach and I vividly recall passing crystal clear lagoons. In these lagoons, swam small 'guppy' fish waggling their beautifully coloured tails. To my recollection, the lagoon was also filled with a school of 'angelfish'. Nowadays, I do not see these blue seas, neither the crystal-clear lagoons with its exotic fishes. I hope this was not a figment of my childhood imagination. Yet, I wonder if the causes of such disappearances may be due to the effects of climate change.

Town boy on Panka Street

My father's parents, Otto Sobion and Clerine Frontin got married on 19th June 1949 in Mayaro. The reception was held at a spanking new building at the corner of Mayaro-Guayaguayare Road and St. Anns Road. Immediately after they wed, Otto and Clerine moved out of Mayaro to settle at house number 8 Panka Street, St. James – *the city that never sleeps.* The Sobion family would remain there until 1962. The house on Panka Street is also still standing and although it has been renovated, it essentially maintains its original form as when it was occupied by the family. In a sense, the decision to move to town would have been tough for a young married couple who were accustomed to growing up in the countryside. However a new adventure was in the making as my father's parents sought to secure better work opportunities in the city.

As soon as the Sobions relocated to St. James, Dad Otto landed a job at the McEnearney company. His employment at McEnearney spanned his entire working career as he moved up the ranks from within the sales department up to middle management. Due to the 'perks' that came along with his job, Dad Otto always seemed to have a new or semi-new Ford vehicle at his disposal.

Clerine was a teacher by profession. Before moving to St. James, Clerine taught at the Roman Catholic Schools at Mayaro and Guayaguayare. Once she relocated to the city, she taught at Mucurapo and Maraval RC Schools in the environs of Port of Spain. Upon her retirement, she was the Vice Principal at St. Anns RC Primary School.

On 15th September 1951 my father wailed his first cry into the world. He was the second of seven children and was born in the house on Panka Street. My father's official birth certificate indicates that he was born on Hyderabad Street, St. James. This however was an error, because Hyderabad Street runs parallel to Panka Street. One reason behind this error was probably that the owners of the property lived on the Hyderabad Street side of the premises.

As a result, the address was officially registered as Hyderabad Street. Notwithstanding this, by being born in St. James, my mother dubbed my father a "town boy" even though both his parents originated from Mayaro.

At birth, my father was given the name Keith Stanford Phillip Sobion – the first middle name being the name of his grandfather. From all evidence, it appears that my father adored the name *Stanford*. For instance when he was admitted to practise law as a Solicitor in 1975, he would sign his name as "K. Stanford Sobion". It was said that he believed the name 'Stanford' was more prominent as opposed to 'Keith', the latter name being a bit boyish and not becoming of a lawyer. In the later years, my father abbreviated his signature to read "K. S. Sobion".

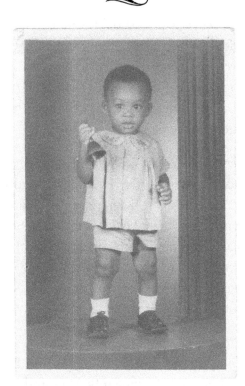

Keith's first birthday.

When I was a child, my father would proudly rattle off his supposedly official name; *Keith Stanford Phillip Sylvester Thellosilous Maximus Sobion the III"*. This was a name that he took very seriously yet it could not be found on his birth certificate. (I later found out that the name *Sylvester* was given to him by a Catholic priest during his Confirmation ceremony at St. Patrick's R.C. Church in Newtown, Port of Spain). It was as if the only person who knew of the existence of this name was he himself. Such a recital was obviously a reference to his bizarre fixation on names that he thought carried a certain degree of eminence.

As if he did not have enough names, I couldn't help but notice that my father was also called 'Skeef' by his elder brother Lennox. The story goes that when my father was around twelve years, he travelled to Martinique on a one-week exchange programme, to learn French. At Martinique, he stayed at the family home of one called 'Michel'. On his return to Trinidad, Michel, his now new Martiniquais friend, accompanied him. Michel stayed with the Sobion family in Trinidad for another week. Whenever Michel was looking for my father at home, he would ask Lennox - *Where iz Skeef?* Michel, for the life of him, could not pronounce the "K" in Keith and the name *Skeef* would more easily roll off his French tongue. Thus the name *Skeef* was adopted as a home name within the family. During Michel's stay at Trinidad, he would also be heard conversing in French with my father's mother Clerine. Apparently Clerine would respond to him using French Creole, a language that she picked up while growing up in Mayaro.

My father's brother, Lennox, was the eldest sibling of the family. The age-difference between Lennox and my father was close, just one and a half years. My father's younger sisters in order of birth were Teresa, Paula, Helen and Patricia. All of the siblings, with the exception of Patricia, were born at home at Panka Street with the assistance of the same midwife. Patricia was born at the Seventh-Day Adventist Hospital in Port of Spain.

There was one other brother who neither my father nor his siblings ever really knew. His name was 'Gary', and he was born between Paula and Helen. My father was a toddler when Gary died of a mysterious illness a few months after he was born. He remembered dressing up and going to church to see baby Gary lying down in a small coffin. That was the only memory he had of his little brother. He was too young to understand the concept of death.

The Sobion family at the home of Austin Frontin at Belmont. From left to right: Dad Otto (father), Lennox, Helen, Keith, Teresa, Patricia, Clerine (mother) and Paula.

My father spent the first eleven years of his life growing up on Panka Street, St. James. Even though the property was an upstairs and downstairs house, the space was fairly small for a large family. The house contained two bedrooms, one of which was occupied by the parents. The second bedroom was shared among the Sobion siblings and their cousin Gerry Frontin. Gerry moved from Mayaro to live with the Sobions between 1951 and 1962 to attend school in Port of

Spain. With seven young kids living in one bedroom, I could imagine the space at No. 8 Panka Street being somewhat cramped.

St. James, a suburb just on the outskirts of Port of Spain, was at one time the home of the Indian indentured labourers in the nineteenth century. The Indian influence is easily spotted by narrow street lanes, bearing names such as, Bombay, Calcutta and Delhi. St. James was and probably still is, the nerve centre of Port of Spain and its immediate environs. Growing up in St. James, in the 1950s would have been quite an experience for my father and his siblings. Compared to nowadays there would not be as many people, noise or commercial businesses lining the streets.

There was the story that my father would repeat about Paula, his younger sister. Shortly after she was born, Paula spent a period of time in Mayaro. When she was about three years old, she returned to Panka Street. This was a time when motorcars were beginning to become popular in Port of Spain. My father, quite jokingly, said that when Paula returned to Panka Street and she heard the roar of an engine of an approaching car, she would scream at the top of her lungs and run inside the house and hide under the bed. He would cackle at himself after he told the story. Up to this day, Paula would deny the full story as told by my father.

Back in St. James, the Sobions came across the *tadjahs* which paraded across the Western Main Road during the Hosay festival. If Carnival was the party, then St. James was definitely the dance floor. At an early age, my father and his siblings were exposed to the calypso music emanating from loud speakers. He and his siblings would have certainly been intrigued to see characters such as the 'moko jumbie', 'fancy sailors' and steelpan bands as they shuffled across the narrow streets of St. James. But the curiosity would stop at the gate on Panka Street. As a teacher, Clerine Sobion was a disciplinarian. It was very unlikely that she would permit her children to partake in the Carnival festivities that primarily catered for the adult folk. The early memories of Carnival on Panka Street would however always linger in my father's mind.

Church and school days

As strict as she may have been, Clerine Sobion had a gentle soul. Her love for her children and grandchildren was insurmountable. Being a devout Catholic from Mayaro, she insisted on a Catholic upbringing for her children. This could be seen in her choice of schools. In the late 1950s, both my father and his brother Lennox were enrolled in Newtown Boys' RC School, one of the more prominent Catholic Primary Boy Schools in Port of Spain. The girls attended Newtown Girls' RC. Every morning, the children would squeeze up in Dad Otto's green Peugeot to attend school.

In 1962, my father passed the Common Entrance Exam enabling him to attend the college of his first choice – St. Mary's College (also known as the College of the Immaculate Conception or simply 'CIC'). A Catholic institution, St. Mary's College is known for its production of national scholars and for its academic excellence. The college stands on prime property on Frederick Street at the heart of Port of Spain. It was the same college that my brothers and I would attend some thirty years later.

My father's siblings also passed for the schools of their first choice. Lennox passed for Fatima College situated on Mucurapo Road. Their cousin Gerry Frontin also passed for and attended Fatima College with Lennox. From Panka Street, Lennox and Gerry used to walk to and from school every day. The girls attended Holy Name Convent situated just east of the Queen's Park Savannah. Holy Name Convent is an all-girls school founded by French Dominican nuns in 1902. According to the history of the convent, these nuns first came to Trinidad in 1868 not to teach, but to oversee the Leper Asylum in Chacachacare, an island situated just off the western peninsular of mainland Trinidad.

My father entered college in 1963. Attending St. Mary's College in the 1960s, the seniority of each student was measured by the length of his khaki trousers. For the first two years at College, my father wore short khaki pants. It was only when he entered Form 4 that the length of his school trousers was allowed to pass the knees and touch his ankles. My father often joked about being heckled and called a "small man" by the older students because of his 'short pants'. It was so frustrating, that my father yearned for the day of donning long khaki pants and thereby becoming an "adult." By the time my brothers and I entered the gates of St. Mary's College in the early 1990s we were able to avoid such emotional challenges as long khaki pants were permitted from the very first day one entered the classroom.

St. Mary's College is a seven-year all-boys school. At the time, it prepared students for the GCE O Level and A Level exams. But St. Mary's College is a very intense and competitive institution. When my father attended college, there was a *streaming* system in place. Under this *streaming* system, a batch of the brightest students in each academic year was placed in an *A* (Special) class. This *A* (Special) class was specially catered for what was thought to be the "more intellectually gifted students". If a student was not listed in an *A* (Special) class, even though he was thought to be intelligent in his own right, he would be placed in a lower level class.

The *streaming* system also permitted second year students in the *A* (Special) class to skip the third year of college and directly enter the fourth year. In 1964 my father, who was in Form (year) 2 A (Special) class, skipped year three and entered directly into Form 4. Two years later, he sat the GCE exams. The subjects which he read were Religion, English Language, English Literature, History, Geography, Mathematics, French and Spanish.

The academic burden and stress of the streaming system had its effects on young Keith. As his grades were not up to par, he had to repeat his GCE O Level Examinations in the academic year 1966/1967. In his second chance around, he improved his grades and was able to pursue his GCE A Level certification. In Form 6, my father read 'Modern Studies', which consisted of General Paper, Geography, English Literature and French. From his academic record, he performed well in Literature and French, receiving 'B' grades over the course of two years in each subject. His performance in Literature was not surprising because my father had a passion for reading. Likewise, on the subject of French, it seemed like his one-week visit to Martinique a few years earlier, had paid off. While in Martinique, his interest in French language grew. This, coupled with the fact that his mother and grandmother spoke French patois also motivated him in being successful in French at St. Mary's College.

Although my father never picked up a French book after college, some three decades later, he would still speak to us in his 'broken French'. On mornings, while firmly grasping his porcelain coffee cup by its handle, he would walk delightfully into the room and greet us in his smooth mellow voice – '*Bon matin tout le monde*'.

Latin, on the other hand was different. Even though my father studied Latin at college between 1963 and 1965, he did not speak a word of it at home. Compared to French, Latin was a more medieval language and for that reason he submerged himself in the French language. Notwithstanding this, his knowledge of Latin at college would have undoubtedly helped him when he encountered Latin maxims while reading Law at University.

Finally, in 1969, after spending six years at St. Mary's, my father successfully completed his 'A Level examinations' and graduated from college.

Checkmate!

While at college, Keith represented St. Mary's in cricket and football. He was also a member of the 6th Trinidad Sea Scouts, the Literary and Debating Society and Secretary of the Chess Club. Out of these extra-curricular activities, two of them struck out to me like a sore thumb. They were 'Scouts' and the 'Chess Club'.

In the mid-1980s my brother Jules was also a Scout – a 'Cub Scout', to be exact. Whether he was inspired to be a Cub Scout or not because of my father, may be a moot point. What truly mattered, was that my father was present one morning

27

at Balandra beach where Jules and his fellow Scouts were camping for the weekend. On that morning my father was taking pictures of the young Scouts on the beach when he noticed one of them having a difficulty in the water. Rushing beyond the shoreline to assist the young Scout, my father not only forgot that he was fully clothed from head to toe, but that he also had his camera strapped around his neck. The end result was that the young Scout was saved, but not my father's camera. The camera was damaged beyond repair. The film was spoilt; but most importantly a life was saved.

Keith as a 6th Trinidad Sea Scout (right) at St. Mary's College with an unidentified friend.

I also did not have to read my father's college transcript to know that he was a lover of chess. At home, there was always a fancy chessboard which served a dual purpose; aesthetics and for playing. This chessboard was always tucked neatly away under a living room coffee table. It would stay there for months, until Dad decided to bring it out for a quick game. His opponent was always my little brother Darien.

Checkmate! That is what we would hear my father shout during every game he played with Darien. Then he would laugh *"kya kya kya."* Darien was always the loser. However month after month Darien watched my father's every move. He was 'reading' those thoughts in my father's head before he moved his rook. His eyes were constantly fixed to the chessboard. His day of deliverance was coming. And it did. One bright afternoon, many years later, it was Darien's turn to say *Checkmate!* My father was amazed. After congratulating Darien, he immediately reassembled the pieces on the board and challenged him to another game. Darien would have none of it. He said he would stop while he was on top and that he retired from chess as the undisputed family champion. My father would laugh at this. But it was Darien who had the last laugh. He never played chess with my father after that.

Religious education at College

At St. Mary's College religious education classes, in the form of Catholicism, were mandatory. Every Sunday morning my father, Lennox, Teresa and Paula used to walk to St. Teresa's RC Church in Woodbrook to attend mass. Mass started promptly at 8 o'clock in the morning. After mass they would go to Sunday School between 10 a.m. to 11.30 a.m. When we were young, my father would only go to church on memorable occasions such as first communion or solemn occasions such as funerals. Outside of these two occasions, he did not attend Sunday mass with us. His excuse was that his parents made him go to Church every week, which amounted to, at least for him, a lifetime. In addition to this, he had to go to mass every day at college. And he had the results to prove it. For the first five years at St. Mary's he received straight 'As' in the subject Religion. As a result of these experiences, my father would say that he had prayed for us for his entire youth. Sundays was now his time to relax. So every Sunday, my mother would be the one responsible for taking the three of us through the church's gate.

Although my father may have been absent from church, we were still brought up in a Catholic tradition. Before bedtime, both my parents taught us the following prayer:

"Gentle Jesus,

Meek and mild,

Look upon, this little child,

Pity my simplicity,

Suffer me to come to Thee."

The reality was, that throughout my life, my father may have given up the Church but not his spirituality. When religion conflicted with pragmatism, he would not hesitate to say so. I would never forget the conversation he had with his father at a family gathering on Christmas Day. Dad Otto, who was in his early 80s, was still taking public transport from D'Abadie to Port of Spain to attend daily mass at the Living Waters Community. One afternoon on his way back home, Dad Otto could not remember the exact location of his house. Dementia was slowly setting in. Eventually he was found roaming the streets of the neighbourhood. When my father heard about this he was furious. He immediately made a demand that Christmas Day. That demand was that due to Dad Otto's age and failing memory, he be prohibited from going to mass in Port of Spain. In total defiance to this, Dad Otto quoted scripture from the epistle of James – *'the effectual fervent prayer of a righteous man availeth much.* This was an argument that my father could not win. Dad Otto continued going to Living Waters but not every day of the week. He spent the last years of his life living with nuns at a home for the elderly on Mount St. Benedict. He survived my father and was ninety years old when he passed away.

However, as he grew older, my father never totally abandoned his Catholic and Christian upbringing. Christmas was a special occasion for him, an occasion which was spent with family and friends. In the early years, Christmas Day was first spent with his parents in Diamond Vale, then later at our household. After my family moved to Jamaica, Christmas Day was celebrated at the home of his sister Teresa – a family tradition which remains today. These gatherings were important to my father as they served to reconnect and strengthen our familial bonds. For him, there was also an inextricable link between Christmas and the reason behind the season. In what was his last Christmas email to close friends, he extended *"a holy and joyful Christmas, in celebration of the Birth of Christ."*

Town boy returns to his roots

While my father spent the first ten years of his life in St. James, he was always eager to point out that he was a *country boy from Mayaro*. My father was a very simple down-to-earth man, – such attributes undoubtedly acquired due to his Mayaro genes. So although he was born in St. James, he never lost touch with his rural roots. As a child, he and his siblings would spend their holidays with their family in Mayaro. My father often declared that he would seek an early retirement in Mayaro where he would pull seine on the beach with his "one khaki pants". To follow through with his *khaki pants dream*, in his later years, plans were put into place to purchase a piece of land in Mayaro. Unfortunately, his dream of pulling seine with a net full of fish never materialised. This dream vanished without warning, without any notice whatsoever. You see, my father never made it to what life defines as "retirement age". He passed away at age fifty-six. At his funeral, as his coffin was being rolled out of the church, I heard the wailing cry of a mourner – *there goes another son of the Mayaro soil!* It was then that the stark reality hit me. My father was a country boy.

Chapter 3

From 121 Emerald Drive to a Revolution

Fond memories

In the year 1962, my father's parents moved from Panka Street to their new three bedroom single flat house situated at No. 121 Emerald Drive, Diamond Vale. Cradled in a valley on the northern range of Trinidad, Diamond Vale is a community which falls within the Diego Martin Region. The houses in Diamond Vale were built by the government in the late fifties for low-income families under the administration of Dr Eric Williams, the first Prime Minister of Trinidad and Tobago.

In the sixties, all the houses looked the same – one-story residences with a fresh coat of a sombre paint colour and a flat roof. This coupled with the number of roads, junctions and football parks made Diamond Vale feel like a labyrinth of a neighbourhood. Although today, the physical structure of most homes has changed, Diamond Vale can still be seen as an enormous maze to persons who are unfamiliar with the area. Nowadays the cost of homes in Diamond Vale has escalated quite drastically. Many years ago, Dad Otto told my father that he purchased the home in Diamond Vale for 12,000 TT dollars. Dad Otto added, with a bit of regret, that if he had known the value of the home would have risen so sharply, he would have purchased two homes in Diamond Vale in 1962. In reply, my father reminded him that back then, 12,000 TT dollars was already a large sum and that my grandfather could not have afforded to purchase two homes at that price.

The move from St. James to Diamond Vale, may have been a matter of economics and space. The Diamond Vale property was a more attractive investment for my father's parents at that time. Diamond Vale was not far from Port of Spain and the neighbourhood was a decent place to raise six young children. Added to that, my grandparents purchased a corner house which made their property one of the larger ones on the street. As first-time owners, the Diamond Vale property was probably one of the best investments that my grandparents ever made.

121 Emerald Drive was not just a corner spot; rather it was a home away from home. It was a home where the Sobion and Frontin family met every Christmas and Boxing Day to exchange gifts, share a meal and discuss matters which took place during the year and reflect upon what the future would hold. Outside my own immediate family home, 121 Emerald Drive was a second home. It was a home where my siblings and I, could freely enter and my grandparents would welcome and greet us with warm and open arms. Even though my memories of 121 Emerald Drive go back many years, these memories still remain very vivid. My impressions of the early days will forever be within me. That is all I have about 121 Emerald Drive- *Fond memories.*

Fond memories. Like when my parents would take us to visit my grandparents at least once a week. On most occasions, this visit would take place on a Sunday after Church. During those Sunday afternoon visits, my mother would talk to my grandmother Clerine about the Church message and the sermon delivered by the Parish priest. On one occasion, my mother told her that during the mass, when the Priest proclaimed; *"The Lord be With You"* I heartily replied *"And also With You,"* then stretched my hands high to the church's ceiling in praise of God. My grandmother chuckled with delight when she heard this.

Whilst my grandmother was vocal in the household, there were times when she would be amazingly quiet. These were the times when she would sit on her rocking chair while concentrating on a board upon her lap which supported a deck of cards. I would watch my grandmother intensely as she focussed on these cards which lay upon that board. I observed keenly the movement of her eyes as they roamed the length and breadth of that board until with one flowing motion, her sturdy hand flipped over a card. Granny remained in deep thought, entirely absorbed in the one-man card game, not saying a word and not even noticing her silent spectator. Sometimes I would try and guess whether she won or lost a game. It was difficult to guess correctly, because after a game was over and she reshuffled her deck of cards, her face remained nonchalant, displaying no expression on the game's outcome. The name of the game she played was called '*Patience*'. As an inquisitive youngster, I remember asking my father why my grandmother played this card game by herself. He quipped – *Because she is patient*. My father was so full of witticism, yet graceful in his remarks. Years later, I understood the pun, his quirky sense of humour and the ease of his temperament.

My grandmother also used to pick these green cherries, which she called c*erise* (which I later learnt was the French word for *cherries)*, from her tree. She would then make a deliciously filled bottle of cherry jam – which she called *cerise jam*. Bottles of this jam with sweet cherries were shared and enjoyed by her children and grandchildren. It seemed like my family was known to prepare these delightful delicacies. Like Tanty Dora, who was famous for her homemade coconut fudge and sugar cakes. The knowledge of this *country cuisine* was handed down to my father's sister Paula who now makes an equally delicious coconut fudge. Aunty Paula's fudge was even served as a dessert at my own wedding.

I would never forget when my father once told me that his mother was the most intelligent woman he had ever met. He said that you could have never deceived her or taken advantage of her kindness. He used the example of the occasions when he and his siblings borrowed money from her. Hoping that over the years she would forget and forgive her debtors, one day she produced a copybook with a list of persons and the exact amount of money owed by each of them. When this book was produced, everyone was surprised and had to scramble for pennies to repay their debts.

In the Sobion family there were the three boys – Dad Otto, Lennox and my father. The boys were outnumbered by the girls – who included, my father's mother and his four sisters. As a youngster, I observed the three Sobion boys carefully. If one were to meet them for the first time on the patio of 121 Emerald Drive, one would think they were best friends who were all outspoken and not afraid to frankly put forward their views.

At Emerald Drive, the boys would often argue about politics or some other national issue over a round of drinks. The outcome of the debate would take various shapes and forms such as an agreement, a disagreement, an agreement to disagree or an adjournment of the debate altogether. Sometimes, my father's cousin Gerry Frontin would take part in this family debate. On Christmas Day, these arguments took a whole different dimension. It would be a good-humoured shouting affair, with the 'girls' also expressing their points of view. If a consensus was emerging, Lennox was the only one to disagree with it.

Poor Lennox! He would always end up in the sole minority defending his arguments. Dad Otto would giggle his trademark giggle at Lennox's arguments which seemed untenable. To obtain my father's attention, Lennox would repeat *"Skeef.... Skeef...listen to me nah."* My father would continue talking. Despite the din, the Emerald Drive disputes were not 'disputes' in the true sense of the word, but rather an avenue for the entire family to bond.

Another interesting fact was that my father would habitually refer to his father as *'Old Man'.* When I first heard this phrase of *'Old Man'* I wondered why my father would use such a term. Was my grandfather really that old? Later I realised that the term *Old Man* was an informal way of referring to someone's father. Moreover, the tone in which my father said *'Old Man'* made me feel that it was a title which carried with it a great respect and deep admiration. It made me understand that Dad Otto was the man who my father wanted to become.

121 Emerald Drive was also a private family school where my brother Jules, our cousin Darryl Frontin and I would do our homework under the supervision of Paula. It was a place where, the next generation of the Sobion family would play, run on the lush lawn, eat lunch and even sleep overnight when the circumstances warranted. Up to this day, there is still a wooden cupboard in one of the rooms which still bears pencil markings of our individual heights when we were little children. These pencil markings have withstood the test of time and looking down at them, my soul has been transported

to those fond memories of the past. Fond memories are memories which cannot be erased and which will always stay with you no matter how old you are or where your weary feet may carry you. These memories often travel with you in the back of your head and at the spur of the moment, when you least expect it would flash in front of your eyes like the speed of lightning.

Another fond memory of 121 Emerald Drive occurred in the late 1980s, a time when no mobile phones existed – at least in Trinidad. My father was at our home in Dorrington Gardens. He called his parents' house on Emerald Drive using a rotary dial telephone. His mother Clerine answers. I could hear her voice on the next line. From my memory, the conversation went something like this:

Keith – Hello Mom, I'm outside using a telephone in my car. Come outside ….

Clerine – Hello….Keith…..is that you??

Keith – Yes it's me. Come outside, I'm right here.

Clerine – You are? …..ok …..(Clerine shouts before putting down the receiver) Everyone Keith is outside….He is calling from his car!

My father's mother and his sisters scampered outside. They searched for Keith, his car and his brand new car phone. They found nothing but silence and a serene street. It was the first of April. My father successfully played an *April Fools' Day* prank on his family at 121 Emerald Drive. It was a prank that they would never forget.

When my father completed college in 1969, he was still living in 121 Emerald Drive. He decided to take one year off to get some work experience and to save to pursue his law studies at the University of the West Indies. I have often wondered what fuelled my father's passion to study law. Maybe it was his liking for classical studies – such as literature, languages, philosophy and history? (He always told me, for some reason, that if you want to study law you should study history). Neither his mother nor father was a lawyer. Maybe he needed to carve a rock out for himself? To be a leader for a cause and to fight for equal rights and justice? It must not be forgotten that in the 1960s and early 1970s this noble profession, which they call the law, was fashioned by Englishmen in England. Maybe he thought it was time for West Indians to shape their own jurisprudence.

Keith's siblings provided some further food for thought on this matter. His sister Teresa felt that Keith's timing to study law was ripe. The Law Faculty at the University of the West Indies was about to open for the very first time in 1970. Besides this, Keith was also argumentative. So it came as no surprise to the family that he wanted to be enrolled in the Law Faculty. Lennox on the other hand offered a different twist. Keith acquired an interest in the law after continuously watching the American legal drama series *Perry Mason*.

To commence his studies, my father had to work and save. He came up with a master plan because he realised that the joint salary of his parents was insufficient to see him through his five years of law studies. He took it upon himself to send out random applications to various companies. Out of all these applications, it was the Royal Bank of Canada at Independence Square, Port of Spain that called him for an interview. He had nothing to lose and much to gain. As 'bold as a lion' and with his nappy afro and beard he went to that interview. The next thing he knew he was the new teller of the Royal Bank of Canada (RBC); a position which not only made him but also his parents proud.

For a young black man profiling an afro and a beard to get a job working in a predominantly white financial institution in 1969 in Trinidad, was like Barack Obama winning the US Presidential election in 2008. My father would tell us that he was probably among the first group of coloured folk who worked at RBC in Trinidad. Yet, despite his colour and his seemingly unconventional approach to a white hierarchal system, he appeared to be well-liked by all levels of staff at the Bank. After spending one year at RBC, my father was able to save a decent sum of money to fulfil his dream – to enrol himself in the Faculty of Law at the University of the West Indies (UWI), St. Augustine Campus. The year was now 1970.

The Revolution begins

In 1970, there was a lot more on my father's mind than attending constitutional law lectures. At that precise moment, his eyes were keenly following the force of socio-political change which was sweeping throughout Trinidad and Tobago. This force was known as the 'Black Power Revolution'. The Revolution was sparked by the manifestation of Black consciousness, a demand for Black economic power which was mainly controlled by the descendants of the white bourgeoisie who settled in Trinidad. My father soon found himself in an almost precarious position – a position, which if he wasn't cautious enough, would have made him lose sight of his immediate academic goals.

The truth is, that my father had a brief introduction to the Black Power movement during his stint at the Royal Bank of Canada. His awareness of the Movement became further refined during his first year on campus in St. Augustine. At UWI, he wasted no time and he soon became a member of a group which published the campus' newsletter. On campus, he was also actively involved in the organisation of meetings, discussions, rallies and demonstrations relating to the Black Power Revolution. As the months went by, less and less time was spent in the Law Faculty class rooms and more time was spent at the Student's Union Guild building, discussing the topic of the Revolution. He soon realised that UWI was not only a place to experience higher learning, but a place where one came to grips with what was actively taking place within the society. What was actively taking place was this: in February 1969, one year before my father entered the gates of UWI, the National Joint Action Committee (NJAC), a Nationalist political party was formed. Not by coincidence, NJAC was formed in the hallways of the Guild of Undergraduates at the St. Augustine Campus. Under the leadership of Geddes Granger, who later adopted the name Makandal Daaga, NJAC and the Black Power Revolution appeared as a serious challenge to the authority of Prime Minister Eric Williams.[4] During this period, a large number of disenchanted sectors of the society, students from Campus and various trade union interests took to the streets protesting for better social conditions. There were several mass mobilizations and demonstrations in Port

---

[4] For more on the NJAC and its role in the Black Power Revolution, one can visit the website at: http://www.njactt.org.

of Spain and as the protest movement gathered momentum, the ruling People's National Movement (PNM) and its middle-class began to fear for the worst.[5] Even the police began to employ tear gas tactics, horses and gunpowder to quell the demonstrations. On 6th April 1970 a protester, Basil Davis, was shot and killed by the police outside the "University" of Woodford Square, Frederick Street. Dubbed a national hero by some, Davis' funeral attracted a very large following, estimated by one reporter to be between 20,000 to 30,000 persons. Mourners at the funeral wore the national colours: red and black. Davis' coffin was also draped with red and black flags and there was African drumming and chanting at the funeral.[6]

It didn't stop there. Ferdie Ferreira, a close confidante of Prime Minister Williams, was quoted as saying that Davis' funeral was the largest one he had ever seen and that the procession of persons with their "Castro berets" reminded him of Fidel Castro's triumphant return from the Sierra Mountains when he marched into Cuba after the overthrow of Fulgencio Batista. All these events fuelled the resignation of A.N.R. Robinson, then Member of Parliament (MP) for Tobago East, a strike by sugar workers and the eventual proclamation of a 'State of Emergency' on the 21st of April by Prime Minister Williams. All this took place during the first half of 1970, just before my father enrolled and entered into the St. Augustine Campus. In fact, my father was working with RBC located in the heart of downtown Port of Spain in the middle of all the mass protests.

---

[5] Selwyn Ryan *Eric Williams The myth and the man* (2009) at pg. 384.

[6] Victoria Pasley *The Black Power Movement in Trinidad: An Exploration of Gender and Cultural Changes and the Development of a Feminist Consciousness*, Journal of International Women's Studies, Issue 1 (2001).

There were a few stories that my father shared with us regarding his own intimate involvement in the Black Power Revolution. Like the time when all the coloured folk working at RBC agreed to wear dashikis or shirt jacks on the same day as a planned Black Power rally in Port of Spain. However, much to his chagrin, when he arrived to work on the day of the rally, he was the only person who donned a dashiki at the office. No one even wore a 'shirt-jack'. (In fact, my mother, who met my father in the Bank a few years later, also admitted to me that she never saw Dad wearing a shirt and tie while at duty at the Bank but rather shirt-jacks).

Then, there was another story, even perhaps a bit more disheartening and one that may have emotionally broken his warrior spirit. My father was taking part in a march, with scores of other persons on the outskirts of Port of Spain. When they arrived in the city, the masses were confronted by the Army which had instructions to shoot as soon as the order was given. A plan was hatched. The masses would march boldly towards the Army while interlocking their hands in an act of solidarity. They were sticking together, through thick or thin. As they moved, closer towards the enraged Army, my father felt a strange uncanny feeling. He looked to the right, then to the left. He realised that he was marching by himself. Luckily he made a singular retreat before a shot was fired.

Jawara Mobota, a dear friend of my father from the Law Faculty, was able to rekindle that fire by giving a brighter perspective regarding Dad's philosophy behind the Revolution. Born Keith Gordon Adams, Jawara joined the NJAC during the 1970s. Jawara accredited my father to the expansion of his own *black consciousness*. Jawara confirmed that my father had a direct interface with persons involved within the Movement.

In 1970, Jawara, my father and a few others were reading Walter Rodney's *'The Groundings with my Brothers'* and *'How Europe Underdeveloped Africa.'* Jawara was quick to point out that *Sobi* (as he so called him) had an intellectual clarity of the Black Power Movement. However as time passed, Jawara detected a shift in his perspective.

After my father graduated from Law School in 1975, Jawara noticed he stepped away from the Movement. Jawara was not clear as to why my father made that shift. Maybe it was the pressure placed on him by his family which had PNM ties. This may have been the reason, given the fact that it was in the interest of the PNM and the established forces to discredit the Movement. Jawara also thought that my father was disappointed with the superficiality in the way the people embraced the Movement. According to Jawara, my father always wanted to write his own story and had he so written it, he would have explained in detail why he distanced himself from the Movement.

His banking stint and the Black Power Revolution would have certainly influenced my father's Pan-African thinking. Although the philosophy behind the Revolution originated before he entered campus, his viewpoint on Nationalism and Black empowerment was sharpened by the time he enrolled to pursue his law degree at UWI in 1970. To put it simply, my father was not the author of the Revolution. He just happened to fall smack in the middle of the story. By so doing, he was able to read and analyse the plot from those who came before him, evaluate his own role and even set goals for a positive outcome. Even though the desired outcome may not have been ultimately what he wanted, I believe that he was excited to be a part of the process. Personally, I am happy his life did not end prematurely when he found himself marching alone towards a menacing army.

Once a revolutionary, always a revolutionary

The events and the upshots of the Black Power Revolution remained with my father for the rest of his life. The struggle remained within him, although I must admit that with maturity he became less of a rebel and more tactful. This is where his West Indian legal training came to the fore. He began to think in a more orderly fashion, for example how conflict management could be used as a tool for resolving disputes. So, even though the Revolution was still residing within him, what changed was the method in which the Revolution could be realised. Even my mother recognised this. He changed his revolutionary silver bracelet and later replaced it with a gold one. He replaced his shirt-jacks with a jacket and tie. The beard however was the last remaining relic of his revolutionary days. As my mother always said – she never knew my father without his beard.

Keith always wore a beard. These words often resonate in my mind. When I think of Revolutionaries, I always think of persons who fought for a cause and wore bushy tufts of hair on their face. The first names which immediately come to mind are Fidel Castro and Ernesto 'Che' Guevara. For me, my father was a Revolutionary and a Pan-Africanist. He was fighting for a just cause, not with arms and munitions as soldiers do, but rather with clarity of thought, humility and his intellectual prowess.

The revolutionary Keith at the Sobion family home at
121 Emerald Drive, Diamond Vale in the 1980s.

Given this background, I could now appreciate why my father
wanted to name me *Sekou* after Ahmed Sékou Touré, the first
President of the West African nation Guinea. Such admiration
was undoubtedly deeply rooted by his history, his views on
the Revolution and his vision for equality of the local black
folk. However, little did my father know, even after four years
of marriage, that my mother was a strong woman. She was
adamant that my first name be "Justin". In the end, my father
accepted that *Sekou* would be my middle name. Even the
parish priest who baptised me felt that *Sekou* was too much an
African name and not a Christian name. But it was too late. A
compromise had been struck. My name was already accepted.
I was to be called Justin Sekou Sobion.

Yet throughout his life, my father would still call me *Sekou, Sekou Touré*, or even simply *Touré*. He would use 'Justin' when he was being stern with me. So when he called me 'Justin' I knew in advance that I was doing, or about to do, something terribly wrong. Later on, my mother would also relent and call me *Sekou*. The only person outside of my mother and father who would call me *Sekou* was my father's brother – Lennox.

Yet, it was not only me who bore an African name. My father, through the suggestion by his sisters, wanted to name my younger brother Darien – *Olatunji*, which is of Yoruba origin. Although my parents did not initially agree on this name, my father and my mother would call Darien by the abbreviated version – *Tunji*.

My eldest brother Jules was never given an African name. How Jules' name came to being had more to do with my father's legal practice. Prior to Jules' birth, my father was doing some searches on a family Deed in Mayaro when he stumbled across the name 'Jules'. My father instantly fell in love with the name even though my mother found it a tad bit old-fashioned. It is interesting that Jules was also the name of the son of Alphonse Sovignon, the first direct line in our family tree who came to Trinidad from Martinique as slaves.[7]

---

[7] The name Jules was also found as a witness in a series of marriages which took place in Mayaro in 1899.
(Source: Trinidad and Tobago Ordinance No. 16-1904).

Chapter 4

Letters to Lenny

In August 1971, my father left his parent's home on Emerald Drive to continue his law degree at the UWI Cave Hill campus in Barbados. This may have been a bittersweet moment for his parents. Bitter, because he was the first of the siblings to leave the home in the pursuit of a higher education. Sweet, because they knew that he was following his dream: his passion to become a lawyer. The fact that there was a Revolution the preceding year and that Dad was somewhat involved also added to that sweetness. This created a window of opportunity for him to escape the current volatile environment in Trinidad and to re-focus on his objectives. Going to Barbados (or "Little England" as it is sometimes called), would have been a big event for the Sobion family. It was not just a 'hop and skip' over the islands. Such a trip, though short as it may have been by aeroplane, required a certain degree of physical and mental planning. My father's parents would have heavily packed his 'grip'[8] with an assortment of groceries and homemade delights such as 'sweet bread' and 'coconut fudge'. The irony was that he was not travelling to England to study law but rather to another West Indian island, where they would have maybe those same delicacies in addition to the sun, sand and cricket. In August 1971, my father's parents would have been extremely proud to see their son off to Barbados to continue his law studies. On

---

[8] A grip is an old-fashioned word for suitcase. The term "grip" is commonly used by older folk in the British West Indies.

that faithful day, my father's dreams and aspirations would have taken off with that airplane to Bridgetown.

Sometimes I wonder how life would have been for my father during his first few months living in Barbados. Besides his two-week stint in Martinique during his college days, it would have been the first time he would have been away from his home and his family for a protracted period. Fortunately, due to some of my father's hand-written letters from Barbados, I was able to extract a sense of how he felt. In all, we managed to find five letters written by my father between late 1971 and early 1973. Forty years later, there I was, reading line by line trying to decipher any hidden meaning or gather a faint hope of understanding his emotions. Interestingly, all these letters were addressed to my father's childhood friend Lenny who was living in Trinidad.

Lennard Jacobs, known simply as 'Lenny', hailed from Green Hill Village, Diego Martin. A former member of the Defence Force and my father's 'best man' at his wedding, Lenny was more than a trusted comrade. He was my father's 'brother'. They met in 1962 in Diego Martin while playing football together at Pearl Parkway in Diamond Vale. When Lenny joined the army, my father nicknamed him *Nam*, short for Viet Nam. This nickname was timely and clearly in reference to the ongoing Vietnam war.

In what appears to be his first letter from Barbados to Lenny in 1971, I could feel a sense of independence. I could also feel his excitement of his new environment jumping out of his words on the faded light blue paper. In order to demonstrate the personality of the individual, the local parlance, the emphasis, the original writing style and the sentence construction are preserved as I found it.

"Lenny Boy,

Is like I am alright. Today is Monday and classes started this morning. From Wednesday, since I reached it has been straight party and lime.[9] A. A [10] I forgot to tell you. We got a pad here and it's something else- ah mean is a straight case of your boy getting up on he own home cooking and you know ah real good at that."

Speaking of his introduction to the Barbados community and his fellow West Indians, he continues:

"Barbados is a real cool place (if you have any bread) to lime- up on campus they have people from all over the West Indies (even places like Tortuga which I ent know nothing about)."

At the conclusion of this letter, one can sense a remote feeling of homesickness kicking in or perhaps a general mood of concern for his family:

"Anyway, until I hear from you- if you pass my way tell them Hello....and you keep good. Right on. Tell everybody else I'm good.

Keith"

On 8th November 1971, my father wrote a second letter to Lenny. By this time he was living in Barbados for close to two

---

[9] "lime" is a common slang or a form of colloquialism originating from Trinidad and Tobago. It is equivalent to the phrase "hanging out" e.g. "hanging out with family and friends."

[10] "A.A" is used locally as a form of exclamation which usually depicts astonishment or surprise.

months. He seemed more settled – at least when it came to partying and going to fetes. He speaks about his law studies and how it is taking a drain on him. Yet despite this physical and mental exertion, he somehow manages to find a harmonious balance by having an active social life over the weekends. Again, he expresses his concern for his family and friends, the 'state of emergency', back home – caused by the Black Power Movement and even his comrades on the block.

Monday 8ᵗʰ November, 71

7:00 am

"Hello Bro,

I hope things are going well with you-I didn't know you were going on holidays so quickly. I thought it would have been somewhere around the end of this month or near X<u>mas</u>. I was saying that you are a real scamp-man to take holidays as soon as ah split. Jennifer told me that you got cut short though- (that's terrible). You wouldn't be able to get it until the <u>S of E</u> [11] finish? Probably 5 months-6 months?

I haven't been writing much these days- and I have only got a few letters. I heard from Lennox last week (early) and from Gerry K about Thursday or Friday. He's going alright- but he had to watch his ass with all this <u>Sedition</u> Bill etc.

Me- I've been trying at least I've been working hard as ass during these weeks. Boy the work never stops flowing in. Weekend- boy it does be real hectic. Every weekend is at least 2 and sometimes 3 fete. This weekend I couldn't take it, I went 1 ½ ….

---

[11] Shorthand for "State of Emergency".

Hope everybody is good at Home. Then all the Bros on the Block. What about Sr. Anne and Bro David- none of them ent split as yet? Keep in touch. I hear Arlene (and) Dawn mom gone. What about the chick? I am keeping cool- no big fuss. You do the same. Tell everybody Right on. Moving on.

Your brother, Keith"

In a letter, written on Friday 19th January 1973, my father shares with Lenny his life as a final year Law Faculty student on the Cave Hill campus.

Fri 19ʰ January, <u>Lunch Time</u>

"Bro Lenny,

I delayed writing you because things were going a bit of a drag the first few days I was here. I was trying to get myself into some work as well and thinking a little about myself and people and all that. Nothing much happened.

What about you? I am alright as usual but up to my neck in activities. We have a little group going and we are involved in some education classes with some fellas on the block. In addition we are working on a steelband scene...right now we are still trying to raise funds.

We doubt whether it will be really going before Carnival. Yes they have Carnival here but only on campus. I was supposed to be in charge of the Carnival Committee (CBD) but I couldn't make that with everything else that I'm doing. School work? Well that is coming along ½ way ½ way but I have some time to really get going."

The letter ended with the usual pleasantries and 'hellos' to his people back home in Trinidad.

"I think I'll push off now. I want to get something to eat and head back up. So tell everybody Home 'Hello' for me and everybody else. Keep yourself good- I'm doing the same. I'm supposed to write David and then I'll probably see about that later.

Be good.

Br. Keith

P.T.O.

1) *ah cyar[12] hear no blasted calypso in this barren place.*

2) *How de mas[13] shaping up?*

I gone."

After my father passed away we found these letters to Lenny in his personal belongings. More than forty years later, I asked Lenny two questions – if he remembered these letters and how come they ended up in my father's possession. In response to the first question, Lenny's answer was forthright – *of course* he remembered them. He added that whenever my father was planning a visit to Trinidad, my father would write to him and let him know the exact dates. As soon as Lenny received that letter he would put aside some cash from his salary to celebrate his return.

In response to the second, Lenny said that while my father was living in Jamaica he asked him to 'borrow' the letters as

---

[12] "Cyar" is a local dialect for "Cannot".

[13] "Mas" is short for Masquerader. In this context 'mas' refers to the annual Carnival parade that takes place in Trinidad and Tobago about forty days before Easter.

he wanted to re-read them. The second response was typical Keith. Reading over the letters that he had written to his childhood friend would have been a source of enjoyment for my father. Maybe he wanted to use these letters to relive his Cave Hill years or to perhaps write his own memoirs. Yes, my father always told me that he wanted to write.

Lenny was a faithful friend to my father although they did not see each other every day, especially during my father's latter years when he resided in Jamaica. Yet whenever they reunited, I saw the magic in their eyes as they greeted each other and I was amazed at how easily they were able to re-engage themselves in an affable conversation as if they were never physically apart.

Lenny's own words, my father's letters to him and their general interaction, sum up the type of friendship that they had. It was one based on trust and loyalty even when they had chosen different career paths and lived in different countries. This was a friendship beyond boundaries. A friendship between a military soldier and a lawyer.

Chapter 5

To become a Lawyer
UWI, Cave Hill, Barbados (1971- 1973)

Politricks, Damages and Family Law

In the Caribbean, the word *politics* is sometimes altered to reveal a double entendre – *politricks*. The first time I heard this ingenious construction of the word was when I moved to Kingston to live with my father in August 1997. This new word was repeated countless times by the Rastafarians and the higglers selling Guinness, Malta and cigarettes on the street-side. *Me nah mix up inna nuh politricks* – they would grumble. The coined term formed a part of the evolving language of the Jamaican grassroots who were fighting against a political system which failed to provide for them. Under this system, politicians told the masses what they wanted to hear when in reality it was far from the truth. *Politricks* was a term of art used to describe these politicians who duped the electorate to get into office and when they did, ignored the promises which they had previously made. As I grew older I understood that the terminology *politricks* had long trickled across the Caribbean islands and formed part of the regional lexicon. But the immediate bias towards politicians may have existed long before that. Aesop was accredited as saying: "We hang the petty thieves and appoint the great ones to public office."

When my father arrived in Barbados, there was a quest to prove wrong that concept of *politricks*. Surely there must have existed selfless politicians within the region. During the first week on campus, my father forged a friendship with a young Guyanese law student by the name of Mayo Robertson. Mayo remembered meeting Keith like it was yesterday. These were his words:

"I first met your father in 1971 in Barbados. It was at a cocktail reception which the University of the West Indies at Cave Hill hosted for students coming from the St. Augustine Campus, Mona Campus and from the University of Guyana. I remember it clear as day. I could see your father now. He had on these silver rimmed glasses. It was him and another fella called Lamy. Both of them came from Trinidad to study law in Barbados. They came up to me and introduced themselves. I remember shaking Lamy's hand first. Then after I shook your father's hand. When I told them I was from Guyana, your father immediately told me how much he liked my Prime Minister Forbes Burnham. And that was it. That's how we became friends. And this was like the first week in our first year on Cave Hill campus."

Mayo and my father spent hours on *Sherlock Hall,* the only student residence on-campus at the time, discussing the Guyanese Prime Minister Forbes Burnham, regional politics and the need for Caribbean integration. It was at *Sherlock Hall* that they agreed that Mayo would return to Guyana to join Burnham's party while my father would return to Trinidad and Tobago and join the PNM. That was what bonded them from the outset – regional politics. Caribbean integration was to start with Trinidad and Tobago and Guyana. One has to understand the depth of these conversations. In 1971, we had two, 20 year-old students talking passionately about Caribbean unification starting off on the South American continent and expanding northwards to Trinidad and Tobago and beyond to the other islands.

Apart from these enlightening political discussions, Mayo also noted how extremely diligent my father was. He remembers episodes of his own habit of sleeping late and missing all his classes. The night before the examination on *'Damages'*, Mayo approached my father with these words – *'Sobes I'm going to fail this exam'.*

My father looked at Mayo like he was stunned. Yet for Mayo it was a look of quiet confidence. My father then suggested that they select four topics to go through together. After the topics were chosen, my father took out his own notes and taught Mayo all he needed to know about *Damages* that night. Mayo could not believe it that when the exam was over he had received an 'A' grade.

Mayo expressed that this memory revealed two things. Firstly: my father's commitment to their friendship in that he could have forgotten about him and instead spent the night studying on his own. Secondly: that my father was an organised student. He further recalls that *Sobes* was his only friend from outside Guyana who came to visit him at home after he graduated. For this reason and others, Mayo thought my father was a remarkable man.

In fact, life is a cycle and 'what goes around comes back around'. This story bears a stark similarity with my own experience; and it was on familiar territory – Barbados.

I fast forward to the year 2000. I was in my small two-bedroom apartment situated in Wanstead Heights, studying for my family law exam that was coming up within the next few days. The topic I was studying was *'Fault-based divorce'*. For some reason, I had a mental block on the subject. All the material was in my possession. I just could not make sense about what was before

59

me. I did what the average 19 year-old would do as the hours ticked away without any results. I panicked. I telephoned my father in Jamaica, crying on line, telling him that I was not ready for the exam. He grew quiet for a short while before asking me what was the difficulty that I was having. When I told him, he started to explain the problem over the phone. Realising that his lecture over the phone was having a minimum impact, he said that he would fly in to Barbados to see me. He vowed to call me back in a *few minutes* so that he could first speak to his travel agent.

So said, so done. In a few minutes he did call me back. He would be arriving in Barbados the next day. He told me not to worry, because in the final year of the LLB Programme, the Faculty of Law tends to overload some courses which had the effect of making a student overwhelmed. He added "it was only natural to feel that way".

The next day, my father arrived at my apartment building. He explained that it was difficult to study everything and I should just focus on a few simple topics. The technique sounded similar. This was Mayo's story repeating itself some thirty years later. So he started with the family law concepts of 'fault-based divorce' and maintenance. Back then – he made it sound so simple. Just his mere presence in Barbados motivated me. I was not the only one whom he taught. In fact, the family law lesson was also extended to my friend and roommate Faye Finisterre and another good friend Kieron Bailey. All three of us were interested in what he had to say.

My father was like that. His mental alacrity was on point. He had the ability of easily captivating an audience and getting them deeply engrossed. And he did it in a very calm and collective manner. In fact, Faye confided in me, years later, that it was during this lesson, and over a few glasses of gin and tonic, my father managed to persuade her to write a paper on *fault-based divorce.*

Eventually, I did the exam and received a Grade B. I was grateful for this result because a couple days before I was thinking of not attending the exam. I was further grateful because my father took time off from his busy work schedule in Jamaica to ensure that I would succeed in just one law course. These are memories of the past. They were good times and actually made me the person who I am today.

The Mighty Threads and The Sags Man

For the two years in Barbados, my father shared an apartment in Stanmore Crescent, Black Rock; known as the 'Carlton Apartments,' [14] with three other students. They were Jawara (Mobota), Ken Sagar and Robin Rajkumar. Sharing an apartment brought about friendships which were shaped and formed by their own individualities. For instance, on campus, my father called Jawara *"Threads"* because he was always impeccably dressed. *Threads* is a name which stuck with Jawara and to understand the origin of the name, one had to be in my father's year-group.

Jawara, Sagar, Rajkumar and Sobi lived in close proximity to *Paradise Beach.* Every morning, they would get up from bed, take a swim, return to Black Rock and then get ready for classes.

---

[14] In his letters to Lenny, Keith's address was written as "Melbourne apartment #B, Stanmore Crescent, Black Rock, St. Michael, Barbados, West Indies."

One weekday, the four friends were on their way to *Paradise Beach* when they stumbled upon Professor Ralph Carnegie. In what would have been a slightly awkward moment, the professor was heading to teach one of their classes on campus, while the four were walking in the opposite direction to the beach. On passing them, with towels over their shoulders, Professor Carnegie muttered words under his breath to the effect that the four were in Barbados on holidays and not as students. This situation did not deter my father and his friends from having an enjoyable time on campus. During the first term of Law Faculty, every weekend an island would have a *fete*. Jawara recalled that by the second year, Trinidad and Tobago students hosted a beach party in Christ Church. Life could not have been sweeter for the four friends and budding lawyers.

Jawara remembers Sobi as a slender fella with 'bat ears' – an amusing yet most accurate description. Sobi also was smooth in the department of *picking up ladies* as sometimes his friends found out about a female companion way after the event. Then there were the calypsos. Apparently my father wrote songs for his friends but would never sing. He would, however, give them moral support and advice during the calypso competitions on campus. So the singing was left to Jawara and Sagar. Jawara laughed out loud when he told me that his name was *The Mighty Threads*. Sagar went by the sobriquet – *The Sags Man*. During one competition, *The Mighty Threads* was providing backing vocals to *The Sags Man*. Minutes before their performance, the four friends were having a drink backstage. Due to the prior consummation of beverages, which perhaps contributed to a temporary loss of memory, *The Sags Man* forgot his lines half way through his performance. When they were looking for my father, he was in the crowd laughing. So much for moral support!

The fact that my father wrote calypsos and would never sing them was not surprising to me. When I was seven years old, my father wrote my first calypso for me. I was attending Holy Name Preparatory School just across the road from the Queen's Park Savannah. I don't remember if I had volunteered to sing the calypso or if he had volunteered me. I still see vividly, the yellow page from his note pad with his handwriting of the chorus and verses. To me it did not take him long to write it. The name of the calypso was *Simple Calypso*. He gave me the melody. He told me how to sing it: like where to pitch my voice high and where to pitch my voice low. It was like a music class. *Simple Calypso* had its own philosophy behind it. My father said that the youths needed music which was not complex, but rather easy to connect with. Today, I still remember the chorus and the melody.

The chorus went like this:

"We need simple Calypso to jump up,

We need simple Calypso to free up,

We need simple Calypso I'm telling you,

So jump how you want, jump how you want.

Calypso for me and you!

Jump how you want, jump how you want.

Calypso for me and you!"

Simple Calypso was an instant hit. All my teachers and classmates at Holy Name Prep got up from their chairs while singing the chorus and dancing. Even I was impressed when I saw this scene from the stage. My calypso placed second and when my father heard about the result after school, he was impressed.

Building on this success, the following year my father wrote me another calypso. The theme of the calypso this time around was more solemn. It was not a message urging to *jump and wave*. Rather, it was a message of the youth taking initiative and leadership. Once again, I only remember the chorus.

"The youths of today (Oh Yeah),

The youths of today (Oh Yeah),

The youths of today – I say,

Must lead the way!"

Your mother working hard to send you to Law School

Every Friday after class, the four would shop for groceries at Carlton Supermarket in Black Rock. They would then each drink a *Banks* beer while they walked home with their groceries in hand. When the friends arrived home, they would sit down and talk about politics. It was like a *Panchayat*, – a meeting of the elders. As a consequence of these discussions, my father was able to persuade Jawara to become involved in the Black Power Movement back in Trinidad.

Sagar recalls playing hard but also studying hard. He further realised that *Sobi* could not afford to fail his law studies. Sagar came to this conclusion after he found out that my father's mother used to send him money every month. Before Sagar came to Barbados, he was privileged enough to have worked four years in the Magistrates' Court in Trinidad. Sagar had savings. He realised that Keith did not. The only source of his income was his mother's remittances. Although it did not occur often, when Sagar noticed that Keith was slacking off in his studies, he would pull him aside and remind him: *"Remember your mother working hard to send you money every month. Don't disappoint her."*

Whenever the money from his mother came late, my father would ask Sagar for a loan. When my father eventually received the money from his mother, he would repay Sagar. That was the way they lived. Sagar was older than Keith and he admitted that he viewed my father as his little brother; and the feeling was mutual. Many years later when I finally met Sagar, my father introduced him to me as – *my brother Ken*. My father was also the best man at Sagar's wedding and Sagar in turn was a groomsman in his. This was a friendship built on solid ground, way before I was even born.

Despite all the fetes, the 'liming' and in my father's case – the uncertainty of financial flows, my father and his friends always kept in mind their ultimate purpose in Barbados. They studied hard. The late nights with the books eventually paid off. By the latter part of 1973, my father returned to Trinidad with a LLB degree from the University of the West Indies.

Hugh Wooding Law School (1973-1975)

Guinea pigs in the system

Back in Trinidad, my father found an apartment in Curepe where he lived with his Guyanese friend Mayo. The apartment was a short distance from the Hugh Wooding Law School

(Hugh Wooding) on Gordon Street and on a daily basis he would commute to and fro by bicycle. It was at Hugh Wooding that my father would spend the next two years of his life receiving practical legal training.

When my father and his classmates graduated from Hugh Wooding in September 1975, they were the first legal graduates from the local institution. Together, with their counterparts from the Norman Manley Law School in Jamaica, these graduates were the first group of regionally trained lawyers.

Prior to 1975, if someone from the English-speaking Caribbean region wished to practise law, they had to be legally trained thousands of miles away in England. One would think that being the first Law School graduates in the Caribbean would come with a barrage of accolades. However the opposite was true. The hardships overshadowed the accolades which they received. In a sense for some, especially the older English-trained lawyers, the Hugh Wooding Law School was, to put it simply, an experiment.

Endell Thomas, a former policeman and a 1975 graduate, was quick to highlight that they were "guinea pigs in the system" and therefore treated as 'inferior' to those lawyers who had graduated from England. Years later, Endell Thomas became a household name for us the younger law students. While studying law at Cave Hill we came across the Privy Council case of *Thomas v The Attorney General*. The details of the case I would not go into here, however it is worthwhile to mention that it shaped the landscape of our Caribbean constitutional law jurisprudence. I was surprised, to say the least, that the same Endell Thomas we read about in the West Indian Law Reports studied law with my father.

Thomas first met my father in 1971 in Barbados. He was older than my father and that factor would have hindered their daily interaction. However two years later, Thomas, in his capacity as a representative of the Student Body at Hugh Wooding, recommended that my father attend a Law School meeting in Jamaica. Principal Aubrey Fraser had no difficulty accepting this recommendation and that was how my father first travelled to Jamaica. The second time my father travelled to Jamaica he did so as a Student Representative of the academic committee at the Law School. He attended the inauguration ceremony of the new building of the Norman Manley Law School which took place on 28th April 1975. The new building was inaugurated by Elizabeth II the Queen of England. It was in this new building that the first Jamaican graduates sat their Law School exams. Prior to that, the Law School was operating out of a temporary building.

There is a picture of my father, as a student, standing by the cornerstone plaque in front of the Law School in 1975. Two decades later, there is a similar picture with my father, with the same pose by the cornerstone. This time he was not a student, but rather, the Principal of the Law School. And this was deliberate. My father wanted to document his transition from being a law student to being the Head of an institution that was responsible for harnessing the legal skills of young Caribbean law practitioners.

While visiting Jamaica as a student, my father was able to revive a friendship with one Dennis Morrison. He was first introduced to Morrison while studying on campus in Barbados. Morrison recalls my father as being part of what was then known as the *"Trini Posse"* which also comprised other goodly gentlemen like Jawara Mobota, Ken Sagar, Kenneth Mckenzie, Gordon Lamming and Ronald Paris. My father had a great deal of respect for Morrison and I am certain the feeling was mutual.

They also happened to share a little bit of history together. My father topped the Law School class in Trinidad while Morrison topped the Law School class in Jamaica. Morrison came 'first' overall in the English speaking Caribbean region. My father came second. It was stated that what separated these two fine gentlemen was one point. But if you ever had an opportunity to meet any of the two individuals, you would never trace a sign of intellectual arrogance. They held no 'airs' or egos. I cannot help but repeat myself, but when I see Morrison, I see also my father.

I can only guess, but I believe that because my father topped the Law School in Trinidad, he was selected by his peers to deliver the Valedictorian speech at the first Hugh Wooding Law School graduating ceremony. This was 22nd October 1975; a day at which both of his parents and family would have been extremely elated. My father was about to begin his journey as a young West Indian lawyer.

Keith, as a student, at the inauguration ceremony of the new building of the Norman Manley Law School in Kingston, Jamaica, April 1975.

Chapter 6

Meeting my mother

Two years before my father graduated from Law School he met the woman who would eventually become his wife and my mother. Her name then was Judith Anne Marie Massy. From ever since I knew my father, he would affectionately refer to my mother by her maiden name *Massy*.

My mother's father was a gentleman called Knolly Massy. During my lifetime I met him about twice. The last occasion was at his home in Curepe where there were a number of chickens strutting through his yard. Knolly Massy was a fair, stocky gentleman with short curly grey hair. I was told that he had Spanish blood in him. Knolly never married my mother's mother – Lucina Connor.

By profession, Knolly was a policeman. Almost every time when we were on a family outing to Mayaro and we drove past the old dilapidated Sangre Grande police station situated on top of a hill, my father would reminisce about Knolly. The story was that Knolly was once driving his bicycle down the hill on his way to do patrol duty. Upon reaching midway of his descent, the brakes of his bicycle had malfunctioned. As a result, Knolly ended up crashing into the drain at the bottom of the hill. Whether he was seriously injured or not was never confirmed.

My mother and father met in 1973 at The Royal Bank of Canada on Independence Square, Port of Spain. Judith, twenty years old at the time, was a full time Audit Clerk with the

Bank. On the other hand, my father was *a little rebel* (according to my mother) who had just completed his law degree at UWI in Barbados. He was at the time engaged as a teller at the Bank for a couple months to earn some extra change before he started Law School at Hugh Wooding. In the words of my mother:

"I first met Keith in July 1973 when I was working in the Bank. The thing with Keith was that he was a super cool guy. He was 'cute' but still like a little rebel. That was one of the things which attracted me to him. He was a radical. He wasn't the ordinary guy wearing a shirt and tie. He always wore shirt-jacks and a thick silver bracelet on his hand. He also sported a beard. To my knowledge he was one of the first black men to work in the Bank in those times."

My mother instantly realised my father's Mayaro connection after he revealed that he was a *Sobion*. Their initial courting was met with some favour as Lucina, a pupil-teacher at the Mayaro Government School, was acquainted with Clerine Sobion who was also a teacher and seven years her senior. Thus, my parents' relationship was founded on a degree of familial association.

My mother noted that my father was 'bright' and 'such a gentleman'. *"Everyone in the Bank liked him, and he would spontaneously bring me flowers and chocolate at work"* – my mother recalled, quite flattered. Even her colleague Elphege Joseph would whisper in her ear - *I feel the guy who is the attorney likes you.*

In September that year, my father left the Bank to complete his law studies at Hugh Wooding. With my father's departure came a void in my mother's heart. Even though she never thought she would see him again, admittedly, she would think of him often. Shortly after, my mother also left the Bank to pursue her dream career as a flight attendant at the British West Indian Airways (BWIA also known as 'Bee-Wee'). This was the beginning of an exciting period for her and day by day, her mind wandered away from my father.

My mother's first flight was to New York City. It was the 1st February 1974. Prior to this, my mother had never left Trinidad nor travelled on a plane. As a result, her eagerness to experience *The Big Apple* and what it had to offer could not be contained.

From what she had heard, New York was a big city lined with golden streets. However, when my mother landed, she was somewhat disappointed. Indeed New York City was glamorous with all its lights and skyscrapers. But it was February, the heart of the winter. Brought up in the tropics, my mother did not fare well in the bitterly cold temperature. Further, if there were any golden streets to be found, they were covered by layers of soft, perfectly white snow.

My mother continued flying with Bee-Wee and travelling the world. In late 1974, she did another Port of Spain to New York flight. On her return to Trinidad she was exiting the arrival hall at the airport in Piarco with her pull-on luggage when she saw someone from the corner of her eyes waving, trying their best to get her attention. That person was my father and it was the last person in the world she had expected to see. At that time, my mother had not seen my father for an entire year.

What are you doing here? – she wondered out aloud. My father replied that he was at the airport meeting a family member. They chatted a bit and then my father asked my mother for her phone number. This was the second time that my father met my mother. Little did they know it would now be for a lifetime.

By late 1974 my parents were seeing each other on a daily basis. In fact, from the first six months after they met at the airport they were inseparable. For dates, they would go to the cinema to watch a movie. Other times, my father would take my mother to UWI fetes at Milner Hall. To her, Keith was a *party man*, a social butterfly. In the relationship, my mother was the more conservative one. Keith was the socialite, the extrovert, with all his friends huddling around him. Despite this, my father was always there for my mother and displayed to her love and affection. This was the aspect of the relationship that my mother genuinely loved.

An example of love and humility, which would be forever etched in my mother's mind, took place in early 1975. My father used to ride a bicycle from his home in Curepe to the Law School in St. Augustine. My mother also used to live in the Curepe area with her mother. When they went on their dates, my mother would drive her white *Mini* to meet Keith at his apartment. At the end of the night, she would drop my father home. This was however not the end of the night for Keith. He would then jump on his bicycle and follow her while she was driving back to her mother's house. Once my father saw that she was inside safely, he would make a U-turn with his bicycle, and return to his apartment in the still of the night.

Marriage is something that they had spoken about early in the relationship. Before my father proposed to my mother, he first had a chat with Lucina. To put it simply, Lucina was totally opposed to the idea. Lucina thought that her young daughter, without a University degree like Keith, was not ready for marriage. My father then took my mother to his parent's home and told them about the marriage proposal. At the Sobions' home, Clerine was almost moved to tears and her voice trembled with emotion. Dad Otto, on the other hand was more serious, but he realised that the couple was in love. At the end, *the Sobions* at Diamond Vale gave their blessings for my parents to wed.

Round Two. My parents went back to speak to Lucina a second time. Eventually, Lucina yielded; although she did make life a little difficult for the young couple. There was an occasion when Lucina locked the couple out of the house one night when they came home late from a party.

My father proposed to my mother in April 1975 – four months after meeting each other at the airport. The engagement ring that they originally wanted to purchase was located at Maraj & Sons Jewellers at the corner of Frederick and Duke Street. Unfortunately that ring was too pricey. Eventually, they found another ring that suited their budget. My mother recalled that they were just so excited to get married that they had no care for the ostentatious part of the ceremony.

Originally the plan was to get married in one year – April 1976. As the weeks passed by, my parents realised that they wanted to become more independent and to live together under the same roof. For these reasons, they brought forward the date of the wedding to December 1975 – eight months after the original proposal and one year after officially courting. My grandmother, Lucina, often repeated this story about my father. She said that when my father initially asked her to marry her daughter, my father did not formally write her a letter seeking her permission (that was the tradition!). Appalled by this fragrant breach of marriage protocol, Lucina sternly asked my father the following question – *Young man what is your intention?* My father's reply was curt yet polite – *My intention is to marry Judith as soon as I graduate from Law School.* So said, so done. My father graduated from Hugh Wooding in October 1975 and married my mother in December that same year.

My parents wed

On 7th December 1975, two months out of Law School, my father married my mother. The wedding ceremony took place at St. Theresa's R.C. Church in Malick, Barataria. The reception was held at a Hall in the Police Barracks in St. James. *Uncle Boysie,* who was the Assistant Commissioner of Police, arranged the venue of the reception. *Uncle Boysie* was the nephew of my mother's great grandmother. He was a 'father figure' to my mother and was chosen to give her away at her wedding.

From all reports, the wedding was a grand affair. My father ordered a case of Johnnie Walker from Antigua since it was the cheapest country within the region to buy liquor in bulk. Everyone was dressed for the part. My father's sisters Teresa and Helen were bridesmaids. The best man for my father was Lenny (it was rumoured that Mayo was originally selected by my father to be his best man but my father changed his mind at the last minute when Lenny approached him with tears in his eyes). Pure merriment was in the air. The three hundred plus guests laughed at the speeches, danced at the music and drank off the Antiguan Johnnie Walker at the bar.

Wedding Bliss, Keith and Judith Sobion, 7 December 1975.

After the wedding, my parents flew to New York for their honeymoon. As a young married couple, my parents could not afford to stay in a hotel. As a result, they spent their time at the home of my mother's aunt, Mabel Massy, in Brooklyn. *The Trinidad Guardian* dated 22nd February 1976, under an image of the bride and the groom, had this to say about the wedding:

Honeymoon in New York

The St. Theresa's R.C. Church, Malick, Barataria was the scene of the recent marriage of Mr and Mrs Keith Sobion.

The bride, the former Miss Judith Massy, daughter of Mrs Lucina Connor-Massy of Bhadase Maraj Avenue, Curepe chose traditional white in a gown of French nylon richly appliquéd with pearl-centered daisies and cut on the Empire line, with slim-fitted sleeves.

She was given in marriage by her uncle, Assistant Commissioner Fitzgerald Henry.

The groom, a lawyer and the son of Mr and Mrs Otto Clerine Sobion, had Mr Lennard Jacobs as his best-man.

After the ceremony, at which the Rev. Fr. Wheelan officiated, a reception was held at the Lucy Beadon's Clinic, Police Barracks, St. James, after which the couple left by plane for their honeymoon in New York.

There are two wedding gifts, which have survived the test of time and which are older than my brothers and I. The first is a blue and white China porcelain set. The second is a Bible given to my parents by my father's first cousin Carl Frontin. The handwritten message on the first page of the Bible reads:

"Presented to
Judith and Keith
By Carl with a hope and
prayer that the Lord will
bless your marriage and
that this word will be a
source of comfort and guidance
Date: Sunday December 7, 1975"

There are two newlywed anecdotes that, for posterity sake, I would like to highlight. Prior to my father getting married, he was awarded a scholarship to pursue a Master's degree in Law in Australia. This scholarship opportunity in Australia arose after he topped his class at Hugh Wooding. It was said that Dr Aubrey Fraser was instrumental in facilitating this scholarship. My father however decided to defer his pursuits *Down Under*. The reasons for his deferral are unclear. One real possibility is that my father, a newly married man, was simply not ready to settle in a country far away from home. One thing that is certain is that the deferral ended up being a complete postponement of his scholarship opportunity in Australia.

But Australia was not the only option he failed to take up. In 1977, my father was exploring an option of pursuing a Masters in Law degree in England. This was the year that my brother Jules was born and there were preliminary discussions about leaving him behind in Trinidad in the care of my father's mother. My mother would not agree with leaving her young baby boy in Trinidad while they were both living in England. This plan was also swiftly aborted.

The second anecdote is somewhat unfortunate yet amusing in a sense. My parents' first vehicle was a Gold Ford Escort. One Friday night, my father was driving in the vicinity of the Croisee (a main junction in the town of San Juan) when his vehicle was involved in a collision with another vehicle. My father emerged from his vehicle to speak with the other driver to view the extent of the damage and to discuss who was liable. What my father failed to realise was that leaving his keys in the ignition in a bustling Croisee area was not a very wise choice. While my father was debating with the other gentleman about who was at fault, an unidentified intruder drove off in his idling car. Upon realising the loss, my father contacted the nearest police station to make a report. The police received a tip-off a couple days later and my parents were escorted by a single, slim, unarmed police officer (well he had a baton) to an isolated bushy area, many miles away from the scene of the accident. There they found the Ford Escort, at the side of the road, stripped beyond recognition. They were only able to positively identify the vehicle when they retrieved my mother's driver's licence lying on the ground of the frame of the car. My mother, knowing the tendency of my father to maintain a focussed argument without due care and attention of his surrounding environment, even late at night at the middle of the busy Croisee, was not too pleased. It is only now, many years after the story, she can laugh while she tells it.

Chapter 7

The Young Solicitor turned Barrister

History was created in 1975 when the first English-speaking West Indian trained lawyers produced by the Hugh Wooding Law School of Trinidad and Tobago and the Norman Manley Law School of Jamaica – graduated and entered into the noble profession. My father, and his peers, would have felt proud and humbled to be one of the first Law School graduates originating from within a regional institution. Despite this sense of pride, it was no smooth sailing by any means. These young West Indian trained lawyers soon realised that Law School was a mere breeze and in the real working world it was a different ball game. On 7th November 1975, my father was called to the local Bar to practise law. This must have been an exciting time for his mother Clerine, as she also celebrated her fifty-second birthday on that day. I can only imagine the emotions running high at the Hall of Justice. A mother on her birthday, witnessing her twenty-four year old son being sworn into the legal profession, must have been an unforgettable experience.

Presiding at the special sitting, was Chief Justice Hyatali and Puisne Judge, Justice Garvin Scott. My father's petition was filed by T.M. Milne and Co., the law firm in which he commenced his legal career. Selywn Richardson was the advocate who presented my father's petition before the court.

Picture taken at the ceremony of the first graduating class of the Hugh Wooding Law School in Trinidad in 1975. Here Keith is surrounded by his parents Clerine and Otto Sobion.

Noteworthy, is the fact that Richardson also hailed from Mayaro and was the older cousin of my father. Not only were Richardson and my father cousins – in later years they both served as Attorneys General of Trinidad and Tobago.

When my father was admitted to the Bar to practise law, there was no fusion within the legal profession. This meant that the new graduates had to decide whether they would pursue their legal careers as either barristers or solicitors. My father opted to become a solicitor, as financially this was the safer and more secure option. Being a barrister, especially the first English-speaking West Indian trained barrister, was too risky.

As a 'new kid on the block', there was no guarantee that one would receive legal briefs especially from the prestigious law firms owned by the highest echelons in the society. My father always held his friend Ken Sagar in high esteem because he was the only lad from the Hugh Wooding graduating class of 1975 who had opted to become a barrister. After being admitted, my father returned to the Law School as a part time Associate Tutor until around 1987. As Associate Tutor, one of the subjects he taught was the Law of Evidence (between 1980 and 1982). Some of the persons he taught were Miriam Samaru (currently the Principal of Hugh Wooding) and Kamla Persad-Bissessar, a former Prime Minister of Trinidad and Tobago.

But being the first barrister or solicitor from a regional institution was a difficult experience. All of their seniors in the legal profession were trained in England. Some seemed to cast doubts on the legal acumen of the 1975 Hugh Wooding graduates. These new generation of lawyers were called names such as *locally assembled*, or *knock down lawyers*. After graduating, they were immediately placed at a disadvantage and had to compete for a space in a competitive legal market – a market which perceived that anything which came from England was of a finer calibre. Given the history of West Indian legal education, it was such a distasteful nomenclature to say the least. Emile Ferdinand Q.C., a 1983 graduate and a well-respected lawyer from St. Kitts and Nevis said that he first heard of the expression *locally assembled* from my father. Ferdinand noted that it was the early graduates, the *Sobions*, the *Sagars*, the *Morrisons* and the *Thomases*, who made swift work in demolishing that pejorative phrase.

An old photo found in my family's archives. It has been suggested that this photo was taken in 1975 when Keith (centre) was admitted as a solicitor in Trinidad and Tobago and the other persons include: Justice Garvin Scott, Shaheed Hosein, Yolande Cumberbatch, Ken Sagar, Kenny Persad, and Chief Justice Isaac Hyatali.

My father's first full-time job out of Law School was as a solicitor with the law firm Milne and Company. It was a small family firm headed by Terrance Milne and was located in Port of Spain. In his four years at Milne and Company he practised civil law litigation before the High Court. How my father's time at Milne and Company came to an end is worth mentioning. One morning, he was "on his legs" making a legal submission before a Judge at the High Court. Present in the Court was Brian des Vignes, a Partner of the reputable law firm J.D. Sellier & Co. (*Sellier*). When Court was adjourned des Vignes, impressed by his submission, invited my father to lunch. My father accepted and few days later, he was sitting across a table having a meal with an influential Partner from a large law firm. In the words of des Vignes –

"I had a feeling that Keith was bright. While interacting with him, I realised that his personality was a good fit for our clients and the people in the firm."

Des Vignes proceeded to ask my father whether he was interested in joining *Sellier*. But des Vignes was taking a gamble. He knew that any offer made to Keith had to be cleared by his other Partners, David Boucaud and Victor Stollmeyer – Victor being the firm's Senior Partner. Keith thanked des Vignes for the offer and said he would get back to him. The waiting game would commence; but it didn't last long.

A couple days later, Keith telephoned des Vignes signalling his interest in joining the firm. Des Vignes, by then having the full authorisation of his Partners, made a formal offer which included the remuneration package. If my father accepted, he could start working within one month. My father's reply was that while he was pleased to work with the firm, under his contract with Milne, he needed to give the appropriate two-months' notice. Des Vignes agreed with this proposition and he even later spoke to Terrance Milne about the offer made to Keith. As an afterthought, des Vignes remembered that it was the simplest of things which attracted Keith to join *Sellier;* such as the fact that they were now setting up a law library with updated law reports.

My father joined as an Associate at *Sellier* in 1979. Under the terms and conditions of his new contract, he was to be made a Partner within two years of joining the firm. On 1st January 1981, at twenty-nine years of age, Keith was appointed a

Partner of the firm after being so invited by Victor Stollmeyer. Also joining as a Partner at the same time with my father was Dennis Gurley. Gurley, later in his career, was appointed Senior Counsel.

Humphrey Stollmeyer, a former Partner of *Sellier* and a retired Court of Appeal Judge, put his own spin as to how Keith joined the firm. Stollmeyer claimed that Keith bested him on an Order 14 (Summary Judgment) application. Given both perspectives, perhaps des Vignes was present at this Order 14 submission when he later recruited my father.

In any event, Stollmeyer handed over his office and filing cabinet, complete with litigation files, to Keith in the firm's Litigation Department. Stollmeyer then took up a new role in *Sellier's* Corporate Commercial Department. Upon his move, Stollmeyer kindly permitted his secretary, Linda Pereira-Joseph to type for Keith on a temporary basis until the firm found him a permanent one. According to Linda – my father was dedicated to undergoing thorough legal research. He loved winning an argument and he fought to the very end. On urgent *ex parte* matters, Linda recalled:

"Your father loved to do injunctions. It brought light to his eyes. Working through the night was fun although we had to rush like crazy."

Linda would work with Keith late evenings even though she was a secretary "on loan". But Linda was not only a secretary; she eventually became a dear friend of my father. So close a friend was she that when Darien was born, my father asked her to be his godmother. When Keith passed away, I remember speaking to Linda on the phone and hearing her sob. She sobbed not only because her friend passed away, but because he died on Valentine's Day, the same day as her birthday.

The roti and red solo case

Whenever I think about Humphrey Stollmeyer, I always remember the serendipitous encounter which took place between him and my father many moons ago. By that time Stollmeyer was a Judge of the High Court in Trinidad and my father the Principal of the Law School in Jamaica. On one of his spontaneous visits to Trinidad, my father found himself randomly roaming the corridors of the Hall of Justice. He opened the Civil Court door slightly ajar, peered in, and spotted his friend Justice Stollmeyer presiding. He then entered and quietly sat in the public gallery observing the trial from a distance. But Justice Stollmeyer was astute. He noticed my father in the gallery and wondered in his mind – *What in heaven's name is Keith doing in Trinidad and much less in my Court!* Yet as the professional that he was, the Judge showed no sign of emotions as he continued his trial. After ten minutes elapsed, my father scribbled down a note on a piece of paper and slipped it into the hands of the Judge's usher. Keith bowed before the Judge and left the Court to go about his daily business. My father's note, written in very flowery language, thanked the Judge for the opportunity to sit in his Court on "a very highly complex matter" involving *"a roti and a red Solo."* [15]

By the time Justice Stollmeyer received the note, Court was out of session and my father had already vanished from the Hall

---

[15] *A red Solo* refers to a red coloured soft drink produced by the Solo Beverage Company in Trinidad. A roti with a red Solo is widely perceived to be a perfect combination for a local meal.

of Justice. Of course what was at stake at the trial was much more than *'a roti and red Solo'*. This was just a simple case of my father being witty with his former colleague and friend without disturbing his Court.

The turn to advocacy

As in Milne and Company my father started off in *Sellier* as a solicitor. As a solicitor one had audience in Chamber Courts on the hearing of summonses. One however could not appear at trials or on the hearing of motions. Eventually, when the Legal Profession Act was passed in 1987, the process of *fusion* took place and solicitors were permitted to become *barristers* or *advocate attorneys* and appear at trials. Keith's transition from solicitor to barrister was explained to me by André des Vignes – his friend and the brother of Brian.

When André joined *Sellier's* Litigation department in 1979, just before *fusion*, the Litigation department comprised Keith, Gurley, André and a young female lawyer named Marcelle Ferdinand. After *fusion*, Keith and André decided to become barristers where they provided in-house advocacy services to the firm's clients being briefed by Gurley and Ferdinand. So the advocacy arm of *Sellier*, led by my father, came into being. This was the middle of 1987 and probably at a time when no other law firm had embraced the concept of internal advocates. The following year, another advocate attorney by the name of Frederick Gilkes joined the Advocacy Department.

André recalled my father as being an excellent advocate, who was very insightful in terms of the essence of what needed to be proved to succeed in a claim or a defence. Working alongside my father, André had the opportunity to see "his brilliance at work." As the years passed by, André believed that my father's career as an advocate was growing and that he was regarded as one of the sharpest juniors on the circuit. André and Keith continued to work together as junior advocates for Michael de la Bastide (who turned out to be my father's mentor), Selby Wooding and Russell Martineau. The work of the Advocacy Department included civil litigation, banking law, contract law, shipping and admiralty, commercial law and alternative dispute resolution. One case I recall my father being an advocate in (probably a pro bono case) while at *Sellier*, involved Lucina Connor, my maternal grandmother. It was a rather unfortunate case to say the least. My grandmother was standing at the side of the Southern Main road in Curepe waiting for a taxi to Port of Spain, when the wheel of a passing car suddenly ejected and crashed into her making her unconscious. My grandmother broke her left leg and it was a miracle that she was able to walk again. My father represented my grandmother in a claim for negligence brought against the driver and the insurance company. An out of court settlement was eventually reached in favour of my grandmother. I recalled that my father preferred the option of a reasonable out-of-court settlement as opposed to an unpredictable assessment of damages before a judge.

As much as my father was a sharp advocate, he was not taking care of his health. Rumours were that at the office he would drink, smoke cigarettes and seldom eat. On the latter I heard stories that my father would willingly give away his lunch, prepared with much devotion by our household helper Martha, to colleagues at the firm. Many years ago, when my father was still alive, Brian des Vignes confided in me that he was worried about my father's health. On that occasion Brian added that my father had a lot to contribute in terms of regional legal education and to that end he would have liked to see Keith live until he was seventy. This was a genuine concern coming from an esteemed friend and someone responsible for bringing my father into the folds of *Sellier.* At the time of this conversation with Brian, my father was living in Jamaica. Not too long later, I disclosed to my father what Brian told me. He was visibly upset. He dropped his head and peered at me over the rim of his glasses. From that angle I could still see his dark bulging eyes. My father replied:

"Why is Brian limiting my life to seventy years? What makes him think that I cannot live beyond seventy?"

The truth is that my father never attained the age of seventy. He died at fifty-six.

Throughout his life, my father would deny that he had a problem – drinking or health-wise. When his friends approached him on this subject, he would find ways to disagree with them and deftly wiggle out of the conversation. Sometimes, if a friend dared to raise it, he would put them on 'cold storage' until, by a stretch of his imagination, he thought they had forgotten. Perhaps this was why Brian had approached me. These were the early warning signs.

My father led the Advocacy department at *Sellier* for about four years. Within that time frame he served as a temporary Senator under the PNM. Shortly afterwards, on the 17th December 1991, my father retired from the Partnership, after being appointed Attorney General and Minister of Legal Affairs of the Republic of Trinidad and Tobago. André was disappointed, when my father decided to venture into politics. For him, Keith should have remained in the profession and continue to build his reputation as an Advocate until he was appointed Senior Counsel. André begged Keith to reconsider his decision to leave *Sellier* for a life of politics. Like others, André's greatest fear was that politics would destroy him. He explained:

"He (Keith) resisted my efforts to convince him that staying on as an Advocate was the sensible choice to make. He was bitten by the bug of altruism and was convinced that he and his party (PNM) could make a difference. He was very much involved in the formulation of the party's manifesto and in the period 1990-1991, he spent less and less time doing advocacy and more and more time preparing for elections. I was bitterly disappointed by his decision to leave the firm and I felt that we had lost a top-class Attorney who would have had a bright future as an Advocate. My personal view at the time was that he had made an unwise choice and I still hold that view."

Twelve years after my father left *Sellier* I entered through the firm's doors as an Associate Attorney in its Litigation Department. The truth is that I grew up in *Sellier*. As a little boy in 'short pants', I would often visit and spend time in my father's office. I knew all the lawyers, the staff, faces and names. The environment was nothing new to me. The only thing different was that now I was a little older with an oversized shirt, tie and slacks. During my tenure, I marvelled at the high degree of respect the firm's Partners and administrative staff had for my father. This respect in some way trickled down to me. I could not deny that my father's reputation was handed to me on a silver platter. I knew, from the very first day, that I had some big shoes to fill. My father would often tell us, as his children, that the only asset you have in this world is your good name. Such an adage was quite applicable to my early days as an Associate in *Sellier*.

I will use one example in which I was able to somewhat reap the benefits of my father's reputation during my time at *Sellier*. One afternoon, I went to the office of the then Senior Partner, David Boucaud, to chat about a probate matter we were working on together. In reality it ended up being about an hour long meeting where ten minutes was spent talking about the matter and the next fifty minutes about life and other things in general. In that ten minutes however, Boucaud did give me some sound advice on how I should approach the case. With that, I returned to my office. Little did I know that this was the last time I would speak to Boucaud. He sadly passed away a week later.

About a month after the funeral, Boucaud's wife paid me a visit at my office with a dark brown briefcase. She explained that she was clearing up her late husband's belongings and thought that she should give me his briefcase. She probably noticed the look of surprise on my face. After a slight pause, she continued. She said that her husband always spoke of the good relationship he had had with my father and myself as a young attorney and for that reason she was pleased to offer me the briefcase. I was most honoured to receive this gift, formerly owned by such a humble human being. I still have this briefcase today as a prized memory.

Chapter 8

My father – some personal reflections

"**K**eith was like a social butterfly fluttering up and down the place." These are the words of my mother and to a large extent they are true. Whilst my father was naturally bright, he also had an engaging personality. He balanced both work and his social life pretty well. When it came to entertaining or being entertained, he was an extrovert by nature. However, when it came to his work, he could easily transform into a cocoon, like a recluse. Anytime he was concentrating, reading or writing he would morph into his introverted world, not wanting to be disturbed by anyone or anything. In his introverted world was where he found his inner peace. My vision of him reading a book, his notes or newspapers on his patio in Kingston personifies this. There was one incident, which I recall, where his introverted and extroverted world almost came to a screeching clash.

It was in the early 1980s and my brother Darien was less than two years old. It was mid-morning and my father was on his way to work. He climbed into his motorcar and headed to his office at *Sellier*. He however had one stop along the way. This stop was *Veni Mangé* restaurant which was owned by his friends, the sisters – Roses Hezekiah and the TV personality Allyson Hennessy. Unknowing to him, a few minutes before he drove out of our Diego Martin driveway that morning, Darien crawled and hid in the back seat of his vehicle. Twenty minutes later, my father arrived at *Veni Mangé* on Lucknow Street, St. James. He exited the vehicle and locked it. (It is important to note that in those days there was no power lock and one had to manually turn the key in the door to lock the car). My father crossed the road and entered *Veni Mangé*. My little brother, still unnoticed and now locked in the car, started to sweat profusely. Recognising that my father had no intention of coming back anytime soon, he opened the door from the inside, by pulling up the nob, crossed the road and entered the restaurant. It was Roses who saw him first. She exclaimed – *"Keith, why is your son crossing the road???"* Barefooted and dressed in his pyjamas, my brother calmly walked into the restaurant, directly to my father's feet. Everyone was speechless. *"Darien....what are you doing here? And where is your mother?"* my father asked, quite confused and perturbed. *"She is at home. I came from the car. I wanted to go to work with you. What are you doing here?"* was my brother's reply. My father almost collapsed.

Meanwhile, at home my mother and Tanty Dora were frantically searching for my brother. When they finally received the news that my brother was with my father (in those days, there were no mobile phones), they were relieved but not pleased. My brother told my mother afterwards that he did not feel hot in the car because he shook the wings of his *He-man* bird toy for breeze. The question however was: what was my father doing at *Veni Mangé* just before he went to work? My father claimed that he had briefly stopped by, for the sisters to sign a document in relation to a matter in which he was acting on their behalf. However, it was quite possible that it was more than work that had been discussed and that he had also spent time socialising with Roses and Allyson. Nevertheless my mother wondered, and rightly so, how my father could have driven his vehicle from Diego Martin to St. James without noticing or hearing young

Darien in the back seat. This was a classic example in which Keith had got caught up in the middle of his two worlds – his daydreaming introverted work world together with his extroverted social side.

Besides my father's introverted and extroverted side, he also exhibited, what I would call, his *playful persona*. When we were young, he would come home from work and feign his fatigue by lying down on the bed in his full work attire. In order to obtain his attention, we would take off his shoes and socks. His eyes were always closed but the mischievous smile, which flashed across his face, suggested that he was playing a game with us. At night-time, he would tuck three of us in bed and tell us bedtime stories with much animation, changing his voice to suit the character he was portraying. I must admit that some of the stories were 'ghost stories' and I had dreadful nightmares when I fell asleep.

Impact Night Club

In the late 1970s, my father was not only practising law but also harnessing his entrepreneurial skills. He was one of the directors and part-owners of the *Impact Night Club* (Impact) located on Frederick Street, Port of Spain (close to the "University" of Woodford Square). Impact was situated on the top floor of a building owned by businessman William Munroe and it was one of the most popular discos in town. Besides my father, other persons who were affiliated with the club were Haydn Joseph, Terry Charles, Mark Superville, Michael Lawrence and Alvin Dorset. Journalist, Peter Ray Blood, a cousin of my mother, recalled that Keith hired him as the manager of Impact. To use the words of Blood:

"We hosted every major artiste to visit Trinidad, including KC and the Sunshine Band, Shalamar, Roberta Flack, Evelyn "Champagne" King, Jeffrey Osbourne and Kool & the Gang. Impact also promoted Blue Boy (later known as "Super Blue") at the start of his career in 1980".

Apparently Impact was so much the centre of attraction that even The Jackson Five, which included the afro-sporting Michael Jackson, made a whistle stop visit one Saturday morning. Blood recalled that Michael Jackson and his brothers did an interview with the Community Dateline Programme during their visit to Trinidad.

On Saturdays, Impact would open during the day to sell soup. The club always seemed to be jam-packed and it was claimed that after Harry Wayne Casey, lead vocalist from KC and the Sunshine Band visited one Saturday he declared – *"I've never seen anything like that"*.

From a managerial point of view, Blood thought that Impact was a gold mine and success story. I however questioned, what caused Impact's downfall. Perhaps it was the competition from other new and upcoming clubs such as *Rolls Royce* and *Palaver Place*. Blood felt that the club's overdraft was allowed to run too high. Blood remembered my father being *'damn vex'* when he saw the overdraft figure.

Despite what sounded like very promising beginnings, the glory of Impact came crashing to an unfortunate demise some four years later. While my father spoke about the good times he spent as a director of Impact, as a practicing lawyer he simply did not have the time to handle the day-to-day affairs of the club. Thanks to Peter Ray Blood, I got to fully understand that managing events were in my father's genes. These genes have been passed on to my brother Jules who now oversees a fortress of an empire in the entertainment world – *Caesar's Army.*

Let's talk about cricket

Even after his St. Mary's College days, my father continued to try his hand in cricket. In the early 1980s, he was a member of the *Slack Pack* cricket team which comprised a few of his friends. He was also a member of the *lawyers'* team which often fielded a side against the *doctors.* On all occasions, they played 'wind-ball' (tennis ball) cricket on the concrete pitches in Chaguaramas, not too far away from the location of the lands which were formerly occupied by the American army. My own impression as a young boy attending these matches, was that the level of competition was almost on par with the level of beer consumed at the side of the pitch. It was clear to me that these sporting encounters were just *fete matches* which brought together friends and members of the two professions together.

In the bowling department, Keith was a crafty spin bowler. He was a fair batsman and because he was so lanky and agile he was able to run between the wickets quite easily. However I witnessed an unfortunate incident while he was batting at Chaguaramas. On that occasion he was running frantically to the striker's end. While doing so, he slid his bat to the crease and tumbled over on the ground together with the wooden wicket. Whether an umpire at square leg would have judged him out, was the least of our concern. My father was in pain. Luckily for him, there were doctors present on the opposing team. After failing to get my father to straighten his hand, a makeshift sling was made. The end result was that he had broken his arm all in an effort to avoid being run out. As my father could not drive, his secretary Linda had to take my brothers and me home. I do not recall my father playing cricket after that incident. A few years later, my father endured the pain of a broken arm once more. This time, he had slipped and fallen in a bathroom in a hotel in St. Lucia.

Despite these incidents, my father continued to follow cricket. He loved watching both Test matches and 'One Day Internationals'. In those days watching and listening to cricket were almost synonymous. My father owned a radio, and when he could not attend a match at the Queen's Park Oval, he would quite happily sit in his armchair at home and listen to the commentary while watching the television on mute. Actually, some traditional cricket fans would even go further and be present at the Oval watching the cricket while at the same time listening to the commentary over a portable radio. Nowadays, there is live streaming of the game over the internet and portable radios have been replaced.

While watching *the gentleman's game*, Keith was pleasantly amused with the antics of Billy Bowden – the international umpire from New Zealand. These antics included Bowden's theatrical *'crooked finger of doom'* out signal and his *hop-jump* depicting the 'six runs' signal. I understood afterwards that Bowden's improvised signals may have been adopted because he suffered from rheumatoid arthritis. Nevertheless, I can surely say that his signals provided extra entertainment of the sport for my father.

Part of what fuelled Keith's passion for cricket was that he saw the sport as being intimately linked with West Indian regionalism. For him, cricket was the sporting arm to regional integration just as the Caribbean Court of Justice was the judicial arm. He loved Brian Charles Lara and used to refer to him by his other given name – *the Prince of Port of Spain.* He watched keenly, ball by ball, when Lara broke the highest individual Test score with 375 runs against England in 1994 and then ten years later with 400 'not out' against the same side. Keith would also spend time talking on the telephone with Duane Allen, one of his students from Jamaica, about Lara's records and whether he had made a wise decision to resign from international cricket.

One afternoon while he was in Trinidad, my father took me for a drive up Lady Chancellor Hill to visit the *Prince of Port of Spain.* Apparently, well so he told me, Lara had a signed West Indies cricket team jersey for him and that he had to urgently stop by the residence to collect it. Keith was ecstatic and smiling from ear to ear as we mounted the hill to Lara's residence. On arriving, my father descended from the vehicle and rang the bell at the gate. The electronic gate slowly opened and he proceeded to walk up the broad driveway. From a distance inside the vehicle, I saw him speaking to a gentleman (not Brian Lara). The gentleman handed him a package, Keith shook his hand and he then returned to the vehicle. Unfortunately the Prince was not in his castle. However, when Keith opened the package, therein lay the original West Indies team jersey signed by the Prince himself. His eyes literally lit up.

On examining the jersey myself, I noticed that it was a little damp. I pointed this out to my father and he replied that the gentleman informed him that Lara had just finished playing a One Day International at the Oval with it, hence the reason why it was so valuable. Keith chuckled. Whether this was in jest or not, my father valued the gift from Lara for the rest of his life. He believed in Brian Lara and was always proud to claim that he was a part of the Manning 1991-1995 Cabinet which decided to pay tribute to the Prince by naming the promenade in Port of Spain after him.

Strike Squad – the greatest national team of all time?

While my father did play some cricket after he left college, his post-college football career never got off the ground. The reality was that my father did not have the physique or make up of a true sportsman. He was slender, a bit awkward and he hardly ate. There was one time in my entire life that I saw my father gaining some muscles in his arms. That was when he decided to work out in the gym with his friends. After a couple months he stopped going to the gym and the little muscles he gained quickly flattened. That being said, my father was more of a fan of sports than an actual sportsman. I have fond memories of his friends, including Richard Camacho, Reggie Armour, Eric Etienne Jr. and Tony Cherry – coming home at Dorrington Gardens to visit him. These friends would also come home to watch the World Cup Final football games. In 1986, during the FIFA World Cup in Mexico it was comical to hear the Mexican commentator scream from the top of his lungs – *"Goooooooooooool,"* every time a ball went into the back of the net. Another recollection was the heated argument which ensued between him and his friends when Diego Maradona scored, what became famously known across the globe as the "Hand of God", against England.

In terms of World Cup, my father, like most Trinidadians, favoured the Brazilians and their style of play. On the local football scene, he was a loyal supporter of our *Strike Squad* team. Not surprisingly, on the 19th November 1989, he was one of the thousands of supporters who formed part of the 'Red Sea' at the Hasely Crawford Stadium. In this last football World Cup qualifier, Trinidad and Tobago needed just one point at home against the United States to qualify for the 1990 FIFA World Cup in Italy. Unfortunately, the local team went down 1-0 in front a full-to-capacity stadium and my father's dream of going to Italy came to a dead halt.

I was eleven then and I remember watching the match 'live' on television and seeing the tears rolling down the cheeks of both male and female *Strike Squad* supporters. My father came home a very disappointed man after the game. A short time after, he said that in hindsight it was probably better that the *Strike Squad* did not qualify for the World Cup that day, because of the massive pandemonium that would have erupted at the stadium by the unmanageable crowd. In his private living room area, my father had pinned up on his bookshelf an original *Strike Squad* team picture together with his whole ticket of the game. How he managed to preserve his ticket fully intact and not just the stub is unclear. The rumour was that outside the stadium, the crowd got so out of control that my father managed to push through the gates without security getting an opportunity to check his ticket. As we moved home many times since then, the picture and the ticket are now lost for eternity.

Many years later, the *Strike Squad* was rebranded as the *Soca Warriors*. One could argue that the only thing the *Soca Warriors* did, which the *Strike Squad* failed to do, was to qualify for a World Cup. In my father's mind, even though the *Soca Warriors* created history, the *Strike Squad* had more raw and natural talent than its successor. Dad was a fan of Dwight Yorke, the former captain and Manchester United striker and Russell Latapy (also known as *the Little Magician*). Coincidently, both players donned the national colours for the *Strike Squad* and the *Soca Warriors*.

The World Cup in Germany took place in the summer of 2006. It was the first time Trinidad and Tobago, led by their Dutch coach Leo Beenhakker, qualified for a World Cup Finals. That summer, my mother and I travelled to Germany to cheer on our national team. A day before we left, my father fell ill in Kingston and was admitted to hospital for a brief period. Although my father initially stated that it was too costly to travel to Germany and that he preferred to watch the World Cup games in the privacy of his home, I was, and still am, of the opinion that had it not been for his illness, he would have preferred to travel to Europe.

While my father was hospitalised, Darien was with him at all times. A couple days later he was released and he and Darien watched the games on television together. I must say that it was Darien who played a critical role in nursing my father back to health that summer. For me it was a wake-up call. Prior to Germany, two of my friends, both students of the Norman Manley Law School, constantly inquired on what they described as my father's failing health.[16] On all occasions I assured them that my father was *"alive and kicking"*. This assurance sounded so convincing, so much like the truth, that after repetition I started to even believe it myself.

Outside of cricket and football, my father keenly followed NBA basketball. The playing skills of Earvin *'Magic'* Johnson of the Los Angeles Lakers and Isaiah Thomas of the Detroit Pistons appealed to him. Then when Michael Jordan came on the

---

[16] The two friends identified are Kerry-Ann Mason from Jamaica and Elisa Montalvo from Belize.

scene for the Chicago Bulls, there was no turning back. My father would stay up late at night (we were not permitted to stay up late to watch television) to watch 'Air Jordan' and the Chicago Bulls play during the playoffs. Around midnight he would scribble on a piece of paper, the final score of the game and how many points Jordan had scored for the Chicago Bulls. This note was stuck on the refrigerator for us to see in the morning when we were getting ready for school. Those indeed were the good days.

The Art Collector

Shortly after the *Strike Squad* failed in their bid to make it to the World Cup, my father met Russell Latapy at *Veni Mangé*. Perhaps the meeting was pre-arranged because my father had on him my painted portrait of the *Strike Squad* star. He presented it to Latapy who signed behind the canvas – "Dear Justin, the sky is the limit – Russell Latapy #10". I remember my father bringing home the painting with the signature behind and I was extremely surprised. This encouraged me to continue painting. Today, this painting remains among our family's private collection.

Being around an art lover like Keith, it was not difficult to gravitate towards painting. As an avid art collector, Dad purchased so many paintings during his life that there came a time when he ran out of wall space. The end result was that some of his owned masterpieces were left on the floor, in storage or in his office at the Norman Manley Law School. One also could not speak about Keith and art and friendship without speaking about Eric Etienne Jr., simply known as Junior. To show how close the pair was, they were born in the same year and in the same month.[17] Junior and Keith first met at St. Mary's College in the 1960s. From college, they attended the Faculty of Law at Cave Hill and Hugh Wooding Law School. To illustrate their dedication to their scholarly years, both Keith and Junior were Class Valedictorians at the Hugh Wooding Law School graduation – Keith in 1975 and Junior in 1976. Friends for over forty years, Keith had a permanent seat at the Etienne's household for Sunday lunch.

Keith and Junior would regularly attend various art exhibitions across the country. Junior recalled times when a 'tug of war' competition and vying for art pieces between them were the order of the day. It was often a case where the highest bidder or the skilful persuader eventually walked away with the grand prize. The end result was that there were many art pieces belonging to my father which, had things been different, would have easily hung on the walls of Junior.

My father loved the works of Carlisle Harris, Leo Glasgow, Dermot Louison, Stacy Wells, Canute Caliste, Ras Dizzy and Earl Darius Etienne among others. With respect to Canute Caliste from Carriacou, Dad was pleasantly amused by the unorthodox spelling at the bottom of his paintings such as – "*Conut* Tree in Hillsborough," "The Jet *living* for London" and "The *Fimily* Wedding in Carriacou." In true Caribbean style my father and Junior made friends with artist Earl Darius Etienne from Dominica in the late 1980s. Earl together with two other Dominican artists came to Trinidad to host an exhibition at the *Aquarela Galleries* in Port of Spain. The story goes that when Earl arrived in Trinidad for the exhibition, his accommodation arrangements were not sorted out. Junior stepped in and offered

---

[17] Years later my father and I became the "joint godfathers" of Miles, the son of Junior and Bette Etienne.

Earl alternative accommodation at his own home. My father and Junior both attended this exhibition and this was how the friendship among the three started.

I will use an example as to how my father became close to Earl. My father struck a deal with Earl whereby the artist would paint him a masterpiece *free of charge* provided that he purchased the canvas and the acrylic paints. So one Saturday, my father carried me to Deltex Art shop to purchase the relevant material. True to his promise, Earl delivered his side of the bargain and the painting now adorns the wall of my mother's home. When my father passed on, I also found an unframed piece done by Earl folded up in a bedroom cupboard. The 1998 painting is entitled *The Sweetest* and portrays a bunch of bright yellow bananas enchantingly surrounded by several green figs using Earl's trademark flambeau style. There was one minor problem – the painting suffered severe structural damage having been stored away for so many years. While on a work trip to Dominica, I brought *The Sweetest* to Earl's home for it to be repaired. I had not seen him for over a decade and naturally we were both happy to see each other. Earl then asked about my father and when I informed him that he had passed on earlier in the year, he held his head in disbelief. He could not imagine that almost a year had elapsed and he had not received the news in his native Dominica.

While my father was alive, he purchased for and on behalf of the Norman Manley Law School, another painting from Earl. The painting portrayed a tree with silhouettes of human beings representing the leaves. My father secured this piece of art work to remind his students that all West Indian people came from the same root. This painting still hangs on the walls of the Norman Manley Law School to this day.

It was Latapy's endorsement and the visit to the Deltex Art shop with my father that aroused my interest in becoming an artist. In addition to this, visits to local art galleries like *Art Creators*, *The Gallery 1234* and even the home of Carlisle Harris had an impact.

In 1988, my father introduced me to art dealer and businessman Peter Kwang. Since then, Kwang has been a good friend and my art adviser. I say all this to make the point that had it not been for my father, I would not have been exposed and sensitised to the world of art. Reggie Armour, a long-standing family friend and an attorney-at-law always had this valuable piece of advice for me: '*Never let the law impede your creative talent as an artist*'. These words I still carry with me up to this day.

Then there was the piece of fatherly advice. Between the years 1992 to 1995 I had a brief hiatus in my painting. I failed to pick up a brush as I focussed all my energies on passing my Ordinary level examinations at St. Mary's College. After these exams, I told my father that I had forgotten how to paint. I would never forget his reply. He said that painting was like riding a bicycle, once you start you would never forget how to do it. I resumed painting in 1996.

J'ouvert morning and Players Inc.

Keith was a lover of Trinidad culture and Carnival. I still have memories of playing *Kiddies Carnival* with him in Port of Spain. He and my mom also played *mas* (the street parade) on Carnival Monday and Tuesday with the bands such as *Harts*, *Barbarossa* and *Poison*. They played *mas* every year and only stopped around the time when my father became a Minister.

Also at home, it was a family tradition to sit down in front of the television in the evening and watch the *Dimanche Gras* – the Kings and Queens of the Bands parade and the Calypso Monarch.

Party Time. Keith playing Kiddies Carnival in Port of Spain with his son Darien, in the early 1980s.

Keith was also a supporter of Lennox *Boogsie* Sharpe's Phase II Pan Groove. In the early years, my mother used to attend the steelpan finals competition *(Panorama)* in the Savannah with my father and his friends. She later admitted that she disliked *Panorama*. The noise of the steelpan was unbearable and the dust floating around the Savannah track affected her allergies.

There was one J'ouvert (opening of Carnival) morning experience which my father would never forget. At the time, he was the Principal of the Norman Manley Law School and happened to be in Trinidad for the Carnival celebrations (for some bizarre reason, Dad always managed to arrange a Law

School meeting a few days before or after Carnival). He was full of paint all over his body, dancing on the streets to the music, surrounded by my brother Jules and his friends. According to one of our female friends, Sian McIntosh:

"We were walking up the street close to Brooklyn bar (in Woodbrook). Out of nowhere these two guys dressed like crime scene investigators in white coats and allergy masks jumped Uncle Keith. I don't even know how they noticed he was wearing that gold bracelet because he was fully covered head to toe in paint. One of the guys hit Uncle Keith in the head from the back and he fell to the floor. Everyone just stood there. I ran after the man and I jumped kicked him in his back and he turned around, knife in hand and I froze....he just looked at me and ran away with the other guy...I think they were shocked I did anything being a girl....after that we just helped Uncle off the ground and went home."

Keith, though clearly shaken up, tried to stir up some humour out of the situation. He said, with his sheepish grin, that he could not believe that out of all the men who were around it was a woman who decided to fight for him. My mother had also warned my father prior to the incident to take off his gold bracelet before going to participate in the J'ouvert festivities. She thought that my father never fully recovered from the strike because he was always rubbing a slightly faded bruise behind his head. To this day, my mother believed it was the same mark caused by that incident on J'ouvert morning.

As he enjoyed mingling with the youth, Keith became popular among our friends. When Jules first displayed an inclination towards the promotion of fetes, he had the full support of both my parents. Around 1994, Jules, teamed up with Kwesi Hopkinson and organised a number of parties in backyards of homes and clubs at various locations in western Trinidad. These parties were promoted under the names *Players Inc.* and *Radioactive*, the latter being the sound system owned by Hopkinson. A few years later, Jules moved on and co-founded J-Cube Entertainment named after the first letter of the name of three friends - Jules, Jerome Brammer and Adrian 'Jah' Navarro. Today, Jules is a successful entrepreneur with his international brand *Caesar's Army* well established in the Caribbean and beyond.

During the *Players Inc.* days, my father often provided advice to the youngsters on how to manage their events. No doubt in providing such advice, my father drew from his past experiences as a part owner of the Impact Club. My father's interventions, though with a good heart, may not have been at all times tactful. It was clear in one instance that his involvement was made to protect Jules, Hopkinson and associates from the predators who were trying to take advantage of their inexperience in the entertainment business. This incident took place in the wee hours of the morning after a *Players Inc.* house party in Blue Range, Diego Martin. Apparently, and contrary to what was previously agreed, one of the disc jockeys, who was older than my brother and Hopkinson, wanted to be paid in cash right on the spot of the venue. A heated debate ensued. Recognising that the disc jockey's request and actions may have posed a security risk, my father decided to intervene. My father assured the disc jockey that he would be paid the following day. With that, my father quickly took control of all the cash that was collected at the door and transported it to our home in Flagstaff, St. James.

But the disc jockey and his men were persistent. Realising what my father did, they immediately drove from Diego Martin to my parents' home in Flagstaff. They knocked on the door, demanding the money. By this time it was around four in the morning. My father could not believe it! He calmly invited the disc jockey and his entourage inside the home. Jules and Hopkinson were also present. Once inside, a further demand was made for the cash. My father, very relaxed, placed the disc jockey's fee on the table and said – *"This is the cash."* Not even one second passed. My father then pulled out his licensed firearm from his pouch and also laid it on the table next to the cash. With a similar relaxed tone my father spoke again – *"And this is my gun. You choose."*

"Goodnight Mr Sobion, we're very sorry to disturb you," the disc jockey replied as he and his men exited our home. The issue was resolved there and then. The disc jockey was paid the following day.

My mother detested the fact that my father walked around with a firearm as she was paranoid that it would go off accidentally causing injury to herself and her children. The truth is that the only reason my father had a licensed firearm in the first place was because as a Minister, he was obliged to carry one. As a result, as soon as he was appointed a Minister, he would go off to the shooting range in Chaguaramas to practice. My mother however was not convinced. She felt that guns should only be used by qualified persons and that my father, despite his training, did not fall within this category. Today my mother would joke and say that she could not see my father using a gun to save his life. To be honest, besides the confrontation with the disc jockey after the *Radioactive* party, I seldom saw my father's firearm. He used to have it well hidden, in a leather pouch that he carried with him wherever he went. It is also true to say that my father never really liked guns. Having one was just a course of his duty. As Attorney General, he did receive death threats;

the seriousness of which I was not privy to. I used to observe his security detail in a room, huddling around each other, dismantling their firearms and inserting bullets. Knowing and respecting her fears, they would never perform these acts in front of my mother.

Wanderlust

Before politics, every July or August, my parents would take a ten-day holiday outside of Trinidad. As my mother was a flight attendant, they were both able to secure inexpensive tickets and they used this to their advantage when planning their final destinations.

For holidays they visited places such as Mexico, New Orleans, London, the Netherlands, Italy, Zurich, Hong Kong and Thailand. This ritual was their yearly honeymoon, a time to unwind away from their three infant children. While on holiday, we were placed in the care of our paternal grandparents and Uncle Lennox was designated to drive us to school every morning. Later on, another couple also travelled with my parents. They were family friends – Warren and Patricia Sookdar.

On a trip to New Orleans my father was head over heels with the French Quarters and a rustic hotel which was recommended by a taxi driver. The Sookdars and my mother were however not so impressed. The hotel had these rickety doors and broken jalousies – all of which appealed to my father. It was also said that the private pool consisted of only dry leaves and twigs. My mother and the Sookdars had to threaten, bully and drag my father out of his paradise. They never spent a night at the hotel however they would never forget how adamant Keith was to stay there. The four friends eventually had a fantastic time especially at Bourbon Street and Pat O'Brien's Restaurant and Bar. It was on the trip to Amsterdam in the Netherlands that Warren Sookdar noticed that Keith had a penchant for reading. Quite fascinatingly Warren observed that each day Keith would purchase a newspaper to read even though it was written entirely in Dutch – a language which Keith was not fluent in, nor familiar with.

As children, it seemed like the ten-days dragged on. We were always eager for our parents' return especially to receive the toys and gifts from their exotic vacations. One year, my parents brought home from London a post card with a black and white photo of Michael Jackson waving his shiny silver glove. Behind the card was a hand-written message by the King of Pop himself and to our surprise it was addressed to "Jules, Justin and Darien". My parents then boasted that they met the King of Pop on their trip and asked him for a personal message. A few years later we realised that Michael Jackson and my father had the same handwriting.

Apart from the honeymoon trips, we also had our fair share of travel. When Jules was about four years old, he travelled to Canada with Granny Clerine. After spending a month in Canada, the joke was that Jules returned to Trinidad asking for a *"soda"* in the *"refrigerator"* in a distinct Canadian accent. My father and mother would often repeat this memory with much laughter. Together as a family unit, we travelled also to Florida where we visited the Universal Studios, Disney Land, SeaWorld and Sawgrass Mills. In Florida we were, more often than not, accompanied by Lucina, our maternal grandmother.

From my memories of Sawgrass Mills – my father disliked shopping and spending endless hours shuffling the corridors of the mall. In fact there were very few items he would shop for and all of them were purchased within minutes. These were a good book, glasses (with his prescription fitted in less than an hour), a pair of shoes and jeans. Outside of work, my father rarely wore short pants but rather jeans. That was why his skinny legs were light in complexion when compared to the rest of his body. His legs were never exposed to the sun. Well so my mother used to say.

Our Caribbean holidays were quite memorable ones. I remember, quite fondly, our visit to Tobago with Dr David Toby and his family. It was there I enjoyed the most sumptuous homemade coconut ice cream as a child. In St. Lucia, my parents carried us to visit the Sulphur Springs in Soufrière and on a Jolly Roger cruise with André des Vignes' family. It was however the vacation in Grenada which stuck out in my mind. This family trip took place around 1985, shortly after the execution of their Prime Minister, Maurice Bishop. My parents rented a rustic cottage, a short distance away from the charming Grand Anse beach. We were to spend one week in Grenada but our holiday was cut short to three days. On the second night we were there, all five of us were huddled together in one big bed in the bedroom of the cottage. In the still of the night we were awakened by the shriek of my mother.

"Keiiiiiiiiiiithhhhhhhh someone is peeking through the door!"

Upon hearing my mother's cry, I noticed the bedroom door slightly ajar and a streak of yellow light emerging from behind the door coming into the bedroom. Keith dashed off the bed in a stupor and cautiously made his way outside the bedroom and into the living room. Trembling, one by one, we followed our father. My father, who was now on the balcony of the cottage then exclaimed – *"Look he is getting away!"* At that moment, I saw someone jump on a motorbike and speed away under the moonlight. On the balcony, my father quickly pointed out to us the fresh footprints on the dirt on the ground below as evidence that the intruder had jumped down from the balcony. On further examination of the cottage, we realised that the intruder may have been just a mere petty thief. Nothing substantial was missing, except a few beers in the fridge, cheese and slices of bread. Some fresh ash deposited in a nearby ashtray also suggested that the intruder had been smoking a cigarette or two. The police were called in and they interviewed both my father and mother. After this incident, my mother was in a state of shock. Although my father was willing to continue our stay in Grenada, my mother was not. The very next day we flew back to Trinidad.

In retrospect, my father may have strategically planned the Grenada holiday. More than twenty years later, we found a huge suitcase filled with newspaper clippings, books and journal articles about Maurice Bishop and the Grenada revolution. Darien found this to be particularly intriguing because based on the volume of literature, collected over all those years it appeared as if he had been planning to write a book about the former Prime Minister. This secret went to his grave because my father never discussed with anyone the possibility of writing a book on the revolution or about the mysterious suitcase.

The honeymoon holidays and our family vacations, like most other things, all came to an end when my father entered into politics.

Chapter 9

Political winds blowing through the air

Why politics?

It's the 11ᵗʰ February 1990. Nelson Mandela is free in South Africa after spending twenty-seven years in prison. My father's eyes are glued to the television where Mandela's release is being broadcasted live throughout the world. I am partly watching my father and the television. On the screen, there was a large gathering of people. Mandela pumps his fist in the air. My father imitates him. *Finally Mandela is Free!!!* My father was constantly observing the international politics in South Africa in the lead up to Mandela's release. However his interest in politics, especially domestic politics, existed long before Mandela's long walk to freedom.

How my father became actively involved in politics is a question that is often asked. My father refuted reports that his relatives Francis Prevatt and Selwyn Richardson inducted him into political life.[18] It is interesting, that both Prevatt and Richardson at one point in time served under the PNM. Both also hailed from Mayaro. When it comes to national politics, one cannot mention Keith and Mayaro in the same sentence without mentioning one Victor Campbell, a former MP for Ortoire/Mayaro. It was Campbell who singlehandedly introduced my father to the key players and constituents of Ortoire/Mayaro. Despite all this, it was the

---

[18] Taken from the 'Keith Sobion' Parliamentary Channel video.

student life in St. Mary's College coupled with the Black
Power Movement in the early 1970s that ignited my father's
interest in politics.

This was first manifested when he became involved in the
Tapia House movement (Tapia) in 1976, which was led by
economist Lloyd Best. At that time my parents were renting
a home on Sierra Leone Road, Diego Martin owned by
Theodore 'Teddy' Guerra, a well-respected criminal lawyer.
This home was used as a meeting point for members of
the Tapia in the lead up to the 1976 elections. During the
walkabouts in Diego Martin, many persons pledged their
support for Tapia. However, this support was not reflected
when the final ballot box was counted. In the Diego Martin
West and East constituencies, Tapia was the first runner-up
notwithstanding the fact that they received approximately
10% of the votes cast.[19] Nationwide, Tapia failed to win a seat
in the 1976 election – an election which was won by Dr Eric
William's PNM. My father was probably disillusioned by this
first political experience.

Then came 1986. My mother and father held several rounds
of family negotiations as to which political party to support.
Needless to say, they both agreed to disagree on which party to
vote for. In the end my father adopted a more reticent approach,
one that did not outwardly reveal where his political allegiance
lied. Sources close to my father suggested that because of his
involvement in the Black Power Movement, he empathised

---

[19] Tapia received 508 and 1029 votes in the Diego Martin West and East
constituencies respectively. Total votes casted in both constituencies were
7226 and 8122 respectively. The PNM candidates who were victorious in
Diego Martin were Hugh Francis and Norma Lewis *(Source: EBC Report on
the Elections to the House of Representatives 1976.)*

with the National Joint Action Committee (NJAC). My view is different. In 1986, he may have thrown his support behind the National Alliance for Reconstruction (NAR). I say this because I believe that at the time he would have been loyal to his cousin Selwyn Richardson, who subsequently became the MP for Ortoire/Mayaro and the Attorney General and Minister of Legal Affairs under the NAR. When all the dust was settled, it was the NAR that handsomely won the 1986 general elections by a landslide victory of 33-3 seats against the ruling PNM. This was the first time that the PNM lost a general election since 1956.

In 1986, the three Members of Parliament for the PNM comprised Muriel Donawa-McDavidson, Patrick Manning and Morris Marshall. From my own observances as a child, my father deeply admired Morris Marshall. Marshall's popularity among the grassroots in Trinidad and Tobago surely appealed to him. In addition to this, Marshall's ability to represent his constituency in the Parliament, in spite of his physical disability, also gained my father's respect. Marshall, who served as the Minister of Public Utilities and was a Cabinet colleague with my father, passed away in 1994.

From all indications, the earliest period in which my father first became officially attached to a political party was around 1988 when he was appointed as a temporary Senator for the PNM during the 3rd Republican Parliament. I have since tried to ascertain how he became actively involved and engaged with the PNM and party politics. On this, I decided to go directly to the political source – Mr Patrick Augustus Mervyn Manning.

A chat with a Prime Minister [20]

Patrick Manning was the person chiefly responsible for appointing my father as Attorney General (AG) and Minister of Legal Affairs. In fact, the former Prime Minister expressed to me that the first thing he did after the election results were declared in December 1991, was to call my father and inform him that he (Manning) intended to appoint him as his AG. Manning added that my father never knew such news was coming and that he was totally caught by surprise. In my opinion, Manning had a vision for the Caribbean region. A West Indian politician was once quoted as saying – *If there was a national disaster across the region, the first man out of the blocks was Patrick.*[21] This sentiment would have undoubtedly struck a chord with my father.

But had Manning known my father prior to 1991? Indeed he did. It was Manning who appointed Keith as a temporary Senator a few years earlier. On this, Manning said that during his days in Opposition, he was looking for *"good talent"* to join his next Cabinet. While searching, it was Manning's secretary who brought my father to his office and introduced him. Manning was forthright – prior to this introduction he did not know my father.

In Manning's own words –

"When I met him, I immediately realised that he had potential."

---

[20] The conversation was via telephone on 19 January 2013 at 12:35 am in Geneva, Switzerland. Manning sadly passed away on 2 July 2016.
[21] *My brother, I have always loved you, Ralph Gonsalves in shock*, 2 July 2016, Trinidad Express Newspapers.

When the news spread that my father was appointed as a temporary Senator for the PNM and had effectively joined the party, some of his friends were shocked. One of these friends was Jawara who remembercd that his greatest surprise was for Keith to run for the PNM. This surprise naturally came about because of my father's involvement in the Black Power Movement in the 1970s – a movement which *trained their guns* on Eric Williams and the PNM. But Jawara was not only shocked; he was disappointed. He gave the credit to my father as the person who expanded his consciousness of the Movement. Jawara's viewpoint was that Keith had the intellectual clarity of the Black Power Movement and that despite his tender years he wanted him to play a leadership role against the establishment. In effect, Jawara wanted my father to lead an anti-establishment campaign against colonial trappings and the formal systems that plagued the Trinidad and Tobago society.

Jawara used the example of when the young Law School graduates of 1975 tried to create a West Indian Graduate Association in order to advance the interests of the local graduates. This Association would have run parallel with the established Law Association of Trinidad and Tobago (LATT). A team, which included my father, was put together and the young lawyers tabled a proposal to Chief Justice Hyatali. Unfortunately, the West Indian Graduate Association never got off the ground. Jawara partly blamed my father for this, as he copped-out on the idea at the last minute. Given the fact that my father was a proud graduate from a regional institution, I had a bit of difficulty coming to terms as to why he would have withdrawn his support from this proposal. I also felt at a disadvantage because I never had the opportunity to discuss his sudden retraction with him. My father's decision to withdraw from the West Indian Graduate Association coincided with a shift in his perspective regarding the Black Power Movement – a shift which also took place in 1975. As noted by Jawara, Keith stepped away from the Movement after he graduated from Law School. These are the reasons why I do not believe that my father supported the NJAC in the 1986 elections.

Today, I still grapple with what caused my father to step away from the Black Power Movement. As previously mentioned, maybe he became disenchanted with the direction in which the Movement was going. It was felt that my father caved in to compromise as his family was rooted in the PNM and it was in the interest of the Party to discredit the Movement. On this point, Jawara recalled that *"Sobi"* never spoke much about the PNM hierarchy in his family.

In the labyrinth of the Supreme Court

On the evening of Friday 27ᵗʰ July 1990, my father attempted to express his own political views in a rather daring manner. I use the word *attempted* because his political message never reached the ears of the intended recipient. In retrospect, it was quite fortunate that his message never reached close enough to the recipient's ears, because if it had, the result may have cost him his life.

On that fateful day, my brothers and I were enjoying a game of *small goal* football with some childhood friends on the street just outside our home on Dorrington Gardens, Diego Martin. From the street, I saw my mother run outside the home frantically. She urged us to come inside immediately. *Abu Bakr and the Muslimeen take over* – she exclaimed at the top of her lungs.

We had no idea who Abu Bakr or the Muslimeen were. Yet the austere gaze on my mother's face made us realise that the situation was grave. We slowly and somewhat reluctantly withdrew ourselves from the game and headed home. Once inside, we were greeted by a television which lit up the already dark living room. On the TV, there was a live broadcast from the Trinidad and Tobago Television Company (TTT). The broadcast depicted a young, armed, slender man, wearing a *taqiyah* cap on his head. He declared that his group of men had overthrown the government and that the Prime Minister was being held hostage in the Parliament. He further advised everyone to keep calm and to stay indoors. I later found out that this man was Yasin Abu Bakr, the leader of the Jamaat al Muslimeen.

Despite the calm and collective words of Abu Bakr, my mother panicked. My father was not home and was attending the Law Association's annual wine and cheese function at the Hall of Justice located just opposite the Parliament (also called "the Red House"). This was the scene that was described to me that evening at the wine and cheese party by *Sellier's* attorney Marcelle Ferdinand:

Maria Wilson (an attorney), stood up on a chair and shouted 'Abu Bakr has taken over the country!' Some lawyers saw fire emanating from the Red House. Justice Carlton Best marshalled and escorted everyone together to the basement of the Supreme Court. Justice Best really took control of the situation in a very professional manner. One female lawyer even had to take off her shoes in order to make her way through the basement. Judges and lawyers exited the basement and came out of the building through Pembroke Street. All throughout the ordeal gunshots were heard firing. Keith, Brian (des Vignes) and some other gentlemen made sure all the women got into a car that took them back to J.D. Sellier on Abercromby Street. Some in the group had their cars parked on Pembroke Street but did not get a chance to retrieve them until after the coup. No one recalled how Keith, Brian and others got back to the office. Eventually they did.

Meanwhile back at Dorrington Gardens, my mother was still terrified. In 1990, mobile phones did not exist and she was completely unaware of what was transpiring in the underground labyrinth of the Supreme Court. After what seemed to be an eternity, we all breathed a sigh of relief when my father's car pulled up into the garage late that night. Inside my father kept on grumbling – *"I cannot believe what is happening!"*

My mother proceeded to lock all the doors of our home while my father kept peering nervously through the windows. The dusk soon turned to complete darkness. A neighbourhood dog howled in the distance. The atmosphere in our home became tense. At that moment, despite the calm and composed words of Abu Bakr, I realised how serious the situation was. My parents decided that we would all sleep together in the living room. Quickly we all sprang into action to construct a temporary bed on the floor comprising sheets and pillows. From that night onwards TTT aired a series of cartoons on the television. Gradually the making of the bed and the cartoons on the television diminished the tension at home. The mood would later erupt again, quite unexpectedly, when my father announced to all and sundry that he was going to pay a visit to Abu Bakr at the national television station.

An argument immediately ensued between my parents. For my mother, it was incomprehensible for my father, or anyone for that matter, to leave their home to seek the ear of the leader of the Muslimeen. Abu Bakr made it clear on the television – *everyone was to remain at home*. But my father was an adamant man, even stubborn at times. He claimed that he knew Abu Bakr and that he wanted to have a word with him with a view to persuade him to cease the armed insurrection. Even from the point of view of a ten-year-old child, my father's plan sounded highly ambitious. It was crystal clear from my father's reaction that evening that he had a deep conviction to prematurely and single-handedly end the armed insurrection. However, before embarking upon such a critical decision, my father ought to have weighed into balance the possibility of success. On the face of it, there was no evidence whatsoever which suggested that he had the sole power to convince Abu Bakr to withdraw his troops. Unless my father possessed a secret remedy, this would have been a futile or worse yet, a life threatening exercise. My poor mother was screaming, fighting and pulling my father away to prevent him from going through that door. My father overpowered her. He prevailed, jumped into his vehicle and sped off in the darkness of the night. My mother could not stop crying. I did not know if it was from the prior struggle, or the thought as to what would happen to my father in the end. My brothers and I tried to comfort her. It was heartbreaking to see my mother cry.

I may have drifted to sleep. From a distance I heard the noise of an engine climbing up into the garage. My father returned. He came back into the house with one of his sheepish grins. He explained that he arrived close to Maraval Road, where TTT was located, only to notice that the army and police blocked off the area. My father informed the armed forces that he wanted to speak to Abu Bakr to persuade him from carrying out the *coup d'état*. Of course, he was not taken seriously and was denied entry. Senator or not, the authorities advised my father to return home.

Almost thirty years later, I cannot help but think that my father placed himself at a serious risk that evening. Even though my father could be optimistic at times, this was a case of him stretching his optimism too far. What transpired during the attempted *coup d'état* was something, which I believe, changed my father's viewpoint on politics forever.

Fire in Port of Spain

The attempted *coup d'état* was a dark chapter in the history of Trinidad and Tobago. While being held hostage in the Parliament our Prime Minister A.N.R. Robinson was shot in his kneecap by the insurgents. It was reported that Robinson was shot after making a heroic appeal to troops outside the Parliament to *"attack with full force."* Robinson went on to survive the *coup d'état* and was a strong advocate for the Commission of Enquiry that investigated the circumstances that led to the insurrection.

After six days, the attempted *coup d'état* came to an end on 1st August 1990. This was the day Abu Bakr and his men surrendered to the national army. Ironically the first day of August was Emancipation Day, a day which commemorated freedom – the abolition of slavery in the British West Indies. One image which continues to float through my head was that of Jennifer Johnson, the Minister of Sport, walking out of Parliament with her right hand pressing on what looked like a handkerchief over her nose. It was thought that she applied the handkerchief in such a manner to mask the scent of dead bodies. Another image was that of Abu Bakr exiting the TTT building. He was obeying strict instructions that were belted over a megaphone by John Sandy, the First Battalion

Operations Officer of the Army. Abu Bakr dressed in white with a black skullcap on his head, walked like a robot as he exited the building. He dropped his weapon (what appeared to be an AK47) on the ground, put his arms to his head and then took a few steps backward. Afterwards, he was whisked away by the members of the Army. There was no real fanfare. That was my own recollection as to how the attempted *coup d'état* ended.

Thereafter, it was like an unspoken piece of advice. The nation was simply told to move on from this six-day nightmare. The curfew, and eventually a limited curfew remained intact for some weeks after the attempted *coup d'état*. This resulted in most of our July/August holidays being spent indoors where we watched cartoons and played videogames. A week or so later, my parents took us to Port of Spain to view the city, or what remained of it. We were not the only persons walking through the capital and despite the limited curfew in place, there were still many other curious onlookers roaming the streets. What I saw was horrific. I could not even recognise Port of Spain! On Charlotte Street, rows of buildings and galvanised roofs looked like burnt charcoal. In the remains of the devastation, smoke still rose like cooking pots which just came off the fire. Windows from businesses and shops were broken – a clear indication of the looting that took place during the six-day siege. In those days my father would share with us a story about a man looting a television and when he arrived home, the screen lighted up but it failed to work. The reason for this was that it was not a television that was looted but a microwave. Persons were pilfering whatever their eyes lay sight on, even objects they did not even know. The truth was that Port of Spain looked chaotic. What was once a relatively promising city was now reduced to nothing more than soot, smoke and ash. We then proceeded to walk towards the Red House on Abercromby Street. As we approached the Supreme Court a few meters away from the Red House, my father made an extraordinary find. At the corner of Abercromby and Knox Street, he unearthed a spent golden-coated bullet shell, which would have been used during the crossfire. I then realised that the very ground we were standing on, the space between the Supreme Court and the Red House, was the battlefield for power.

It was reported that some twenty-four persons died as a direct result of the attempted *coup d'état*.[22] For the purpose of this narrative, I would like to make mention of two of those persons who passed away during the insurrection. The first was special reserve police officer Solomon McLeod who was the sentry at the Police Headquarters at the time the building was bombed. McLeod was reported as being the first person to die during the attempted coup. Then there was Leo des Vignes the Member of Parliament (MP) for Diego Martin Central. Des Vignes was the only MP to lose his life as a result of the attempted coup.[23]

Shortly after des Vignes succumbed to his injuries, there was a by-election in the constituency of Diego Martin Central. It was rumoured that my father was looked upon as a possible candidate to run in that by-election, however this never transpired. In the end, Kenneth Valley (also called Ken Valley) was nominated as the PNM candidate and he successfully brought home the Diego Martin Central seat. The story goes that on the night of Valley's victory celebration, my father was so filled with jubilation that he embraced the new MP and

---

[22] Jada Loutoo *24 persons died in 1990 attempted coup*, Trinidad and Tobago Newsday, 22 May 2013.

[23] Trinidad and Tobago Parliament website: www.ttparliament.org.

gave him a golden hand bracelet as a gift. Little did Valley know that my mother, and not my father, was the true owner of the priceless bracelet. The next day when my mother found out about my father's generous display of affection, she went straight to Valley's wife in an attempt to have it returned. The bracelet was amicably returned on the grounds of being an innocent misunderstanding. There is an old Chinese proverb that is quite apt to this story – *"make no promises when you are seized by joy"*. Despite this awkward moment, my father and Valley remained very close friends. Both shared a mutual respect for each other; both had a dream for Caribbean integration. I am very pleased that I got to know Ken Valley through my father. Valley passed away three years after my father's demise. To date, we share a very amiable relationship with his son Sean. I wish to add that my father and Sean also shared similar relations.

To run for Ortoire/Mayaro

Just like the Black Power Movement in the 70s the 1990 attempted coup played a critical role in shaping my father's interest in national politics. In my view, 1990 was the breaking point as the events of that year solidified in my father's mind that he wanted to make an active contribution to the development of Trinidad and Tobago. But Keith must have known that he was going to contest a seat in the Parliament prior to July 1990. In the early part of March 1990, my father flew to Grenada to observe that country's general election. While in Grenada, he closely followed the campaign of politician Wellington R.L. Friday, the father-in-law of his friend Eric Etienne Jr. There, Friday contested the St. Patrick West constituency on behalf of the Grenada United Labour Party (GULP). It is a fact that

St. Patrick West is a rural district, somewhat like Ortoire/ Mayaro. It was for this reason that Keith wanted to witness how Friday ran his election campaign. Even though in the end, Friday lost his seat, the first-hand experience must have been invaluable to Keith. The details of this trip to Grenada therefore seem to suggest that as early as March 1990, my father *may* have had some knowledge that he was being seriously considered as the PNM candidate for Ortoire/Mayaro. It could also have meant that he had a significant interest in running for Ortoire/Mayaro. If this timeline is accurate, my father had more than a year and a half to prepare, mentally or otherwise, for the December 1991 general elections. My mother on the other hand, recalls that Keith was officially given the nod by the PNM screening Committee to run for Ortoire/Mayaro, some six to nine months before the 1991 general elections. One individual, who worked closely with my father during the December 1991 election, suggested that Keith was groomed for the Ortoire/Mayaro seat since 1990. This fact confirms in my head that my father's campaign would have started in earnest at least one year before December 1991.

My father's final decision to enter into party politics was not an easy one. Indeed my father had some challenges in convincing his immediate family. His sister Teresa recalls that the entire family was not comfortable with Keith entering into politics. The Senator position was thought to be a temporary stint and running for Ortoire/Mayaro was the furthest thing from the family's mind. My father's mother was certainly opposed to it. They had long arguments about his political involvement at the family home in Diamond Vale. Despite Ortoire/Mayaro being her birthplace, she was strongly against my father entering into politics as she felt that politicians in general had unsavoury reputations. She persuaded Keith to remain as a Partner at

J.D. Sellier & Co. One has to remember that Keith's mother was the one responsible for financing his legal education. I got to understand that while my father was in Cave Hill, his mother sent him $200 TTD (Trinidad and Tobago dollars) every month. This was estimated as being almost half of his mother's take home salary. My grandmother therefore did not raise a politician, but rather a lawyer. In brief, politics was not an option for Keith. My father argued that he had a role to play in the development of his parent's community and to a larger extent his country. Furthermore, he was of the view that being a lawyer would properly equip him as he embarked upon his political journey. This was a typical case where two stubborn mules were fighting against each other. In very rare circumstances, my father failed to listen to his mother's advice. In the end, and to the great dismay of my grandmother, my father decided to leave his legal career behind and enter into the uncertain realm of politics.

Ortoire/Mayaro was arguably the largest seat geographically in the December 1991 elections. It covered areas outside of Ortoire/Mayaro proper, such as Rio Claro, Indian Walk, Tableland, Princes Town, Barrackpore and Moruga. In fact, I remember as a little boy campaigning with my father in Princes Town that he would explain to us that one side of the road fell under the constituency of Princes Town, while the other side fell under Ortoire/Mayaro. But why Ortoire/Mayaro? Even though my father was born in Port of Spain, he was deeply rooted in Mayaro. He spent all his school holidays in Mayaro. Both his parents were born and bred in Mayaro. His mother was a *Frontin*, a popular family name in Mayaro. The fact that my father had family ties in Mayaro was a significant factor. A friend of my father called Oliver Alexander, who worked tirelessly with him during both election campaigns, described Mayaro people as very "clannish". Both *Sobion* and *Frontin* were Mayaro household names. Once voters understood this link in a surname, half of the battle was already won for my father – at least in Mayaro and environs. Alexander explained that the party wanted someone from Mayaro or at least someone with strong familial ties with the community. This, plus the fact that my father was a Partner in a prominent law firm in Port of Spain made him a natural choice for the PNM.

Such a strategy in choice was however not exclusive to the PNM. Both his contenders for the Ortoire/Mayaro seat hailed from Mayaro. Firstly there was Keith's older cousin, Selwyn Richardson, the NAR candidate, an attorney-at-law and the current MP at the time for the constituency. Then there was Christine Anderson also an attorney-at-law and the candidate for the United National Congress (UNC). It was a three-way fight for a seat with each candidate having a similar profession and a fairly equal *home-court* advantage.

The Ortoire/Mayaro campaign (1991)

I was not even a teenager, yet it was an exciting time to follow the campaign of my father in the 1991 Ortoire/Mayaro general election. There were many persons who I would say were my father's core team support members within the constituency. Over the period of time, I have forgotten some names and even faces. These are the names which immediately come to mind – Nizam Stephen Bassarath, Cecil Bessor, Marlene Henry, Roger Lewis, Victor Campbell, Matthew Pierre, Denzil Jemmott, Oliver Alexander, Amoy Mohammed, Junior Hackett, Umilta Saunders, Suresh Seecharan and Bunny Mahabirsingh. Had my father been alive, he would have supplied me with many more names and stories. Thus, I am fully cognisant of the fact that my list is incomplete.

At this point I would like to make mention of one team member. Nizam Stephen Bassarath was one who believed in my father.[24] The self-dubbed *Mayor of Palmyra* worked assiduously behind the scenes with my father in the Ortoire/Mayaro constituency. Due to the proximity of Palmyra to Princes Town, Bassarath was readily available and accessible. What I admired most about Bassarath was that he always kept in touch even after my father's defeat and exit out of politics. One thing I have learned is that – no matter who you are or what you did, no one really wants to associate themselves with a defeated politician. There is always a tendency to gravitate towards persons who are in government. Bassarath proved to be the exception to the rule. Even years after my father's four-year stint in politics he would still call him. Just to check in. Such telephone calls took place even when we lived in Jamaica. Bassarath was shocked to hear when my father passed away. But life is transient. Little did we know that a few years later Bassarath would also suddenly pass away.

The campaign trail was a rough one. Much ground had to be covered because geographically the constituency was quite a large one. While the *Sobion* and *Frontin* surname was popular in Mayaro, my father was *an unknown* in areas such as Rio Claro, Tableland and Moruga. Cecil Bessor, my father's campaign manager advised him that if he wanted to secure the Ortoire/Mayaro seat, he had to concentrate most of his energies in these three areas. Bessor lived in Mayaro and he had a better

---

[24] Nizam Stephen Bassarath, a faithful friend of my father, passed away in 2012.

understanding than my father of the political landscape of the entire constituency. My father realised this, and without hesitation he readily accepted his advice. Mayaro was the home base. It was the location where he had his main constituency office and where he met with his advisors. It was in Mayaro that all the strategising took place. Mayaro was the engine-room where all the walkabouts and the motorcades were planned. Nevertheless, my father knew, from early on, that a special focus had to be placed on what I call *the big three* – Rio Claro, Tableland and Moruga.

Early on in the campaign, my father set out to work in the areas of unfamiliar territory. One of his stops was Moruga which lies on the south central coast of Trinidad. Moruga is historically recognised as the arrival place of Columbus, who named the country *La Trinity* after spotting three mountains that became famously known as the Trinity Hills.[25] There was one exchange which he had with one resident in Moruga which I found to be quite interesting. Her name was Marlene and her family owned a bar in the village. It so happened that Bessor and Victor Campbell (my father's adviser) brought Keith to the bar to introduce him to Marlene. Campbell presented my father as "a young, brilliant lawyer who was to fight the Ortoire/Mayaro seat in Moruga for the PNM". My father then took over the discussion. He proudly explained to Marlene that he was called to the bar to practise law in 1975 and that he married and raised three children. He described why he was interested in contesting the Ortoire/Mayaro seat. He wanted to know more about the people in Moruga. He wanted to know their wants and needs. No sooner had the conversation started it came to

---

[25] Laurence Bergreen *Columbus the Four voyages 1492-1504*, pgs. 235-237.

an end. My father exited the bar with these words – "Ok young Henry, thanks for the chat, we will see you again."

After that initial conversation, Marlene wondered to herself how my father knew her surname was *Henry*. She did not know my father before and she also was not familiar with the two gentlemen who brought him into the bar. A few minutes afterwards she realised that my father, while talking to her, was directly facing the bar licence which hung wobbly on the wall. The licence bore the name *Henry* – the name licensed to sell liquors and spirits. It was clear that my father read this sign while he was conversing with *"young Henry"*. From that day onwards, Keith would visit the bar every time he came to Moruga. Marlene remembered the black *Ford Telstar* that he drove from Port of Spain to Moruga. She also recalled that my father would often tell her that my mother did not want him to enter politics. It was not long after that, he asked Marlene to be his Office Manager to oversee the functioning of the PNM office in Moruga. This was an offer that she did not refuse.

In my own view, my father selected Marlene to be his Office Manager for two reasons. Firstly, as one of *the big three*, he wanted to have a firm grip on the votes coming out of Moruga. Secondly and directly connected to the first reason, he realised that Marlene was intelligent and had a pulse of what the people in Moruga wanted. Marlene recognised that the average person in Moruga was different from the others. In her own words:

"Moruga people don't want what people in Diego Martin want. Your father kept abreast of what was taking place in the country. He was intelligent. He would talk and ask me certain questions like – What is it that Moruga people really wanted? What should I say when I go on the platform? I of course gave him my own views. He would listen and then form his own opinion. I got to realise that the conversations we were keeping, he would use for his own information."

Soon Marlene found out that everything she told Keith, he would repeat it on the political platform. There were other things that Marlene noticed about my father. One of these things was that he was a family man and not a politician *per se*. She even reminisced how he was highly protective of his older brother Lennox.

During the campaign trail I found Marlene to be always warm and welcoming. Her mother owned a small grocery shop in the village and as young children we were often treated with goodies from the shop. While campaigning in Moruga, we would on some occasions, overnight at Marlene's family home. My family was quite amazed one night when before we retired to our beds we noticed the front door of the home was left wide open. Marlene would then explain that all Moruga people were family and there was no crime in the village. I was surprised somewhat by these words and I am not quite certain this "open door" policy still remains the same today.

It will be amiss of me if I failed to mention Roger Lewis, my father's *right-hand man* during his election campaign. How Lewis and my father met is intriguing. In April 1991, Lewis received *a tip off* that a Mr Sobion was *'looking for him'*. Having known who he was but yet never having the opportunity to meet the gentleman, Lewis went into his car and drove around Mayaro looking for him. When he finally found him he came up straight to Keith and said – *"Sir, I am Roger Lewis, I heard that you were looking for me"*.

My father replied in the affirmative. He said that he (Lewis) was highly recommended to him to be his Operations Manager for his campaign in the Ortoire/Mayaro constituency. Lewis, taken aback, replied that he was not interested in politics and questioned why he would want someone like him on his team. My father's response was that he needed a new face in the politics and repeated the fact that he came highly recommended. In the end, and with some persuasion, Lewis accepted the offer. Up to today, it was never revealed to Lewis who recommended him.

My father and Lewis struck it off immediately. Lewis became the point person for the campaign. My father trusted him with all the bank accounts and the monies received which funded the campaign. Being so close to Keith, Lewis realised that my father was not one who would conform to the norms. He witnessed many occasions when hours before my father was to speak on a political platform in Mayaro, party officials would come across to hand him an envelope. In that envelope contained a piece of paper that outlined key talking points for his speech. Lewis noted:

"As soon as they handed the envelope to him, he would open it, quickly skim through the contents on the paper which was inside and then hand it over to me. Keith would never say what they wanted him to say. He explained that he did not want to say something which was untrue or a promise which he knew he could not deliver. For instance, he would not say that he was going to build a school when he knew that it would not become a reality. He simply ignored the contents inside the envelopes. We had a good laugh over this. I think because of that, he was viewed within some circles within the party as someone who would not want to toe the party line."

Due to his somewhat defiance to party orders, Lewis noticed that most of his speeches made during the campaign trail were delivered ad-lib. If however, it was a general party meeting outside the Ortoire/Mayaro constituency, speeches were normally screened. In those situations, my father would write down talking points on a sheet of paper.

The 1991 campaign consisted of a number of late night cottage meetings held at various locations deep in the southern part of the country. These cottage meetings usually took place in small poorly lit makeshift rooms. These rooms, which appeared to be living rooms of party supporters, were temporarily rearranged with wooden benches and chairs. My father would sit at the head table with other party group leaders. The rooms were terribly small and on at least one occasion I recall people standing up and spilling over onto the steps outside. On an average I think there were forty to fifty persons who attended one cottage meeting. The purpose of these cottage meetings was to strategise and mobilise. There, my father and his team prepared for rallies, motorcades and constituency walkabouts. The pens and pencils popped out and persons wrote on their pieces of paper. Things were discussed and questions posed. An average night of a cottage meeting typically sounded like this:

Who printing t-shirts? Who is responsible for distributing these t-shirts? How many flyers to print? How many buses are needed for this party group? Who will provide the music? The entertainment? Where would the next public meeting be held? What topic should Mr Sobion address at that meeting?

On the topic of t-shirts, the print thereon bore the image of the *balisier* flower, the symbol of the party, with the catchphrase – *It's just a Matter of Time for Ortoire/Mayaro.* Even though on most occasions I fell asleep at these cottage meetings, the background noise and questions still remained alive in my subconscious.

When on the road, the team hired vehicles for the campaign which were outfitted with walkie-talkies. This permitted team members to provide updates while travelling through the diverse and vast constituency. To ensure confidentiality or in the event that messages were intercepted, each team member, including my father, had a code name. As a child, hearing the words *"Over and Out"* or *"Roger"* made me feel like we were embarking on a special mission like one seen in a James Bond movie.

Keith (centre, front) leading his supporters during the campaign in Ortoire/Mayaro, October 1991.

From the beginning of the campaign up to the end, there was no clear indication as to how the Ortoire/Mayaro seat would pan out. Decision day arrived when the polls were closed and the ballots counted. Just before midnight on 16th December 1991 and perhaps after one year of campaigning, my father was declared as the winner of the Ortoire/Mayaro seat. Even though there was much pandemonium in the PNM Ortoire/ Mayaro camp when the result was announced, the team on the ground was surprised by the results of the other two candidates. Selwyn Richardson, who was the incumbent and expected to be my father's main challenger, received only 2,563 votes. Christine Anderson gathered 6,013 votes – much more votes than my father's team anticipated. My father won after receiving a total of 7,578 votes.[26]

The results suggested that the Ortoire/Mayaro seat was a marginal constituency. Even though my father and his team were in a jubilant mood, in the back of their minds they realised that there was no room for complacency. Much work needed to be done on the ground if the PNM was to retain the Ortoire/ Mayaro constituency in the next general elections. This was the thrust of my father's victory speech in Mayaro after the elections were over.

Back at Emerald Drive, my father's mother was in mixed moods. She was content that her son won his seat in her hometown Mayaro. She was still however not convinced that he was better off being a politician. Mere days after the election Clerine Sobion fell ill. She was diagnosed with cancer. When my father was appointed in the new Cabinet as AG and Minister of Legal Affairs, she could not attend the swearing in ceremony. She was

---

[26] Report of the EBC on the Parliamentary elections held on 16th December 1991.

bedridden and watched the ceremony live on a television which my father's sisters had to install and roll into her bedroom. Clerine Sobion succumbed to cancer on the 20th January 1992, about a month after my father's appointment as AG. The beloved teacher from Mayaro flew away home to paradise to meet her Maker. At least she lived to see my father appointed in his Ministerial portfolio. My father blamed himself for her death. He thought that his determination to enter into the realm of politics caused and even accelerated her demise. My mother once whispered to me – it was the first time she ever saw my father cry.

Keith being sworn in as Attorney General and Minister of Legal Affairs by H.E. President Noor Hassanali at the President's House in December 1991. (Photo provided courtesy the Office of the President of the Republic of Trinidad and Tobago).

Chapter 10

Enter the young AG

Our new life in Federation Park

In compliance with our Constitution my father was the second Minister, after Prime Minister Manning, to be formally appointed in the new Cabinet. Thus, in the second half of December 1991, His Excellency Noor Hassanali, the President of the Republic swore in my father as AG and Minister of Legal Affairs. President Hassanali has often been cited as being the first Indo-Trinidadian to hold the Office of President and the first Muslim Head of State in the Americas. So devoted a Muslim was Hassanali that, according to my father, he never served alcohol at official functions at the President's House. Within a matter of days after being sworn in, a large army truck came at night to our home in Dorrington Gardens to transport all our belongings to the official Attorney General's residence.

Trinidad Crescent, Federation Park was a bourgeoisie neighbourhood. It was very much different from Dorrington Gardens where the children roamed the streets carefree. I immediately missed the Hackshaws and the Wards, my childhood friends at Dorrington Gardens. Directly opposite our new residence lived Justice Jean Permanand and her husband, a lawyer, called Sach. As a young boy, I remember the Permanands as kind-hearted souls who always smiled when they saw us. Next door to us lived Stanford Callender, a new Government Senator and my father's colleague from Tobago.

Our new home in Federation Park was huge and more spread out when compared to our family home in Dorrington Gardens. Upstairs there were three bedrooms, two bathrooms and a library. Downstairs was an enormous living room, with a special section reserved for my father's own use and relaxation, and a kitchen. On the western side of the house there was a maid's living quarters where Martha mainly occupied. My brothers and I also shared this area with Martha to play *Nintendo* and *Sony* video games. On the eastern side lay an open terrace which my father had easy access to since it was directly connected to his section of the living room. Annexed to the terrace was a vast expanse of land made up of lush green lawn. On the land, there was a large mango tree and my mother together with Martha later planted a beautiful garden at the edges of the lawn. At the front of the garden and the property was a ten-foot wall. There was also a dilapidated swing on the land which served as a goal post for our football games. Needless to say, soon our home in Federation Park became known as a place where our friends would assemble to play a game of football. Later, on the western side, my parents installed a hoop and backboard which allowed us to play half court basketball. From my childhood memories, Federation Park was like our own playground!

We were settled in to the Federation Park residence by Christmas 1991. From my recollection, in 1992 – the year my grandmother died, our annual family Christmas celebrations were shifted from my grandparents' home in Emerald Drive to the home in Federation Park.

Too young for office

It is true to say that many eyebrows were raised when my father was appointed AG and Minister of Legal Affairs. At forty years of age, many political experts and those in the legal fraternity thought that my father was too young to hold such a noble office. Many thought that Prime Minister Manning would have chosen Desmond Allum as he was more senior than my father – both in age and years standing at the Bar. But Manning made it clear to me many years after his decision. He was not looking for a Queen's Counsel (Q.C.) or someone with Q.C. status to be his AG. Rather, Manning was looking for raw, young talent. This was Manning's reason for appointing my father as AG in his new Cabinet.

While undergoing research for these *Memoirs*, I had the opportunity to speak to three Senior Counsels and a Judge about my father's appointment. Douglas Mendes S.C. found the decision to appoint Keith as AG *controversial* to the extent that the public anticipated that Allum was going to be so appointed. However on reflection, Mendes thought that my father was a suitable candidate and that the AG's Chambers operated quite effectively during his tenure. This view was similarly articulated by Russell Martineau S.C., a former AG under George Chambers. Martineau however did not use the word *controversial* but instead thought that Allum was the natural appointment given the fact that he was more senior and well known in the legal circles than Keith.

Queen's Counsel Michael de la Bastide, a former Chief Justice and President of the Caribbean Court of Justice also experienced initial surprise at the appointment. Once appointed however, de la Bastide found that compared to some politicians, Keith was more prudent in the way in which he acted and the way he spoke publicly. *"As Attorney General, he never compromised his impartiality"* – were the words of de la Bastide. Although these three eminent Caribbean jurists used different words, the common thread which united them was that Keith did a fairly good job as AG and Minister of Legal Affairs.

Reggie Armour S.C., one of Keith's closest and best friends gave a philosophical perspective on the situation. Armour reasoned that Allum understood that he would have been appointed to the top post and that he (Allum) was hurt when he was not appointed AG. Armour added that even though Keith was Allum's junior, Keith had a wider knowledge of constitutional law. Allum on the other hand was more steeped in equity and fairness. The next thing that Armour said tugged at my heartstring. This was that after Keith was appointed AG, he was always concerned about the situation involving Allum.

Then there were the political points of view. Colm Imbert, a senior member of the PNM and a former Cabinet colleague spun a different twist to the story of Keith's appointment. Imbert first met my father around 1990 when they were both involved in a think tank strategising on how to return the PNM back into power. Other members of this think tank were Ken Valley, Keith Rowley, Ralph Maraj and Wendell Mottley. This group, which was under the overall supervision of Manning, delivered an input into the party's 1991 elections manifesto and the drafting of national policy. Imbert believed that my father's involvement in the planning of the party's central policy gave him the edge over Allum.

In the words of Imbert:

"Your father was more senior (to Allum) in terms of politics and policy-making. With that in mind, Manning had the experience working with Keith. He would have trusted him and had confidence in him as well."

Imbert further recalled that after Keith was appointed AG and Minister of Legal Affairs, no one ever challenged his knowledge of the law or fitness in office.

Camille Robinson-Regis, another Cabinet colleague remembered the times when she acted for my father as AG and Minister of Legal Affairs when he was on duties out of the country. Upon his return to office she would brief him on what transpired during his absence. Working together with him, Robinson-Regis found Keith to be very meticulous and knowledgeable in all areas of the law. Robinson-Regis recalled instances where she would re-read his debates in the Parliament. She found them to be very solid and difficult for the Opposition to respond to and that the Cabinet was at all times confident in his legal advice.

I also broached the subject with Roger Lewis, Keith's right-hand man in Mayaro. Lewis was more exuberant in his views on the subject of my father's appointment. Lewis was not at all surprised by Manning's choice. Actually he, together with most of the constituents from Mayaro, expected that my father was going to be appointed AG. In fact, Lewis thought that at the time Keith "was the best legal mind in the Caribbean".

When Manning appointed his Cabinet in 1991/1992, Desmond Allum did not take up a Ministerial portfolio. This left Allum, the Member for Port of Spain North/St. Ann's West, sitting on the backbenches for the duration of the Parliament. *The Trinidad Guardian* reported that prior to the PNM winning the election, Allum was offered the post of Attorney General.[27] Another assertion was that Manning offered Allum another Ministerial position. Allum refused. With the passing of time, we may never be able to determine the accuracy of these claims.

At the end of the day, the question as to who was fitter to hold the position of AG and Minister of Legal Affairs is rather academic. What is interesting is that in 1993, Keith in his capacity as AG recommended Allum to be appointed Senior Counsel (*Silk*).[28] This gesture in itself illustrated that Keith respected the professional abilities and intelligence of Allum. That was the type of person my father was. He would never bear malice towards anyone and if he thought Allum was deserving of *Silk*, he would not refrain in making a recommendation.

During his tenure my father was proud to work with a talented group of Cabinet colleagues. One evening I sat down at a dinner with a senior public official who revealed to me that the Manning 1991/1995 Cabinet was often referred to as *the Dream Team* as it included the likes of Wendell Mottley, Gordon Draper, Keith Sobion, Ken Valley, Keith Rowley and Augustus Ramrekersingh. Only history would be able to judge whether this assertion was also correct. Yet being a part of a good team

---

[27] *Desmond Allum dies from Cancer,* Trinidad and Tobago Guardian, 18 June 2010.
[28] Andre Bagoo *Manning Vetoed Silk,* Sunday Newsday, 15 January 2012. According to this article other persons who were bestowed with Silk around that same time period were Russell Martineau, Sonny Maharaj, Theodore Guerra, Desmond Allum, Trevor Lee and Rolston Nelson. My father also recommended Clive Phelps to receive Silk but this nomination was not accepted.

did not necessarily imply that a political life was all smooth sailing.

A few months after Keith took up his Ministerial portfolio, himself and Reggie Armour went out for lunch together. At lunch, Armour recalled an image of stress that would forever be etched in his mind.

"The first year that Keith was AG, we went out to have lunch at a restaurant. His cell phone rang and he answered. While speaking, his phone was in his left hand and his right hand was scratching his head. I did not know whom he was speaking to, but clearly it was a work related conversation. Keith told me after the conversation ended that he was instructed not to go anywhere without his cell phone and that he was on call 24/7. I will always remember that image of stress. I really felt sorry for him."

Whilst we will never know who was on the other end of that particular telephone conversation, the signs of stress reared its ugly head at the early stages of his job. And this was expected. The life of an AG, or any politician for that matter, is one filled with high stress levels and overflowing tensions. Yet my father's case was a special one. He held the portfolio of AG, Minister of Legal Affairs and also had to service Ortoire/Mayaro, one of the largest constituencies in Trinidad and Tobago. During his tenure, there was always a conflict between his mammoth Ministerial portfolio and the colossal constituency that he represented.

Marlene Henry delivered a telling account about the demand and conflict of Keith's two offices as a Minister and MP. At the time, Keith was on his way to visit his constituency in Moruga. Upon arriving at Princes Town, some 29 kilometres from Moruga, Prime Minister Manning called him. The Prime

Minister advised that the national dollar was going to be floated
and he needed his legal advice. Keith was instructed to urgently
return to Port of Spain. My father had no choice but to request
his driver to turn around and head back north to Port of Spain.
The Trinidad and Tobago dollar was originally floated with
the US dollar in April 1993. This agreement to float the dollar
was sealed, when top executives of the Central Bank met with
leaders of the commercial banks over the course of the Easter
weekend. This move was reported by the *Daily Express* as being
a "historic weekend in the annals of economic policy-making
and public sector co-operation in this country".[29] Bearing this
in mind, this account of Keith being advised to return to Port
of Spain while en route to Moruga would have taken place
just before or during the Easter weekend in April 1993. This
is just one example where Keith's duties towards his country
conflicted with his duties towards his constituency. As Imbert
rightly divulged – one of these duties had to be sacrificed. There
were other critical national issues that would have conflicted
with my father's constituency time such as the Clint Huggins
hoax, Glen Ashby and the limited state of emergency placed
upon Madame Occah Seapaul, the Speaker of the House of
Representatives. The latter two of these issues will be discussed
here in greater detail.

The hanging of Glen Ashby

My father was a friend to many. Yet if I were to attempt to
zero in on persons who were the closest to my father during his
entire lifetime these persons would be – Eric Etienne Jr., Mayo
Robertson, Reggie Armour, Lenny Jacob and the Pantin family

---

[29] *Floating of the TT dollar: 20 years later*, Daily Express, 2 April 2013.

from Cameron Road, Petit Valley. On a more personal note, I would never forget that moment when my father confided in me that if anything should happen to him, I should reach out to two persons – Armour or Etienne Jr. At this juncture, I would like to describe the relationship with Armour. So fond my father was of Armour that he would forever call him *Tertius* – one of Armour's middle names. Unfortunately, Armour and Keith had a legal spat which temporarily ended their friendship. It had to do with the execution of convicted murderer Glen Ashby in 1994. The outcome of the Glen Ashby case would lead to the two friends not speaking for many years. As Armour once told me – *"But for the Glen Ashby case, Keith was certainly the best choice for AG."*

There is no doubt that the execution of Glen Ashby remained a grey cloud that hung over my father's tenure as AG and Minister of Legal Affairs. Even long after he demitted office, this situation pained my father. He reflected on it and struggled with it both professionally and personally. Professionally: because he had to take tough action that ultimately was driven by political considerations. Personally: because throughout his private life he tried to justify why the action taken was correct. My father and I spent many long periods discussing Ashby and I found that something particularly disturbed him about the matter.

On 14th July 1994 at about 6:30 a.m. Glen Ashby, a convicted murderer and death row prisoner, was hung in Port of Spain, Trinidad.[30] While Ashby was being executed, the Court of Appeal was hearing an application by his lawyers for a stay

---

[30] *Report of the International Commission of Inquiry into the hanging of Glen Ashby by the Government of Trinidad and Tobago*, Caribbean Human Rights Network, St. Michael, Barbados (1995).

of execution of his sentence of death. At the same time, but in London some thousands of miles away, the Privy Council was also hearing an appeal by Ashby for a stay of execution. From all reports, Ashby was hanged within minutes of the Privy Council ruling in favour of the stay of execution. My father, as the AG of Trinidad and Tobago was involved in the case. Armour was one of the Counsels who appeared for Glen Ashby at the Court of Appeal in Trinidad. I also spoke at length with Armour about this case. What he explained was chilling to say the least.

"As I recall it, the lawyers for Glen Ashby were myself, Chris Hamel-Smith, Douglas Mendes and Gregory Delzin. We received information in less than twenty-four hours that they were going to hang Ashby. We then swiftly filed for a constitutional motion on behalf of Ashby for cruel and inhumane punishment. This hearing came before Justice Lucky and he dismissed us summarily. We then received word that Chief Justice Bernard assembled a Court of Appeal team to hear the matter. We asked the Registrar of the Court to fix the Court of Appeal matter by 10 p.m. that night in order to give room for the Privy Council to hear the case – in the event that we had to appeal the Court of Appeal decision. All our documents were lined up and ready to file. Later we received news that the Court of Appeal moved to sit at 4 a.m. instead of 10 p.m. Thus, if the Court of Appeal refused us, it would be difficult for us to obtain a Privy Council sitting as Ashby was to be hanged at 6 a.m. that morning. We therefore bypassed the Court of Appeal and had two matters running parallel at the same time. The Privy Council sat at 8 a.m. London time which was 4 a.m. Port of Spain time. We briefed our lawyers in London to appear before the Privy Council.

At around 4 a.m. we received a phone call from the Court stating that we must come to the Court of Appeal to justify why our lawyers were before the Privy Council. The Court of Appeal thought that this was a contempt of Court and we needed to justify our actions. At 4:20 a.m. we were before the Court of Appeal. At Court, the Court of Appeal was more concerned as to why we bypassed them to go straight to the Privy Council. This was the question which was put by the President of the Court, Chief Justice Bernard. I argued that we took this decision because we did not have any time to appeal, if it arose, to the Privy Council.

Suddenly the doors opened. The media came in. Frank Solomon, my Senior came in and he sat at the front of the bar table. Then the doors opened a second time. Allan Alexander, another Senior Counsel entered and sat in the same fashion. Then lo and behold, the doors opened a third time and in came Philip Hamel-Smith. I realised that all of these senior lawyers came into the court to be witnesses in case we were all arrested for contempt of court. My argument was that this was not about the Counsel representing Ashby. The issue was about a man who was going to be hanged. I remember the Chief Justice Bernard getting irritated with me. Realising this, we had to rely on a strategy. I asked that Registrar Sherman McNichols be present in Court since the hanging could not take place without him being present as a witness. This was around 4:45 a.m. We were told that McNichols could not be found. Then I knew something was terribly wrong....

Around this time, our attorney, James Dingemans was arguing the case before the Privy Council in London. There he received an order for a stay of execution of Ashby's sentence. I remember Gregory Delzin running, as fast as he could, into the Court of Appeal, with a faxed copy of the order. The Chief Justice was angry. Sometime later in the morning we learnt that Glen Ashby was executed.

When it was understood that Ashby was hanged, I asked the Court of Appeal to order an immediate enquiry as to the factual chain of circumstances when the matter was filed up to the hearing of the matter. The learned Judges refused to grant the order. As the time in Court elapsed, I had a strong suspicion that there was collaboration between Keith and the Registrar regarding the execution."

This was the reason why my father and Amour did not speak for many years. How they rekindled their relationship is worth mentioning. Armour said that it was my father who first made the overture.

"He called me many years later out of the blue. At that time he was the Principal of the Norman Manley Law School and was living in Jamaica. He was paying a visit to Trinidad and he invited me for a drink".

So it was a drink and a reminiscence of good times that brought these two goodly gentlemen back together once more.

Two decades later, Armour was contrite. He admitted being angry and emotional after the Ashby case. In retrospect, he explained that he should not have been angry with Keith as in politics one was not a free agent. Armour knew that the Ashby case affected my father even though they never spoke about it. In fact he regretted that they never spoke about the case. Keith was one of the closest and best friends he ever knew – Armour said. I looked at a pensive Armour. I told him that the feeling was mutual.

What really transpired?

The hanging of Ashby in 1994 stirred up a constitutional and death penalty debate in Trinidad and Tobago. My father was severely criticised by many in the legal circles for his alleged role in the execution. Some, like Michael de la Bastide, thought that the Glen Ashby incident was unfortunate. However, de la Bastide went on to explain that from what he was told, my father may have been wrongly blamed as he (Keith) had been unaware that the execution was carried out until after the event.

Russell Huggins, the Minister of National Security at the time, explained that as the Chair of the Mercy Committee he was the one who oversaw the process leading up to Ashby's execution. My father, as holder of the Office of Attorney General, also sat on the Mercy Committee. When Ashby's case was before the Court of Appeal, Huggins was in England and Gordon Draper was acting as the Minister of National Security. While in England my father telephoned Huggins asking for his advice on how to proceed. My father took Huggins' advice.

For Huggins, my father wrongly received the full brunt of the outcome of the matter involving Ashby. Huggins recalled that after Ashby was executed he spoke to Armour and informed him that the decision made was not that of the AG but was that of the Chairman of the Mercy Committee.

Besides a media release issued by the Office of the AG, my father never publicly commented on Ashby's execution.[31] He did however have private discussions with us as to what actually transpired. He was constantly building a case, and I get the impression that he was trying to convince himself, that the execution was carried out legally. My father's personal opinion was that all of the procedures and the requirements of the law were justified. On that morning of the 14th July 1994, the Registrar of the Court called him for his advice. He then politely asked the Registrar to read the final line of the warrant which

---

[31] *Keith Sobion* Newsday Archives, 16 February 2008.

was signed and issued by the President, H.E. Noor Hassanali. To which the Registrar replied:

"And this (the execution) you (the Registrar) are by no means to omit at your own peril." [32]

In other words, the Registrar as the Marshall of the Court would be personally liable if he failed to comply with the President's warrant.[33] The Registrar thereby promptly carried out the President's instruction. This was Keith's version.

The issue as to whether Ashby's execution was legal or illegal was thoroughly debated and even examined by an International Commission of Inquiry. It is not my desire to arrive at a particular conclusion but rather to point out the controversial nature of the decision and the effect it had on my father.

One theory that emerged regarding the so-called *haste* to hang Ashby was that the government wanted to send a strong message to the people of Trinidad and Tobago that murders would no longer be condoned in the country. The government was operating in a climate where crime was spiralling out of control and the majority of the population was in favour of the death penalty. Indeed, on the 11th July 1994, three days before the execution, the country was jolted with the gruesome murder of two women. This murder took place in the middle/upper-class neighbourhood of Westmoorings. Shortly after, one of the persons charged with the murder was Chuck Attin, a sixteen year old. Trinidad and Tobago was in an uproar

---

[32] Media release from the Office of the Attorney General faxed on 19 July 1994 at 12:14 pm.

[33] Ibid. at pg. 3.

as a number of influential persons in the society staged a protest which went as far as the Prime Minister's residence.[34] An urgent solution was needed. To illustrate how tense the climate was, a frustrated Russell Huggins privately expressed to my father: *"What do they want me to do? Put a policeman to guard everyone's front door?"*

It was in this environment, that Glen Ashby was taken to the gallows. As one politician told me quite confidentially – *when Ashby was executed there were no murders in the country for six weeks.* How accurate that statement is I am not certain, but the gist of it was that hanging acted as a deterrent to crime – even if it was in the short-term.

Ashby goes international

The hanging of Glen Ashby did not go unnoticed regionally and internationally. News of the execution created shock waves in Geneva, Switzerland. On the 13th July 1994, the United Nations (UN) Special Rapporteur (for New Communications) at the Human Rights Committee in Geneva transmitted a request to the authorities of Trinidad and Tobago not to execute Ashby while his case was under consideration by the Committee.[35] Notwithstanding this, Ashby was executed the next morning.[36] Upon receiving this news, the Human Rights

---

[34] *Chuck Attin – Killer most Brutal*, Sunday Newsday, 16 November 2003.

[35] The UN Special Rapporteur for New Communications transmitted a request under rule 86 requesting Trinidad and Tobago to take interim measures to avoid irreparable damage to the alleged human rights violations of Ashby. (Source: UN General Assembly Report, 21 September 1994 from paragraph 410).

[36] Ibid.

Committee ('Committee') swiftly transmitted a diplomatic note to Trinidad and Tobago's Permanent Mission stationed in Geneva. The purpose of the Note was to receive *"clarifications about the circumstances surrounding the execution of Mr Ashby."* [37] The first meeting on the subject was called for on the 20th July 1994. No authorised representative from the country was present at that meeting but a Media Release issued by the Office of the AG concerning the circumstances surrounding the execution of Ashby was transmitted to the Committee.[38] After examining the contents of the Media Release, the Committee concluded that the State did not reply to the initial questions it posed.

A public meeting was subsequently held at the UN Office in Geneva on the 26th July 1994.[39] Again, no representative from the government was available to explain its position to the Committee.[40] In its decision the Committee found, *inter alia*, that Trinidad and Tobago failed to comply with its international obligations under the *International Covenant on Civil and Political Rights* and its *Optional Protocol.* The Committee also urged that situations similar to that of Glen Ashby do not recur in Trinidad and Tobago.[41] Apart from this, private persons from Austria wrote letters to the Prime Minister, the Minister of National

---

[37] *Note Verbale 580/1994*, 15 July 1995.

[38] Opening paragraph of Note Verbale from the UN Human Rights Committee, 21 July 1994.

[39] Press communique issued by the Human Rights Committee.

[40] *Report of the International Commission of Inquiry into the hanging of Glen Ashby* at pg. 3, paragraph 5. Also see pg. 71 of the UN General Assembly Report, 21 September 1994.

[41] *UN General Assembly Report*, 21 September 1994, pg. 71.

Security and the AG condemning the execution.[42] One of these letters, addressed to my father read as follows:

The Honourable

Keith Sobion,
Attorney General,
Red House, Port of Spain,
Trinidad and Tobago

19 July 1994

Dear Attorney General,

I was seriously indignant to learn of the pricipitous (sic) execution of Mr Glen Ashby on 14 July 1994. You are certainly as dismayed as me at the fact that this execution was carried out not only despite appeals pending at national and international level, but also despite your personal undertaking to exhaust all possibility of obtaining a stay of execution before the latter would go ahead.

Given this flagrant violation of Trinidad and Tobago's national law, as well as of international standards, I call on you most urgently to arrange for an (sic) thorough investigation into the execution of Mr Glen Ashby, and that appropriate action is taken against those responsible for ordering it. Further, I am gravely concerned about the life of all other prisoners under sentence of death in Trinidad and Tobago; that is why I respectfully urge that no further executions be carried out in Trinidad and Tobago. I appreciate your attention to this important human rights issue and remain,

Very truly yours,

H.P.

Austria

---

[42] Courtesy the archives of the Permanent Mission of Trinidad and Tobago to the United Nations in Geneva, Switzerland.

Regionally, the Caribbean Human Rights Network together with the Organisation of Commonwealth Caribbean Bar Associations (OCCBA) appointed a Commission of Inquiry to inquire into and report upon the circumstances surrounding the execution of Ashby.[43] The Commission sat in Barbados on the 21st and 22nd August 1994 and its terms of reference were detailed.[44] The terms of reference of this regional Commission included whether Ashby was legally hanged and whether there was any impropriety committed in the conduct of the proceedings.

With respect to the latter mandate, focus was placed on the role of the AG, the lawyers involved in the case, the Registrar of the Court and the Government of Trinidad and Tobago.[45] The Commission comprised five eminent Commonwealth jurists namely – James Davis, the Chairman and a retired Justice of Appeal of Trinidad and Tobago, Dennis Daly Q.C. of Jamaica, Miles Fitzpatrick S.C. from Guyana, Anthony Scrivener Q.C. and Leonard Woodley Q.C., the last two from the United Kingdom. Noteworthy was the fact that none of the main actors on behalf of the State of Trinidad and Tobago accepted the sponsors' invitation to attend or testify. Indeed my father did decline the invitation to participate before the Commission. The correspondence from the Office of the AG to the Secretary of the Caribbean Human Rights Network dated the 18th August 1994 read:

---

[43] *Report of the International Commission of Inquiry into the hanging of Glen Ashby* at pg. ix.

[44] Ibid. pg. x.

[45] Introduction of *The Report of the International Commission of Inquiry into the hanging of Glen Ashby.*

Dear Mrs Clarke (Secretary),

The Attorney General of Trinidad and Tobago is unable to accept your invitation to participate as a witness in your proposed Commission of Inquiry into the execution of Glen Ashby.

The matters suggested in the Commission's terms of reference are issues which fall to be determined by the domestic law of the Republic of Trinidad and Tobago or by way of such international obligations whereby the sovereign State of Trinidad and Tobago is bound.

In the circumstances and quite apart from the procedural impropriety of your request, the Attorney General on his own behalf and on behalf of the State of Trinidad and Tobago declines your invitation.

Yours faithfully,

Keith S. Sobion

(Signed for) Attorney General

In his written response, Russell Martineau, Senior Counsel on behalf of the State also cited similar reasons for his non-participation before the Commission of Inquiry.[46]

The Commission, wanting to be seen as fair and without breaching the principle of natural justice, noted in its final report:

"...we were therefore denied an opportunity of receiving evidence and/or explanations of the events from those sources which would be likely to have an interest in contradicting the narrative which did emerge".[47]

---

[46] Ibid. Appendix 1 at pg. 26.
[47] Ibid. pg. x.

The Commission's report went on to deliver some scathing remarks on my father in relation to his handling of the Ashby case.[48] In the end, the Commission, like the UN Human Rights Committee in Geneva, found that the circumstances in which Trinidad and Tobago executed Glen Ashby constituted a significant disregard both for the rule of law and the country's international treaty obligations under the International Covenant on Civil and Political Rights.[49]

The death penalty – personal and political considerations

The natural question that then arises is whether my father was in favour or against the death penalty. Separate and apart from Ashby – the death penalty is an issue which we spoke about several times. My last conversation with him on this topic was when we were living in Jamaica. He held a middle ground view which was that the death penalty should be reserved in only the most heinous acts of murder – for example acts of cold-blooded murder without any remorse. Society has changed and so have human beings. I often wonder if his views on the subject would have been the same, had he been alive today.

As already expressed, the execution of Ashby was something that bothered him throughout his life. Maureen Lindo, his secretary at the Norman Manley Law School in Jamaica shared with me her story.[50] Lindo first met my father in August 1996

---

[48] Ibid. pgs. 5 and 7.

[49] Ibid. pg. x. See also *IN THE MATTER OF AN APPLICATION BY SS (by her kin and Next Friend KAREN MOHAMMED)*, Trinidad and Tobago Civil Appeal No. S 244 of 2015.

[50] This conversation with Ms Lindo took place on 2 February 2015.

when he took up his position as Principal. She claimed that from the very first day he saw her, he wanted her to work with him. From that day onward and for the next twelve years she served my father with great admiration and devotion. While working together, my father helped her develop academically (for she obtained her Masters under his tenure), mentally and professionally. With her touching words, she even disclosed that out of his own pocket, my father secretly paid the fees of the less fortunate law students who were in arrears. Lindo knew about the Ashby case because he often spoke to her about it. In the words of Lindo:

"The Glen Ashby case deeply affected him as he was not the type of person to take a life. That (Ashby case) affected him very badly. The fact that he was part of the process for which a man was executed, he took that very personally. Having been around him for all those years, I knew it was not a decision he would have made given his personal choice."

One of my father's closest colleagues at the Law School also thought the same. This person, who I wish to remain anonymous, spoke to my father "every day, several times a day". This colleague felt that when one is responsible for making legal decisions, such as an AG, their personal views must not come to the fore and they must act within the confines of the law. My own interpretation of this conversation was that perhaps my father was against the death penalty yet because of his office he was constrained to act in accordance with the law of the land.

While undergoing my research on these *Memoirs*, I had the opportunity to interview the Imam Yasin Abu Bakr. The Imam went straight to the point – the hanging of Ashby would not have been my father's decision since he did not have the authority to execute the former prisoner. Abu Bakr reasoned that my father was young and new in the party and he was put there to carry out policies rather than make policy decisions himself. He added – "when you are young, you have limitations on the things you can do". On this issue, my father was compared to Karl Hudson Phillips Q.C. another former AG who Abu Bakr opined had more political clout. Abu Bakr, like many others I have spoken to, felt that the Ashby outcome had a direct impact on my father losing the Ortoire/Mayaro seat in the 1995 general election.

Others, such as Huggins, believed that Keith was *for* the death penalty. Despite holding this position, it was perceived that he had the ability to bring a sober approach to the subject. Drawing an analogy, Huggins said that unlike others who were *for* capital punishment, Keith would not directly put forward his views. What he thought and how he said it depended on the audience he was addressing. In some instances, where persons would bluntly put forward their views on capital punishment, Keith would take you around *the mulberry bush* – a tactic which he deftly used to evade the answer all together.

Today my father would have to face a slightly different environment where there is now a more concerted thrust, especially among developed countries, towards a moratorium and a complete abolition of the death penalty. This is a movement that, at the time of writing, does not share a similar zeal among the majority of the population in the Commonwealth Caribbean.

Parliamentary picong, the Gurley Report and the Bail Act

As a Senator and MP, Parliament was a place which stimulated Keith intellectually. It was a place where my father, over the years, would enhance his legal and oratory skills. Parliament was also a breeding ground for fresh knowledge. Straightaway, young Keith took it upon himself not only to learn the Parliamentary rules and procedure from senior politicians but also those employed within the Parliament itself, such as Jacqui Sampson a then Parliamentary Clerk II.

In 4th Republican Parliament all the PNM MPs, my father included, wore the signature black tie with the party's *balisier* symbol. (The use of the *balisier* tie was a tradition adhered to since 1956, by the party's founder Eric Williams. Nowadays, this tradition has changed since it was felt that once a person is elected into public office, that person is a representative of all the citizens of Trinidad and Tobago, including those who did not vote for the PNM). The 4th Republican Parliament was also remembered for its debates on matters of intense national interest and orators who spoke off the cuff. Notwithstanding this, this particular Parliament Chamber was not void of the traditional Parliamentary *picong* and controversy. After delving into the *Hansard,* I have found cases where my father used political banter within the Parliament's walls. A classic example was the House of Representatives debate on Friday 27th May 1994 on a motion moved by A.N.R. Robinson, the MP for Tobago East with respect to an independent inquiry on the Prime Minister's vehicle. While reading, it is clear, that the Member from Tobago East had some difficulty with his microphone.

Mr A.N.R. Robinson: What has happened? I am speaking in the normal way, Madame Speaker.

Mr Sobion: Speak up!

Mr A.N.R. Robinson: Why is it that the sound system suddenly failed? I am using my normal voice. On a previous occasion the lights had failed; on another occasion the police headquarters were blown up!

Madame Speaker: Would the Member proceed with the Motion at hand please.

Mr A.N.R. Robinson: I am using my – in fact, I am speaking at a higher level than normal.

Mr Sobion: You are losing your marbles.[51]

The thing about Parliament, well at least in the Parliament of the Republic of Trinidad and Tobago, is that every honourable Member is subject to *picong*. Thus as it goes, my father even fell on the receiving side of the fence. This time it was not a microphone problem but a problem with the lighting. The following words were extracted from the *Hansard* transcript during the debate on the President's Statement (State of Emergency) on the 11th August 1995. My father was moving the motion in the Parliamentary Chamber when suddenly the lights started to dim. Trevor Sudama's interjection was epic. Sudama was the Opposition MP for Oropouche.

Hon. K. Sobion: Mr Deputy Speaker, I think the electricity is failing.

Mr Sudama: The whole Government is failing.

Mr Deputy Speaker: May we suspend for 10 minutes until the situation is corrected.[52]

---

[51] *Hansard*, Friday 27 May 1994 at pg. 1042.
[52] *Hansard,* Friday 11 August 1995 at pg. 535.

On a more sober debate, my father made a passionate statement in the Parliament relating to the backlog of court cases awaiting trial in both civil and criminal jurisdictions. There the *Hansard* quotes him as saying:

"Madam Speaker, there is a truism in the world of jurisprudence which is expressed in the oft-heard phrase "justice delayed is justice denied". We the people of Trinidad and Tobago have for many years now felt the full impact of that statement as the slow pace of the legal process becomes a source of frustration to persons in all walks of life." [53]

He went on: [54]

"Madam Speaker, there are also those within the walled prisons, hundreds of frustrated young persons accused of crimes who are denied the opportunity to answer the charges laid against them. The fact of arrest is not a determination of guilt. Under our system, a citizen is innocent until proven guilty. A system which denies a citizen the early opportunity to have his status determined is a system which breeds the lawlessness which it is intended to curtail."

In alerting the national community to this state of affairs, my father stated in the Parliament that this matter "demands the highest priority on the national agenda". As a result, swift action was needed. In order to achieve this, the Cabinet appointed a team which included six lawyers, a Magistrate and two public servants. Members of the team were Dennis Gurley (Chairman), Christie-Anne Morris-Alleyne (Deputy Chairman), Lloyd Skinner, Byron Henriques, Teasley Taitt, Wendell Kangaloo, Gilbert Peterson, Mohan Gopee and Neville Palmer (Secretary). Under the terms of reference, the team was asked to, *inter alia*, advise on systems to

---

[53] *Hansard,* Friday 15 May 1992 at pg. 186.
[54] Ibid. pg. 188.

reduce existing delays in the administration of justice. The report, which later became known as the *'Gurley Report'*, was submitted to the government on 26th June 1992.[55] After its submission, the *Gurley Report* received considerable media coverage over a period of several weeks. Although one of the recommendations of the *Gurley Report* called for a general review of the Rules of Court to facilitate the expeditious determination of civil matters, the actual implementation of the New Civil Proceedings Rules did not come into effect until September 2005.

Apart from the *Gurley Report*, between the period 1991 to 1995 Keith as AG and Minister of Legal Affairs, moved a total of 41 Bills through the House of Representatives and the Senate.[56] Most of these Bills eventually became law in Trinidad and Tobago. For the purposes of these *Memoirs*, I would like to refer to two Bills at this point. The first was the *Indictable Offences (Preliminary Enquiry) (Amendment) Bill* which was assented to on September 1994. Upon becoming law, this Bill was thereafter referred to as "an Act to amend the Indictable Offences (Preliminary Enquiry) Act (Act No. 20 of 1994)." The intention of the 1994 amendments was to speed up preliminary enquiries in the Magistrates' Court by, for instance, permitting a Magistrate to commit an accused person to trial on the basis of written statements submitted by the prosecution.

The second Bill was the *Bail Bill* which subsequently became the Bail Act (Act No. 18 of 1994).[57] The purpose of the Bail Act,

---

[55] *Gurley and court delays* Trinidad Newsday, Sunday 7 October 2012.

[56] Information provided courtesy the Parliament of the Republic of Trinidad and Tobago (see Annex II).

[57] Assented to on 15 September 1994.

according to its long title, was "to amend the law relating to release from custody of accused persons in criminal proceedings and to make provision for legal aid for persons kept in custody and for connected purposes." The Bail Act also established a list of offences for which bail would not be granted to a prisoner. These offences were for murder, treason, piracy, hijacking and any other offence for which the death penalty is fixed by law. One person who I interviewed described "Keith's Bail Act" as a "draconian" piece of legislation. This person's viewpoint was probably influenced by the presumption of innocence of a prisoner and empathy towards persons who felt they were wrongly detained. Whereas the concern of the Government, in a post-1990 *coup d'état* climate, would have been more geared towards the reduction of crime and the preservation of public order.

Speaker under House arrest – another curfew in Port of Spain

There was another situation developing within the sacred walls of the Parliament during my father's tenure as AG and Minister of Legal Affairs. This was a rather tense situation that involved the Speaker of the House Occah Seapaul. The truth is that the first time I was introduced to the concept of Standing Orders of the Parliament was back in 1995 when I was fifteen years old. In those days, *'standing orders'* became a household expression used by my father in Federation Park. I often heard him repeat these words on the telephone with one of his parliamentary colleagues or when such colleagues visited him at home. A constitutional crisis was brewing in the Parliament and the conversations sounded urgent. I suspected that my father was nervous as to the outcome.

In January 1992, Madame Occah Seapaul made history when she was elected as the first woman Speaker of the House of Representatives of Trinidad and Tobago. However, more than three years later, she found herself at odds with the Manning-led PNM government. In early July 1995, the Government filed a Motion of no confidence in the Parliament against the Speaker.[58] There was then an attempt by the Government members to have the Speaker step down from The Chair while the no confidence Motion was being debated. The main thrust of the Government's argument was that the Speaker should not be a judge in her own cause.[59] In fact it was thought by the Speaker, and perhaps those in Opposition, that the purpose of the no confidence Motion was to force her to resign or to vacate office.[60]

The later reflections of Hedwige Bereaux, former MP for La Brea, attempts to clarify why the Government pursued such action against the Speaker:

Government had gotten wind that the Speaker, who was appointed as a result of Government votes, had formed some kind of alliance with the Opposition to suspend persons from the Government benches enough to allow the Government to be defeated if a Motion was brought. As a result of that, the Government decided it was dangerous or unhealthy to its majority if we continued to hold Parliament if the Speaker was in the Chair.[61]

---

[58] *Hansard,* Wednesday 12 July 1995 at pg. 257 (Keith Sobion allegedly spoke to the Speaker on 30 June 1995).

[59] *Hansard,* Wednesday 12 July 1995 at pg. 243 and 4 August 1995 at pg. 410.

[60] Ibid. pg. 246.

[61] *Parliamentary Exceptions Occah Seapaul – House Arrest of a Sitting Speaker of the House* (Video).

The Opposition members counteracted. Led in the Parliament by the voices of Ramesh Lawrence Maharaj (Chief Whip) and A.N.R. Robinson, the view of the Opposition was that under the Constitution, the Office of the Speaker is independent and could not be undermined.[62] Accordingly, a Motion of no confidence could not be used to remove a Speaker.[63] On the 12th July 1995, the Speaker herself rejected the no confidence Motion as being *"entirely out of order"*. [64] The Speaker also intimated that she would have to consider whether my father and Augustus Ramrekersingh, the Minister of Education, had been in contempt of the Chair and the Parliament.[65]

Less than two weeks later on the 24th July 1995, Ken Valley, the Leader of Government Business, took the floor of the House and stated that there was a cloud hanging over the Parliament and the Office of the Speaker. The use of the word *'cloud'* was perhaps in direct reference to the Government's belief that the Speaker was more supportive towards the Opposition members of the House. In response to Valley, the Speaker of the House noted that it was a good session and that she saw *"no cloud hanging over anything."* [66]

The rift between Valley and the Speaker intensified. It got so heated that at one point in time my father, who sat next to Valley in the Parliament, was forced to switch off Valley's microphone just as he (Valley) got up to respond to the Speaker.[67] But my father did not take off the microphone

---

[62] *Hansard,* Wednesday 12 July 1995 at pg. 257.

[63] Ibid. pg. 254.

[64] Ibid. pgs. 243 and 266.

[65] Ibid. pg. 266.

[66] *Hansard,* Monday 24 July 1995 at pg. 343.

[67] *Valley dies at 63,* The Trinidad Guardian Newspaper, 7 May 2011.

when it mattered the most. As the Speaker rose from the Chair and was on her way out of the Parliament Chamber, Valley was heard to have uttered: *"You can run, but you can't hide."* [68]

Although Valley later apologised for his outburst at the next sitting of the House on the 28th July, the Speaker suspended him from the Parliament for six months.[69] Valley filed an action and three days later he was granted a Conservatory Order by the High Court allowing him to continue sitting in the House of Representatives.[70]

For those on the Government benches, the suspension of Ken Valley was the proverbial straw that broke the camel's back. On the 3rd August, the Government reacted by advising the Acting President of the Republic to proclaim a state of emergency limited to the city of Port of Spain. Madam Occah Seapaul was also placed under house of arrest at her residence.

The next day, the 4th August, the Deputy Speaker presided over the Parliament. Basdeo Panday, the Leader of the Opposition and MP for Couva North, immediately took the floor on a point of order. Of course knowing what transpired overnight, his line of questioning was relevant and as usual witty. For these two reasons, I wish to highlight it here.

Mr Basdeo Panday: Mr Deputy Speaker, on a point of order, please, Sir. Section 58(2) of the Constitution says that this Parliament shall be presided over by the Speaker. That is confirmed by Standing Order 5(1). May I ask you, Sir, where is the Speaker? You cannot

---

[68] *Hansard*, Friday 28 July 1995 at pg. 350.

[69] Ibid. pg. 351.

[70] *Hansard*, Monday 7 August 1995 at pg. 516.

sit, Sir, unless we know what has happened to the Speaker. Where is the Speaker? [71]

The Deputy Speaker, Dr Rupert Griffith, tried to allay the fears of Panday by referring to Standing Order 5 (1) which stipulated that the Speaker, or in his absence the Deputy Speaker, shall preside at sittings of the House. Panday would not budge. He was not satisfied with the answer of the Deputy Speaker. He was, for the opening five minutes, a thorn in the Deputy Speaker's side.

Mr B. Panday: Mr Deputy Speaker, has the Speaker applied for leave? The Clerk announces that she is absent, but has she applied for leave? Has she been restrained from coming here today, and by whom? These things are important. The Speaker is not just restrained and the Deputy Speaker assumes office. The question is: Has the Speaker applied for leave? She did not turn up. If she did not turn up, where is she? [72]

Like Panday, the Deputy Speaker did not budge. As the Deputy Speaker ultimately held the reins of power he ruled on this matter thoroughly relying on Standing Order 5(1). The Deputy Speaker then asked the Clerk, once again, to proceed with the order of business for this House.

It was my father who broke the ominous news to the Members of the Parliament:

Mr K. Sobion: Mr Deputy Speaker, the Government, last evening, advised the Acting President of the Republic to proclaim a state of emergency, limited to the City of Port of Spain. Subsequently, an order of detention was served on the Speaker of the House of

---

[71] *Hansard*, Friday 4 August 1995 at pgs. 403-405.

[72] Ibid. pg. 403.

Representatives, Madam Occah Seapaul. Madam Seapaul will remain in detention at her residence, No. 9 Mary Street, St. Clair until further order.[73]

No sooner than my father ended this statement, a fuming Panday cried: 'Bad John! Bad John Manning!'

In reality, the state of emergency was limited in its effect. As my father explained to the Parliament – no curfew was in effect in Port of Spain or in any part of the country. The normal day-to-day activities of citizens were to remain unaffected. The only activity that the regulations restricted was the holding of public meetings, without permission, in the city of Port of Spain.[74] This fact, however, should not detract from the national and international implications which are attached to the proclamation of a state of emergency. My father made it a point to express that the Government chose to exercise the state of emergency as a last resort after all other courses of action, including private and confidential discussions with the Speaker, failed.[75]

The Opposition benches disagreed. *This is the first time I have ever heard that a state of emergency be declared for one person –* was the bemoaning cry of Panday.[76] To put it briefly, the Opposition members believed that in the circumstances, the state of emergency was rather excessive and drastic. In the end, the Deputy Speaker sat in the Chair until October

---

[73] *Hansard,* Friday 4 August 1995 at pg. 409-411.
[74] Ibid. pg. 411.
[75] Ibid. pgs. 410, 411.
[76] Ibid. pg. 428.

that year, when Prime Minister Manning called an early election.[77]

As the legal adviser to the Government, the relationship between my father and the Speaker of the House would have definitely been strained. But my father was never the one to bear a grudge, especially after he exited politics. Seapaul was someone whom he knew outside of the Parliament. She was a lawyer and his senior. He even appeared before Seapaul when she was a Master of the Court. As time passed by, the same could have been said about the former Speaker. She bore no bitterness or resentment towards my father. On hearing about his passing, she made this dignified tribute to the *Daily Express*:

What a brain! Keith was such a brilliant boy. When I was Master of the High Court and he appeared before me, I am (sic) always impressed with his thinking and he was a good advocate. Yes it was him who put me under house arrest. But he did what he had to do. What a man does, his duty – right or wrong – you can't hold that against him.[78]

Like Glen Ashby before, the Seapaul incident was one that tested my father's knowledge of constitutional law. These experiences would serve him well as constitutional law grew to become his forte.

---

[77] These circumstances lead to the amendment of s 50 of the Constitution which established a procedure for the removal of a Speaker in the form of a resolution signed by the majority of the House (Act No. 17 of 1995).
[78] *Sobion dies at 56*, Daily Express, Friday 15 February 2008.

Some official duties and private visits

As a Minister, my father had to travel abroad to represent the country at official meetings. One of the travels, my mother recalls, was a trip to a Latin American country to represent Prime Minister Manning at the swearing in of that country's President.[79] In this country they were greeted at the airport with a lot of fanfare and had been escorted by a heavy security detail. Whilst in Office, my father also travelled to Atlanta on a United States' government sponsored programme. Following him throughout his entire journey in Atlanta was an elderly white gentleman wearing thin-rimmed glasses. He was medium built and just under six feet tall. Keith's cousin Kenny Frontin, who was residing in Atlanta at the time, had a strong feeling that the gentleman was an undercover CIA agent. If it was correct that gentleman was a member of the CIA it could be said that it was a rather low-key and easy assignment.

On that Atlanta visit, Keith took it upon himself to visit the birth home and tombstone of Martin Luther King Jr. Arising out of this opportunity my father developed a very good relationship with Brian J. Donnelly, the United States Ambassador to Trinidad and Tobago. Those were the days when we would mount the steep hill to the Ambassador's residence at Flagstaff Hill, St. James for the annual 4th of July celebrations.

There was another occasion when Keith, as a Minister, also paid a private visit to his cousin Kenny in Atlanta. Early one morning when Kenny went off to work, Keith, all alone, decided to take a stroll around the garden. Unknown to Keith, Kenny soon received a telephone call from his neighbour who informed

---

[79] This Latin American country could not be specifically identified. It was suggested that it was either Costa Rica or Uruguay.

that there was an intruder on his premises. The description of the intruder was – a brown skinned, slender man with glasses, smoking like a chimney. On hearing this description, Kenny's fears were put to rest. He immediately told his neighbour that it was his cousin Keith. At first, I would smile at this story, but soon remembered that it was the smoking of cigarettes that contributed to the rapid deterioration of my father's health.

Back at home, in June 1993, my father opened the Devil's Woodyard – a mud volcano park located in *Hindustan*, which in those days formed part of the Ortoire/Mayaro constituency. A few months later in November, my father together with Chief Justice Clinton Bernard, opened the permanent building which now houses the San Fernando Supreme Court. This fact was acknowledged in Bernard's Memoirs *Beyond The Bridge* where he wrote:

In consultation with Keith Sobion who was the Attorney General during the 1992-1995 [80] period, I proceeded with the construction and refurbishing of all courts in the country. The first to be addressed was the San Fernando Supreme Court.[81]

Keith was also present at the inaugural Summit of the Association of Caribbean States (ACS) which was held in August 1995 at Port of Spain. At this Summit, Member States reaffirmed their commitment to the development of free trade and opposed all policies which were inimical to achieving that end.[82] This declaration was a historic one because it was seen

---

[80] Keith Sobion was actually the Attorney General and Minister of Legal Affairs from 1991 to 1995.

[81] Clinton Angelo Bernard *Beyond the Bridge, the Legal Journey of Clinton Angelo Bernard TC, SC* (2018) at pgs. 74-75.

[82] *Declaration of Principles and Plan of Action on Tourism, Trade and Transportation* signed in Port of Spain, Trinidad in August 1995.

(although not directly mentioned) as rejecting policies that restricted the development of member nations such as Cuba which was at the time still under the United States' economic embargo.[83]

Within the margins of this meeting, Keith together with his friend Christie-Anne Morris-Alleyne had the opportunity to meet the Cuban communist leader Fidel Castro. Morris-Alleyne remembers the meeting as being a memorable experience and, had mobile camera phones been easily accessible then, wished they had all taken a picture together. As my mother once said – Keith was *"ah ole socialist"*. Putting these words into context, I am certain that my father also thoroughly enjoyed the *rendezvous* with Castro.

With all of these ministerial duties, my father still had a large constituency to serve some 96 kilometres away from Port of Spain. When he did actually make it to his constituency, my father would overnight at premises arranged by his team or at the old Amoco complex then located on the Guayaguayare Mayaro main road.

As an MP, my father remained humane. At his Mayaro constituency office, persons would often visit asking him for written recommendations. Roger Lewis was responsible for overseeing the screening process of persons who required such recommendations from my father. Lewis recalled that the tone of each recommendation was similar and that everyone was treated equally despite his or her social status. Another interesting fact that Lewis remembered was that Keith did not use a typewriter and every single recommendation was penned

---

[83] Adria Cruz *Caribbean Summit opens with Trade call,* 17 August 1995 (UPI Archives).

with his own hand. My initial feeling on this was that my father was averse to the use of modern technology. However, Lewis then explained that he preferred for his recommendations to be handwritten in order to give them his personal touch.

Chapter 11

Memories of an Attorney General

My college 'bodyguard'

When my father was appointed AG and Minister of Legal Affairs I had just turned twelve years old. At that age, I was not mature enough to comprehend the significance attached to that particular Office. In this respect there are some intimate teenage memories that are worth sharing.

In 1993, while attending St. Mary's College and like my father before, I skipped from Form Two to Form Four. As a young student in an older class, I had a classmate who became my *'bodyguard'* and protected me from being bullied by the senior students. He assured me that he took up this role voluntarily out of respect for my father and his position. In the early days of my father's tenure, he had one driver and a plainclothes police officer assigned to him. My college *bodyguard* would whisper in my ears to disclose that the role of the plainclothes officer was to *take a bullet for my father if necessary.* I would coyly smile at this but never thought for a moment that what was being uttered was true. Looking back now, perhaps the words of my college *bodyguard* were, to some extent, true.

One day, we invited a few friends, including my college *bodyguard* over to play football at the residence at Federation Park. During the game, the ball went over the wall on to the street and my *bodyguard* elected to climb over the ten-foot wall to recover the ball. And what luck he had! A police jeep was parked up outside waiting to change the shift of an officer. When the officers noticed what happened my *bodyguard,* quite ironically, was thrown on the ground, frisked and a gun placed on his head. When nothing suspicious was discovered on my *bodyguard* and he explained the situation to the officers, he was released. They admonished him and reminded him about the danger in which he placed upon himself and the fact that he should at all times respect the AG's property. This drama unfolded outside unknowingly to us. My college *bodyguard*, who was embarrassed, told me the story later at school. I never repeated this story to my father, who if he had known would have been upset with my college *bodyguard* and by extension us his sons. I am not certain if the police officers ever told my father about this incident. Maybe they did and he just silently took note. Today my college *bodyguard* and I are still best of friends.

Making new friends, tea parties and fashion shows

Living in Federation Park opened up a network of new friends. In the neighbourhood we befriended Carlton Alfonso Jr. also known as *Fuzzy*, whose father was the Chief Brigadier in the Army. *Fuzzy* lived a few houses down the street from us on Trinidad Crescent and would often visit us to play basketball in his army green t-shirt, a trait which he undoubtedly acquired from his father. Later on *Fuzzy* would follow in his father's footsteps and join the army. There was also Gregory Brooks who lived on Barbados Road. Brooks also was always around the home in Federation Park. Brooks' father was a High Court judge and also well known by my father. Both *Fuzzy* and Brooks got along quite well with my parents. Other new friends who frequently visited the home and became 'adopted' children of my parents were Louville Moore and Kieron Bailey.

Then there were others, who came out of nowhere overnight, who we called friends yet to my parents they were not. Over time, some of them my parents accepted but they still warned us to be vigilant. My mother would utter words like – *remember your father is the Attorney General so be careful with whom you keep as your company.* On reflection, I now understand that she was trying to steer us in the right path lest we go down the road of folly. I admit that back in those days we did hang out with some 'undesirable' company. They were *'friends'* who wanted to be friends because of our father's position. Yet I also admit, there were some who were not as privileged as us and who did not have the strong family support structure that we had. These friends admired us and would do anything to protect the sons of the AG. It was these friends who turned out to be the most genuine persons we would ever come across in our life.

While in Federation Park, through the *Alliance Française*, we hosted two French West Indian students who came to Trinidad to improve their English. The first student was called Hervé from Guadeloupe. A year later, in 1995, we hosted Lionel Corbion from Martinique. My parents always supported this exchange programme with *Alliance Française* and were quite happy to open our home to these students. Lionel however recalls rarely seeing my father. His last impression of my father was one of a very busy man who left early for work in the morning and came back late in the night. Today, Lionel still resides in Martinique and is a very good friend of the family.

One thing that was certain was that we had an open door policy at the home in Federation Park. As already mentioned, for us Federation Park was a playground. On any given day – football, basketball and video games would be played simultaneously with our friends and acquaintances. There was one caveat to these fun and games. All sports would have to promptly stop at seven in the evening to enable my father to watch *Panorama news* on the television. Even the armed police officers stationed at home around the clock enjoyed the freedom at Federation Park. At lunch and dinner times, Martha would ensure that the officers on duty had something to eat and drink. Officers would often chit-chat with Martha during the day, and as a result she made many police officer friends over the years. Not surprisingly one of the officers confided in her that there was always a fierce competition among them to be posted at the AG's residence. I could attest that, life was relaxed and stress-free for a police officer on duty at Federation Park.

Federation Park was also the home of fundraisers in the form of tea parties and fashion shows. One year my mother together with her friend Patricia Sookdar hosted a tea party and fashion show to raise funds for my father's Ortoire/Mayaro constituency. The event was so successful that a second one was planned and came off the following year. Throughout my father's tenure as a Minister, my mother always provided him with physical and emotional support. The proceeds from these events went towards the purchase of two stoves for elderly homes in Mayaro and Moruga. My brother Jules would always say that it was these tea parties and fashion shows that first inspired him to become "an Event Architect".

The doghouse fiasco

In the game of politics, you must be careful with everything you say and do. Yet it is difficult to remain in politics without being smeared with some form of bad publicity. About a year after we moved into Federation Park, the Ministry of Works and Transport constructed a kennel for our four dogs at the back of the property. One of the weekly newspapers got wind of it and published an article claiming that my father built a doghouse at the AG's residence for $10,000 TTD. In 1992, this was an enormous sum of money (and I am sure for some, it still is today). The gist of the article was that my father was squandering taxpayers' money and unlawfully using financial resources to provide shelter for his mixed breed dogs. The truth was that the figure published in the newspaper was very much inflated and the relevant Ministries involved approved the financing. These were the aspects of the politics, which my mother never really liked – the fact that you were exposed to untruths and constantly under the public radar.

Sometime around the *doghouse* incident, we asked our father to pave a section of the driveway where we played half court basketball. The driveway was uneven with gravel and we tried to persuade him that in its current state we exposed ourselves to serious injury. After considering our pleas, my father indicated that since it was government property he would have a word with Colm Imbert, the Minister of Works and Transport at the time. Months and years dragged by and there was no evidence that the Ministry took our proposal seriously. We continued playing basketball on the stony, unpaved driveway. Thinking about it today, it is quite possible that my father never spoke to Imbert about paving the driveway. Or maybe he did. However with the *doghouse* incident still fresh in his mind, my father probably decided not to press the matter further in order to avoid being in the public spotlight once again.

As children, we too fell under the public radar. Like when my brother Jules sported a brand new pair of Michael Jordan sneakers at college and was heckled by his classmates. I distinctly remember one student who constantly teased my brother with the following words – *remember it is my parents' tax money which paid for your sneakers!*

I have spoken to many persons, both in public and private life, about my father. One thing that is commonly agreed upon is that my father never used his Ministerial Office for private gain. A public figure once told me that he knew many politicians and if there is one thing he was certain about was that Keith Sobion was never corrupt or involved in any underhand dealing. For myself, I know that my father did not have a corrupt bone in his body. This reminds me, once again, of one of his favourite sayings to us – *the only asset you have in this world is your good name.*

Those quirky moments

My father was quite a quirky character at times. This trait portrayed itself quite evidently in our early days at Federation Park. My mother used to say that my father was politically naive. To justify this reasoning she recalled an instance when he invited journalists home on a weekend to interview him. My father dressed rather casual for this interview, wearing a plaid short sleeved t-shirt and a pair of white slacks. That was however not the worse part – he was barefooted. My mother argued. She knew it was weekend, however she thought he could have dressed more formally. She was blunt with him – *suppose they take a picture of you and put it in the newspapers?*

But my father was not only a bit naive; he was also stubborn. He stuck to his argument that he was appropriately dressed for the occasion and he wanted the journalists to feel relaxed in the comfort of his home. My mother begged him to at least put on some shoes. My father refused. He was so caught up in his grassroots persona and the fact that he was entertaining the media; some of whom he said were his dear friends. My father said that if the media took any photos, they would only take the top half of his body and not his feet. And so the argument ended.

The next day, the media published a photo in the newspapers with Keith reclining on his armchair with his two eyes closed catching him, in a split second, in the middle of a thought. His right hand is gesticulating upwards as if he finally analysed his thought processes and was about to execute his point. It was a full picture and not an upper body photograph as my father expected. The media got his bare feet and they stuck out like a sore thumb. My mother was irate!

Being *politically naive* must be contrasted with being *politically careless*. While a Minister, my father was paid every month by government cheques. Many times my mother would find in random places at home his monthly cheques, almost stale-dated, that he never cashed. When she enquired of my father about it he would act surprised, then admit that he forgot to deposit them. My mother could not understand how my father could forget to deposit his monthly cheques especially with three children to take care of. This demonstrated to me that my father could be negligent and that money was not the motivating reason for him accepting public office. Even many years later after my father passed away, my mother found sums of US Dollars in the pockets of more than one pair of his trousers.

There were other moments, which were far from quirky but more startling. Like the first time I opened the freezer and saw these huge claws or teeth smiling back at me. I soon got to learn our freezer was used to store *wild meat* such as agouti and tattoo (armadillo). Wild meat is a scarce and expensive delicacy that was usually given to my father by his constituents as a token of appreciation for his work.

Colm's bridge

On a daily basis my father would speak to Cabinet colleagues whether it was face-to-face at home in Federation Park or on the telephone. Out of all these interactions, one stood out to me. It was a telephone conversation he was having with Colm Imbert. Exactly what they were speaking about I cannot recall, but it was clearly a matter of national interest. Soon the conversation got a little heated. I could not hear what Imbert was saying on the next line but it was clear on my side that my father's patience was being tested. After a few minutes into the telephone conversation my father blurted out – *"Look Colm, why you don't go build a bridge in Maraval?"*

This rhetorical question must be taken into context. Firstly, Imbert was the Minister of Works and Transport and his Ministry had the overarching national responsibility for building bridges. Secondly, Imbert was the MP for Diego Martin East, which included Maraval. Thirdly, in reality there was no bridge to be built in Maraval and the point my father was trying to get across, in jest, was for Imbert to leave him alone. On reflection, my father would have many telephone conversations and personal visits by Imbert. Both colleagues always appeared to have a very close relationship when it came to the affairs of the Government.

On matters affecting Ortoire/Mayaro, my father relied on the
expert advice of Imbert on the construction of the La Ruffin
spring bridge in Moruga (which collapsed in 1993)[84] and the
bridge on the Manzanilla/Mayaro Road.

Tit for tat with Basdeo Panday

Something a bit embarrassing happened to me weeks before
the general elections in 1995. At that time Basdeo Panday, the
Leader of the Opposition, was a member of a panel which was
invited to a national school debate on politics at St. Mary's
College. The actual theme of the debate fails me due to the
passage of time. For this same reason, I cannot recall the names
of the other panellists. However, I do remember the event being
a grand affair as female students from St. Joseph Convent were
also present at the College's Centenary Hall. All during this
time I was the son of the Attorney General.

After each panel member delivered their opening remarks, the
floor was then opened to ask questions. I am not certain what
motivated me to take the microphone that day, but I proceeded
to ask Mr Panday a question. My question was prolix. To be
succinct the gist of my question was – *If elected Prime Minister
what would you do to make life better for each and every citizen?* Panday
smiled. He then asked me my name. As soon as he heard my
last name he paused, reflected a bit and then smiled again.
After what seemed like a million heartbeats Panday replied:

"Young Sobion, who wrote that speech for you? Perhaps it was your father?"
The entire crowd laughed. I was mortified and immediately

---

[84] *Mooring of boats on to Moruga bridge weakening supports of the last 'spring bridge'
in Trinidad*, Daily Express, 8 May 2014.

turned red. At that moment, I wished I had never asked the question. The laugher continued and only died down after much prompting from the teachers. In all fairness Panday answered my question. Yet I was distracted, as all eyes were on me. Clearly the *Sobion* name had spent some time in the public domain. The very next day, the exchange between Panday and myself was brandished all over the daily newspapers – *Panday heckles AG's Son* (or words to that effect). Everywhere I went with my father after that, be it to political rallies in Mayaro or private functions, people would ask him – *is this your son which asked Panday the question?* This made me realise that the name *Sobion* was no longer my own.

Having the *Sobion* name as our surname was akin to attaching my father by the hip. When my brother Jules came on as a substitute for St. Mary's College during an *Intercol* football match, he came on to play, in my opinion, primarily because his friends were behind the benches jeering and urging the coach to bring on *"Sobion's* son." When Jules' eventually did come on the field to play, it was remarkable how his picture ended up in the Sports section of a daily newspaper. I am not discounting the talent of my brother but perhaps his picture made it for the wrong reasons. He did not score the winning goal but his picture was there in all its glory with the reference – *"Jules Sobion, the son of the Attorney General Keith Sobion".* Every time we made the news – be it for sport, art, education or entertainment you were sure to read in the caption the famous phrase – *son(s) of the Attorney General Keith Sobion.* And when a story was published after he left public office, the newspapers would yet refer to us as – *The son(s) of the former Attorney General Keith Sobion.* This aggrieved my father. Especially as we grew older and he no longer held public office, he felt that we had a right to our own identity. Fortunately, times have changed and my brothers and I have gained the individual respect we deserve in our respective fields. Or so we hope. Years later and despite all our earnest efforts, today in the news we are now graciously referred to as *"the son(s) of the late Attorney General and Minister of Legal Affairs, Keith Sobion"*.

Monitoring our movements

When it came to our movements, our father knew everything. On more than one occasion, my brother Jules would take our father's Isuzu Jeep (registered PBA9), while my parents were sleeping, to go party with friends at the *Base Night Club* or *Club Coconuts*. To move the jeep without making any noise, my brother would put the vehicle in reverse gear without starting the ignition. We would then push the jeep from the front and allow it to roll down the garage with my brother steering the wheel. Once out of earshot, my brother would start the ignition and his friends would jump in the jeep. They would then drive off into the middle of the night.

One morning, my father asked my brother if he used his vehicle the night before. My bother denied. We also supported my brother and claimed we had no knowledge of the subject. We however did not take into consideration that we were inexperienced in life and worldly matters. At first it appeared that my father believed our denials to his accusation. Then he changed the course of his argument. He wanted us to explain to him how it was possible for a police officer to spot his Isuzu Jeep in the parking lot of the *Base Night Club*. Our jaws dropped. We underestimated the strength of our father's office and police network. The officer, possibly someone who worked with him, identified the vehicle by the easily recognisable licence plate number. Looking back at it, the police officer was just doing his job. As my father would often repeat – *"Just remember I was once your age."*

Broken Traditions

Life as the son of an AG was not all a bed of roses. As a son of a Minister much was expected of us both in and out of the classroom. Further I felt that by choosing politics, my father sacrificed his family time with his wife and children. Before we moved to Federation Park, every Sunday the Sobion family would sit around the table to share a home-cooked lunch meal. During Sunday lunch, one of the five of us would volunteer to say the *Grace before meals* as we offered up to the Lord our week and the hands that prepared the food. As soon as my father was appointed a Minister, his seat at the head of the table became conspicuously empty. He was always at meetings, the office, Mayaro, or simply out of the country. Shortly thereafter the family tradition simply broke down. We moved from the lunch table to eating in front of the television. There would be no family interaction and exchange as before since we were now entertained by cable TV. On lazy days, when my mother was too tired to cook we would order Chinese food from *Sunday Kitchen* on Cipriani Boulevard. In short, our Sundays lost their intimacy. Things became lacklustre with the absence of my father.

Despite the absences I genuinely believe that my father did his best, given the circumstances. I say this because there was a tradition which he kept, albeit for a few years, while he was a Minister. Every Christmas Eve, he would take his sons to the *Original Drag Brothers Mall* (the People's Mall or simply *the Drag*) on Frederick Street to purchase our gifts. I knew that this was a tremendous sacrifice for him because he had no patience for the traffic on the road and the rush which came with last-minute Christmas shopping. At *the Drag,* we would start on the Frederick Street entrance and walk through the labyrinth of the street mall until we exited on Henry Street. Once within the labyrinth, my father would buy us sneakers or items of clothing of our liking. This stirred up some attention among the vendors because back then, *the Drag* was not a place where politicians or the upper echelons in society would frequent. If my memory serves me correctly, the tradition of Christmas Eve shopping in *the Drag* was broken during his last year as a Minister. The mention of *the Drag* also brings me back to my father's midnight escapades downtown on Independence Square where he would purchase daily newspapers from street vendors. On odd occasions we would wait outside *Express House* with him at night to purchase the newspaper straight off the printing press. For some strange reason, the purchasing of newspapers at the stroke of midnight brought a sense of joy in my father's life. Roger Lewis and Johnny St. Clair (my father's driver) joined my father on these midnight adventures. They remember Keith as a Minister openly interacting with the street vendors in the middle of the night without his security detail.

My memories at Federation Park were one of a carefree life where at any given moment we had scores of friends socialising at the home. Although my father did receive death threats, I never seriously thought that his life, our even ours, were under danger. Today I believe that the life of a child whose parent is a Minister would be a drastically different one to the life that we experienced.

Whenever I pass by Trinidad Crescent on Federation Park I still remember those good 'ole' days. The lot is still there but the physical home is no longer standing.

Chapter 12

The lost election

I haven't seen my constituency in months

Two months after the Occah Seapaul incident, my father received the surprise of his life. On the afternoon of Friday 6th October 1995, Prime Minister Manning unexpectedly announced in the Parliament that General elections would be held in Trinidad and Tobago on Monday 6th November 1995 – one year earlier than expected. During his announcement, the Prime Minister indicated that he advised the President to dissolve Parliament immediately upon the conclusion of the sitting.[85]

It was alleged that only a couple selected Government members knew that the Prime Minister was going to call a snap election. It was also widely speculated that some Opposition members got previous wind of the early election date and used it to their advantage. My father however was not privy to such information and the first time that he found out about the early election date was right there and then in the Parliament chamber. An MP in Manning's Cabinet told me that when the Prime Minister announced the snap election in the Parliament most members were taken by surprise, including my father. It was also said that upon hearing the Prime Minister's announcement my father while holding his head, whispered: *"Oh shit... I haven't seen my constituency in the last five months."*

---

[85] *Hansard*, 6 October 1995 at pg. 1170. Nomination day was announced as Friday 20 October 1995.

There could be some veracity in this statement. Throughout his stint in politics, my father had a challenge in balancing his heavy Ministerial portfolio and his duties as an MP. What also perpetuated this challenge was the size and the distance of his constituency from Port of Spain. Years before the new election date was called, my mother used to advise my father to visit his constituency office at least once a month. In politics, the optics was essential and if you were seen regularly in your constituency, half of the battle was already won. As one of my father's advisers once said – *people does get vex with you if dey don't see you.*[86]

My mother went further and even offered her services to represent my father as a proxy at his constituency office. My father declined my mother's offer. For him, the people wanted to see the elected MP, not his spouse. The irony was that the MP was missing in action in Ortoire/Mayaro. Today my mother would boldly declare that had Keith listened to her on this point, he would have retained his seat in the 1995 elections.

When the snap election was announced my father and his team had exactly one month in which to campaign. He and his advisers immediately sprang into action by drafting a manifesto for the constituency entitled *"Ortoire/Mayaro into the 21ˢᵗ Century with Keith Sobion – PNM."* Although his team was involved in the drafting, the style of writing inherently represents that of my father. In the opening page of the manifesto my father wrote –

".... four short years later, we can point to some achievements (in Ortoire/Mayaro) in the national effort and we now stand poised to gather the returns from those years of sacrifice and investment."

---

[86] Interview with Oliver Alexander.

From reading the above extract and indeed the entire document, I get an underlying sense that Keith was disappointed in the calling of an early election as he had a lot of unfinished business to be done in his constituency. There were constituency projects that my father wanted to further advance such as – the investment of oil and gas opportunities in Guayaguayare and the utilisation of the Lagon Doux estate for eco-tourism.[87] Sources close to my father also said that he had a legislative agenda he wanted to complete before his term as AG expired.

At the launch of the one-month campaign my father knew he was fighting an uphill battle.[88] Roger Lewis admitted that at the outset he and my father agreed that it was difficult for him to win Ortoire/Mayaro in 1995. Lewis advised that in order to win, they had a lot of groundwork to do in the constituency in such a short space of time. The strategy that was therefore devised was not to do anything to lose. So for the next month my father and his team set up their base in Mayaro. My father was so preoccupied in the short campaign that he did not even get the opportunity to leave Mayaro to go to vote in Diego Martin where he was registered on the electoral list.

Along with the manifesto, the campaign team printed thousands of t-shirts for immediate distribution. Looking back at it, the 1995 campaign t-shirts were a comical sight! At the front of the t-shirt was the phrase *"Sobion Again"* with a tick underneath representing the public endorsement of my father's bid for re-election. When one further examined the t-shirts the tick clearly resembled the *Nike Swoosh* logo. It was

---

[87] *Ortoire/Mayaro Into the 21st Century with Keith Sobion – PNM* at pg. 5.

[88] Technically it may have been a much shorter than a one month campaign. My father (like all other candidates) was officially given the nod to contest his seat sometime around nomination day on 20 October.

Jules who first pointed this out to my father and this brought some amusement to us. Notwithstanding this, the t-shirts were popular with the constituents despite its flagrant breach of *Nike's* intellectual property. What was equally amusing was how my father pronounced the word *"Again"* while on the campaign trail. There was an emphasis on the second *'a'* which resulted in him dragging out the catchphrase making it sound like – *"Sobion Agaaaaaaaaaaaain."* The accentuation on the second *'a'* transmitted a confidential message which was that *Sobion was in Ortoire/Mayaro to stay, regardless if you like it or not!*

The cottage meetings, the walkabouts, the public meetings and the motorcades continued. It was like a family affair with everyone coming together to assist with the campaign. Even my father's friends from Port of Spain came to lend a helping hand as we took the campaign to the road. One was Tony Cherry, an attorney, who loaned us his bright red sports car which Jules drove with much pleasure. At this juncture, I would like to mention the public meetings. Every night during the campaign, my father would travel to a different town such as Basseterre, Grand Chemin, La Lune, Marac, Tableland, Rio Claro and Mayaro to deliver an address on a political platform. At one of these meetings, my father was advised that for security reasons, the general public should not stand behind him while he was on the platform delivering a speech, as was previously practiced. After that, he addressed the crowd with the public facing him directly head-on.

I loved to see my father in action as he delivered his address with a few talking points or sometimes ad-lib. I admired the way he would speak, standing in one position yet rocking his legs in a dancing motion with his right index finger pointing up to the heavens. The crowd would laugh or clap, depending on what he said. In a distance I would hear a voice coming out of nowhere, rising above the din '*True talk Sobi*'. I felt proud of my father just knowing that he could stand there, with little or no notes, delivering a speech in front of hundreds of people who had their eyes glued on him as if he was a television. Sometimes I wanted to ask to join him on the platform and say a few words too but in mid-thought I changed my mind. Just the thought of it made me nervous and I could see myself getting stage fright in front of all those peering eyes. Needless to say, I thought my father was an impressive orator.

Compared to the 1991 Ortoire/Mayaro election campaign, the duration of the 1995 campaign was not only much shorter but there was also one less candidate in the race. In 1995, the NAR failed to field a candidate in Ortoire/Mayaro thus making it a two-way race between my father for the PNM and one Razack Ali for the UNC. But who was Razack Ali? Not much was known about him in my father's team except that he was a farmer and a local government Councillor in the Rio Claro/Mayaro Corporation. Razack Ali was born and raised in the constituency – Rio Claro to be exact. Ali's home advantage and familiarity on the ground was a critical factor for which my father paid a heavy electoral price.

Keith's entry into Mayaro – it's too late!

In Ortoire/Mayaro, not only were the UNC quickly mobilising their troops but also the independents. A week before the elections, my father and his team were in a vehicle passing by the Mayaro junction. As his convoy bent the corner, what he saw distressed him. Abu Bakr was on a podium by the junction speaking to a crowd of persons that swelled over onto the adjoining pavements. Upon noticing this, my father turned to his team member Oliver Alexander and simply said –*'it's too late'*. Abu Bakr was a powerful and persuasive man and this sight confirmed to my father that his political career was in jeopardy. When this news reached his adviser Victor Campbell, he too was moved with emotion that he shed tears while constantly repeating my father's sentiments – *It's too late!* Abu Bakr walked the corridors of Mayaro as an independent campaigning against Keith and the PNM. His campaign was mainly against the incident involving Glen Ashby and pamphlets on the subject were distributed widely throughout Mayaro.

Yet Abu Bakr was not a total stranger to Keith (to this day it still baffles me that my father attempted to speak to him during the 1990 short-lived *coup d'état*). As Attorney General, my father would have overseen the legal matter regarding the compensation of the Muslimeen property on Mucurapo Road. From what my father described, I had a feeling that he and Abu Bakr were playing mind games, with one trying to outdo the other with a wily move. Who won at the end of the day is difficult to say, but my father often repeated Abu Bakr's opening remarks during one conversation:

"Minister, I am so delighted to see you, I was passing by your home in Diego Martin the other day and I noticed it had some cracks on the wall, perhaps it needs a little touch of paint…anyway about the matter on Mucurapo Road…"

Despite all these warning signs, my father and his team continued the fight in Ortoire/Mayaro. As short as the 1995 campaign was, Lewis remembers it taking a heavy toll on my father. To survive during the day my father developed a strategy whereby he would go temporarily incognito by parking his vehicle in a hidden garage in Mayaro and then walk to Lewis' home to take a power nap. As his vehicle was well known in Mayaro, if anyone saw it parked in front of Lewis' residence, they would know exactly where he was. By using his vehicle to conceal his whereabouts, my father was therefore able to get some rest in the middle of the day.

On election night, 6th November 1995, my father and his supporters were at the Moruga constituency office eagerly listening to every result as it poured out the television set or radio. The scene was one of anxiety. Everyone was either at the edge of their seat or biting their nails nervously. As a vote came in, an elderly woman would swiftly mark down the number with a piece of chalk on a blackboard attached to the wall. I heard the enthusiastic clapping of hands when the Mayaro results trickled in. Like 1991, the districts of Ortoire, Mayaro, Radix Village and Guayaguayare did not pose much of a problem for my father and the PNM. There was however one exception and that was in the polling station at Plaisance Village, Mayaro where my father lost with 177 votes to Razack Ali's 202 votes.[89] This news came as a disappointment, as in 1991 my father won at this polling station with 178 votes.

Moruga was the district that brought a thunder of desk thumping and whistles from my father's supporters. There my father won in all nine polling stations with handsome victories

---

[89] Nariva/Mayaro Civic Centre, Plaisance village, Mayaro (polling division no. 2425).

in Basseterre (355 to 46 votes)[90] La Lune village (237 to 23 votes)[91] and Marac village (298 to 37 votes)[92]. Marlene Henry did not hesitate to remind me that my father did better in Moruga in 1995 than in 1991. The statistics are true on this point. Keith amassed 1,984 votes in Moruga in 1991 while in 1995 (with the relatively same 69% voter turnout), he ran away with 2,176 votes.

Then in came the Rio Claro votes. At the end of the night my father won only one of the twelve polling stations in Rio Claro.[93] My father suffered a setback in the rural village of Libertville, losing by 79 votes to 243 votes.[94] When one compares the votes in Rio Claro my father again received more votes in 1995 than in 1991. However the fact that the NAR was absent in the 1995 Ortoire/Mayaro race may suggest that Ali retained the core UNC base while at the same time acquiring the swing NAR votes.[95] Henry could not have explained it better – *Keith got licks in Rio Claro!* My father also lost very badly in the three polling

---

[90] St. Augustine R.C. School, Moruga Road, Basseterre (polling division no. 3440).

[91] La Lune R.C. School, La Lune village, Moruga (polling division no. 3455).

[92] Marac Baptist School, Marac village, Moruga (polling division no. 3460).

[93] This was also the case in 1991. In 1995, Keith's sole victory in Rio Claro was at polling division 2570-01, Rio Claro Junior Secondary School, Naparima Mayaro, Rio Claro. There my father received 290 votes while Razack Ali received 207 votes.

[94] Polling Division 2580-02, Muslim League School, Libertville, Rio Claro.

[95] In 1991 Keith received 1,580 votes in Rio Claro. In 1995, his tally in Rio Claro slightly increased to 1,628 votes. Voter turnout in Ortoire/Mayaro in 1991 and 1995 was stable at 69.5% and 69.4% respectively (Source: EBC).

stations at Poole.[96] The loss was expected, but not the margin. It always proved difficult for the PNM to win in this district. Poole was the beginning of the end of my father's attempt to successfully reclaim the Ortoire/Mayaro seat.

Winston Churchill was once quoted as saying – *Now this is not the end. It is not even the beginning of the end. But it is, perhaps, the end of the beginning.* For my father the beginning, the 21st century vision which he had conceptualised for Ortoire/Mayaro, came crashing down with the results of Barrackpore. *Hurricane Barrackpore* swept through the office, ferociously shaking the windowpanes and the very foundation on which we stood. Every time a Barrackpore result was released I heard the gasps of *"Ohhhh!"* and then *"Ahhhh!"* from my father's camp. It was as if a dagger was stuck into their hearts and the intruder was taking all the time in the world to withdraw it. In one polling station in Barrackpore, my father's 30 votes paled in comparison to Ali's 601 votes.[97] In Kanhai South Trace, Ali secured another landslide victory – 352 votes to a paltry 11 votes.[98] Long after these results were released my father would say in jest that he gave out more t-shirts in Barrackpore than he received votes. Putting all the humour aside, it was the Barrackpore votes which sunk the hearts of many of my father's supporters that evening.

---

[96] At Poole River Presbyterian School, Fonrose village (polling division no. 2585) Keith received 43 votes to Ali's 405 votes. He also lost at Poole R.C. School, Naparima Mayaro Road, polling division no. 2595 (54 votes to 269 votes) and at another polling division (no. 3425) at Fonrose Village, Poole (28 votes to 205 votes).

[97] Kanhai Presbyterian School, Kanhai South Trace, Barrackpore (polling division no. 3480-2).

[98] Kanhai Presbyterian School, Kanhai South Trace, Barrackpore (polling division no. 3480-1).

The results coming out of Tableland just added salt to the open wound. There my father lost in all three polling divisions (392 to 58 votes, 200 to 103 votes and 269 to 59 votes).[99] Everyone was quiet after that. You could even hear a pin drop!

Just before midnight, my father lost his bid to recapture the constituency of Ortoire/Mayaro.

My father, looking quite dejected, delivered his conceding speech to about forty or so supporters in the Moruga constituency office. My memory fails me regarding the full contents of his ad lib speech. But I do remember one thing he said, and that was, that even though he was no longer the MP for Ortoire/ Mayaro, he would always be there to assist the people in whatever way he could. After his speech we went to a back room where my mother cried openly. She was duly consoled by her friend Patricia Sookdar. A few minutes later, the security whisked away my father, family and his small entourage. The destination was Mayaro. In our vehicle, everyone was more or less sombre, staring into the darkness through the window.

But the night did not end there. What happened next remains forever in my memory. About a half an hour into the journey my father's entourage met up with a UNC victory motorcade coming from the opposite direction along the dark winding road. Noticing the PNM flags on our vehicles, the UNC crowd went up into a jeer. My father ordered his driver to stop. When he alighted from the vehicle the crowd got even more unruly. I think it was because at the time they thought that it was a convoy of solely PNM supporters. In the darkness, the crowd did not

---

[99] Polling divisions no. 3510, 3515-01 and 3515-02 respectively.

realise that my father, the now former MP and Minister, was actually a part of the convoy. *Keith what are you doing!* my mother gasped. It was too late; my mother's voice was lost in the din as my father headed towards a man standing in the open tray of van. This man wore a cap with the image of the rising sun, the UNC symbol. For some strange reason, in the darkness of the night, he also wore sunglasses. Maybe because the sun was rising everywhere – on caps, vehicles, t-shirts, posters and flags. That man was Razack Ali, the new MP for Ortoire/Mayaro. My father, wiggled through the crowd, went straight to the van and shook Razack Ali's hand. As soon as this happened, the crowd again went up in an uproar. The tassa drums started to beat louder, people started to clap. The atmosphere no longer seemed tense but more festive. The shaking of hands was the final ritual. It symbolised the peaceful transfer of power from the PNM to the UNC in Ortoire/Mayaro.

I understood my mother's fear. Keith had put himself at risk by coming out of the vehicle into the middle of a crowd during an election night. From all accounts, my father knew what he was getting himself into. Lewis, who was in our convoy, confirmed that just before he exited the vehicle my father handed over his firearm to him and said – *"watch the boys"*. Lewis further recalled that my father's security, a gentleman called William Mckay, was also taken by surprise by my father's sudden exit. Mckay immediately took precautionary measures in case something went awry. In less than two minutes, my father returned to the vehicle. It was a long way home to Mayaro. Slowly, I closed my eyes reminiscing on all the events that recently unfolded.

During the early morning of the 7th November we learnt that the general election ended in a political stalemate with both the PNM and the UNC sharing 17 seats, while the NAR, led by A.N.R. Robinson, held on to the 2 Tobago seats – Tobago East and Tobago West. Questions soon arose as to which party would form the next government. Later that day we returned to Port of Spain knowing that our time expired at Federation Park. When we arrived at the home, we were taken by surprise that the security post was vacant. Slowly but surely we were being reminded that my father was no longer an MP or a Minister. Even back at college, I became a recluse for a few days and shied away from my friends to avoid speaking to them about my father's defeat at the polls. I must mention that my now *'former college bodyguard'* was still loyal to me, even though my father was no longer the Attorney General.

Picking up the pieces

Shortly after the elections, the Elections and Boundaries Commission (EBC) confirmed that Razack Ali won, albeit by a small margin. According to the official results, in Ortoire/ Mayaro my father obtained 8,201 votes whilst Ali received 8,944 votes.[100] Ali won by a margin of 743 votes in a constituency where 7,673 registered electors elected not to vote.[101] In fact 1995, witnessed the lowest voter turnout in the history of Ortoire/Mayaro.[102] It was felt by some PNM members that

---

[100] This should be compared to 1991, where in a three-way race for Ortoire/Mayaro, my father captured 7,578 votes an estimate of 46.9% of the votes cast. In 1995 my father received 8,201 votes which was 47.08% of the votes cast.

[101] Out of the 25,092 electors in Ortoire/Mayaro, 17,145 ballots were accepted and 274 rejected. The total non-voters (7,673) includes the rejected ballots (Source: EBC).

[102] The voter turnout in 1995 was 69.4%. The year 1991 witnessed the second lowest voter turnout at 69.5%. (Source: EBC).

the party should have moved to contest the vote and call for a recount within Ortoire/Mayaro. My father expressed his disagreement to this idea and the result was left as is. Ortoire/Mayaro was officially labelled a *'marginal'* seat post-1995.

In terms of the overall election result even though the ruling PNM party won the popular vote the UNC used its 17 seats to form a coalition with the NAR to have a majority in the Parliament.[103] Basdeo Panday became the first national of East Indian descent to become the Prime Minister of the country. This was not the only piece of history which stemmed from the 1995 election. Less than two years later, A.N.R. Robinson was appointed President by the Electoral College making him the first active politician and first Prime Minister to be appointed to the highest office of the nation. Even though these two gentlemen were on the opposite side of the political fence to Keith, my father would have equal respect for them, especially in his later years.

The election results crushed my father. Not only did he lose his parliamentary seat, but his party was no longer in Government. I sensed also that my father was disappointed that Manning called a surprise election which did not permit him sufficient time to efficiently prepare for his campaign in Ortoire/Mayaro. My mother always encouraged my father not to be upset with Mr Manning. She felt that at the end of the day it was Manning who had unwavering faith in him when he appointed him AG. Through all this, Manning remained the Leader of the Opposition after the elections.

---

[103] The PNM won the popular vote with 48.76% of the votes (Source: Report of the Elections and Boundaries Commission of the Parliamentary Elections held on 6 November 1995).

Keith also felt a bit isolated because his friends within the party – like Gordon Draper, Keith Rowley and Ken Valley all went on to win their parliamentary seats, although they were now serving in the Opposition. Oliver Alexander, once explained to me that what truly hurt Keith the most with the 1995 election was that he was no longer in a position to help the youths of Ortoire/Mayaro. According to Alexander – *Keith was a people's person.* This was a man who would issue handwritten recommendations for his own constituents and, to use Alexander's testimony, *fix up a constituent's passport in one day.* It was then I realised that Keith used the office of MP as a vehicle to promote and develop the youths of Ortoire/Mayaro. He was a role model for some and now that he was no longer an MP, he felt that his purpose had vanquished.

I have heard many reasons which sought to explain why my father lost his seat in Ortoire/Mayaro. Manning's view was simple – *"he (Keith) tried to serve well, but it just did not work out".* Other views were much more direct like – *"Mayaro people did not come out to vote".* While this may have been true to some extent to obtain a clearer analysis one needs to dig deeper beneath the surface. In my opinion, the main difficulty that plagued my father for the four years that he served as a Minister was the fact that he had little or no time to service his constituency. My father held a massive Ministerial portfolio – AG and Minister of Legal Affairs (a portfolio which is split nowadays into two separate Ministries). Additionally, my father represented one of the largest constituencies, in terms of geographical size, in Trinidad and Tobago. One party supporter recalls that due to the geographical size of Ortoire/Mayaro, a recommendation was made to appoint a Senator within Keith's Ministry to assist him. This recommendation never came to fruition.

I turned to Colm Imbert who expressed sympathy for Keith and described him as being a victim of the circumstances. Imbert acknowledged that it was impossible for Keith to perform his Ministerial duties and also represent a constituency far away from Port of Spain. In addition to this, and given the vastness of Ortoire/Mayaro, Imbert concluded that Keith could not have been effective as AG/Minister of Legal Affairs and as an MP for Ortoire/Mayaro. Sadly, one of the roles had to be sacrificed. In hindsight, Imbert thought that things would have been less of a burden on Keith if he had contested a constituency like for example Port of Spain North/St. Ann's West, which was not only a more convenient location but also a PNM safe seat.

I searched the *Hansard* and found out that Imbert had been saying this at least since 2005. During a Parliamentary debate on an Elections and Boundaries Commission Order, Imbert spoke about the size of three constituencies; one of which was Ortoire/Mayaro. His views back then are so applicable that it ought to be repeated here:

There are three seats: the Ortoire/Mayaro seat, the Nariva seat, and the Toco/Manzanilla seat which take up one-third of the land mass of Trinidad and Tobago.

If I remember my geography correctly, if you take a line from Matelot and you come down to the Moruga area, along that whole eastern coast, as far as I could recall, those three seats take up one-third of the land mass or, at least, a quarter of the land mass of Trinidad and Tobago, but there are only three Members of Parliament.

Another reason is that in terms of the quality of the representational function, and in terms of the kind of attention that an MP could give to his constituents, I think those constituencies are just too big in

Trinidad and Tobago, with the kind of support systems that we have at this point in time, in terms of assisting Members of Parliament.[104]

As a result of this debate and many other debates that ensued thereafter, the size of the Ortoire/Mayaro seat has been significantly reduced. The seat traditionally known as Ortoire/ Mayaro is now simply "Mayaro". Moruga and Tableland, which used to fall under the Ortoire/Mayaro constituency, are now lumped under the seat Moruga/Tableland. Nowadays Imbert believes that a candidate for AG should ideally come through the Senate.

On the 10th November 1995, Basdeo Panday, the new Prime Minister, appointed Kamla Persad-Bissessar as his AG making her the first woman to be ever appointed to that position in the history of the country. *The Trinidad and Tobago Newsday* featured a picture on its front page the very next day. The picture illustrates the new AG dressed for work in a formal navy blue outfit with white pin stripes. My father is seen behind her, dressed in white slacks and a burgundy nehru collar shirt, a dress code suggesting the ease at which he was stepping out of public life. My father is gesticulating, making way for Persad-Bissessar to take a seat on his former office chair.

The Newsday appropriately titled the photo – "HAVE MY SEAT". The short description read:

Former Attorney-General Keith Sobion graciously handed over his office and his job to the new AG, Kamla Persad-Bissessar yesterday. As her former teacher, Sobion promised his help with legislation if she needed it.

---

[104] Colm Imbert, *Hansard*, Monday 6 June 2005 at pg. 272.

Front page of the Newsday, Keith with Kamla Persad-Bissessar.
Originally published in Newsday. Reprinted with permission.

Another appointment of interest was Razack Ali, Keith's
Ortoire/Mayaro rival. Ali was appointed as a Parliamentary
Secretary in the Ministry of Local Government.

The end of 1995 heralded an end to a Ministerial fairy tale for
my family. We had to vacate the Federation Park home. As my
parents did not foresee an early election, much less a loss, we had
nowhere to live as my parents had sold their Dorrington Gardens
home. We needed to find somewhere to live and fast. My mother
went down on her knees and prayed. Within a few days, we found
a townhouse to rent in Flagstaff Hill, St. James and we moved
in at the end of the year. Financially my parents were in a bind.

With both parents out of work, I wondered how my parents were able to afford the rent at Flagstaff Hill. Around this time I noted that my father grew more and more conscious of the fact that he neglected us during his time in politics. In fact he put it in writing to my mother. In a secret letter dated 2nd January 1996 he wrote that he was now "trying to change" his life and that he could not continue "with the torment of knowing that" he "wronged all of us". My father begged my mother, and by extension us, for forgiveness. The end of 1995/early 1996 was a trying time for the family as we tried to put aside the loss, hurt and neglect while ushering some stability into our lives.

By January 1996, the new Government began its work in earnest. For my father, he also needed to follow in the footsteps of the new Government. His old law firm, *Sellier* invited him to return as a Partner. He thought about this offer for a long time and eventually declined. His reasoning was that he felt that his name was tarnished by politics and that he did not want to place that unfair burden upon the firm. At one point, he was engaged in separate discussions with colleagues Russell Huggins and Ronald Boynes for a possible collaboration, but nothing tangible ever came off the ground. So for the next seven months, my father worked out of the cramped living room in Flagstaff Hill. My mother always said that psychologically, Keith was affected by the result of the 1995 elections. In those months after the election, he found it difficult to re-acquaint himself with the legal profession. He received a few legal briefs, some from his former Partners at *Sellier* and his other lawyer friends. He appeared as an Advocate in Court occasionally. Notwithstanding this, his mind still lingered in the politics.

The money was trickling in however I sensed it was not enough to pay the rent. Times were difficult living with a self-employed ex-politician and a mother surviving on a VSEP package from the national airline. My mother thought that instead of paying rent we should buy a home. But how could we do that given the financial strain? My mother then said that she was going to the office of the developers of Flagstaff Hill to explore options. My father replied that she was wasting her time. My mother always claimed that God was in front of her when she walked into the office that day. Hours later, she returned home with good news. The family was allocated an end unit townhouse, metres from the townhouse which we were renting. The price was a bargain of a lifetime. Even my father could not believe it! We gathered our belongings to move a second time. This time it was something more permanent.

Jamaica opens her arms

Just as we were starting to enjoy some stability, something else happened. In the first half of 1996, my father was shortlisted for the position of Principal of the Norman Manley Law School in Jamaica. He had to travel to Kingston to be interviewed and my mother accompanied him on that trip. I remember meeting them at the airport (the old airport in Piarco) on their return from Kingston. My father looked glum. Upon inquiring how the interview went, he said although he gave it his best shot, he had a gut feeling that he was not the successful candidate. My mother adopted the approach – 'what is for you is for you'.

Once I read an article whereby a researcher proved that your gut instinct is right 90% of the time. On this occasion, Keith's gut instinct yielded to the 10% of doubt. Shortly thereafter, my father received the news. He was selected to be the new Principal of the Norman Manley Law School, Jamaica. He was on Cloud Nine; especially since he was now the first West Indian trained lawyer to become the Principal of the Norman Manley Law School.

Despite my father's elation, there were some who felt that he was too young, and by extension unfit, to be appointed Principal of the Law School. Actually it was the same recycled argument used when he was appointed AG. I have seen many situations where those with the power to promote or hire someone have refused to do so because of that person's youthful age. There are other criteria worthy of merit such as intellect, trust and aptitude. I was happy that my father was able to defy the odds. These are the same odds that continue to inspire me daily.

Principal Sobion at Kingston, Jamaica

One issue which I have often considered is whether venturing into politics was a grave mistake on my father's part. One viewpoint seems to suggest that my father's entry into politics was a disappointment especially if one takes into consideration the further contribution he could have made to the practice of law and the development of trial advocacy. This school of thought was unreservedly expressed by André des Vignes, his colleague and dear friend. There is another view, such as that of Mayo Robertson, which plainly suggests that Keith's decision to enter into politics was a good one having regard to the interest he had in social justice and creating social change. On the converse, Mayo acknowledged that in pursuing an active career in politics, my father felt that his principles were sacrificed and as a result he suffered some degree of disappointment.

At the end of the day, if one was to juxtapose the two views, the development aspect was constant and remained the core. André des Vignes' view focused on the development of the law itself, in a more private landscape. Under Mayo, the notion of development was more grounded in country and civic duty. One thing that was certain was that neither my mother nor my paternal grandmother thought that Keith should have been involved in frontline politics. My mother would go so far to say that politics destroyed the family relationship.

In a sense, one cannot now reverse the hands of the clock or erase history. The fact remains, even with all its flaws, that if it were not for politics, my father would not have been the person who he was.

To Silk or not to Silk, that is the question

Shortly after my father's tenure as a Minister questions were raised, by lawyers and politicians alike, as to whether he was eligible or entitled to *Silk* (elevation to Senior Counsel). The award of *Silk* is perhaps the highest honour in the legal fraternity that can be bestowed upon any advocate or Attorney at law. After Trinidad and Tobago became a Republic in 1976, lawyers who received *Silk*, were then referred to as Senior Counsel (abbreviated as S.C.). Prior to that year, lawyers who took up *Silk* were called Queen's Counsel (Q.C.) or, when appropriate, King's Counsel (K.C.). At Law School I was taught that the expression *Silk* referred to the silk gowns that Senior Counsel wore when they addressed the Court. To be granted *Silk* there are several criteria which ought to be satisfied, some of which include: a distinguished practice, high ethical standards and legal skill and acumen before the Courts.

In my country, there have been instances where former Attorneys General were elevated to *Silk* while in office. There is a school of thought which reasons that an Attorney General, as the titular head of the bar, should automatically be appointed *Silk*. In other words, once a person is appointed Attorney General he or she should be conferred with *Silk ex officio* – by virtue of the office. If this line of reasoning is to be accepted, another school of thought argues that appointments of Attorneys General should pass the stringent *'Silk material'* test.

My father never 'took *Silk*' as Attorney General, or during his lifetime. He was however once recommended. The anecdote given by him was that while he was Attorney General, a recommendation was made to Prime Minister Manning for him to be appointed *Silk*. After discussing this recommendation with the Prime Minister, the Prime Minister advised that it would not be appropriate for a sitting Attorney General to take up *Silk*. The matter ended there. Manning's account, given many years later, was a bit different. Manning explained that he did not endorse Keith taking up Silk because he thought that at the particular point in time, he did not have the required length of service at the Bar.

Many years after his exit from politics, certain eminent legal minds that I have spoken to found that Keith was "Senior Counsel material". Reginald Armour S.C. for instance considered factors such as my father's indelible contribution to legal education, the fact that he was a genuine leader in the profession and also that he was concerned in developing legal education for people in the Caribbean.

Michael de la Bastide, Keith's mentor, remembers my father as a young lawyer operating out of *Sellier*. *"Keith would instruct me from time to time,"* said de la Bastide with a croaky voice which immediately brought forth that Queen's Counsel allure. There was at least one instance where my father and de la Bastide did a case together, with my father appearing for the litigant on the other side. From early on, de la Bastide was impressed with my father referring to him as a young lawyer who enjoyed trial advocacy. Yet Keith and de la Bastide also shared a bit of history outside of the courtroom. Between 1988 and 1990, Keith served as the Secretary of the Law Association working closely with de la Bastide, the Association's first President. All of these interactions led de la Bastide to conclude that my father was very competent as an advocate and "certainly Senior Counsel material."

Russell Martineau S.C. was a bit more reserved. Martineau did not wish to delve into a debate as to whether or not Keith was deserving of *Silk* after his demise. I interpreted this to mean that to write about my father, I should probe deeper into who the man was rather than letting him be constrained by an artificial concept such as *Silk*. I paused for a second to think about this. My father was a man who recommended lawyers to take *Silk* while he was AG. He was never thrilled about receiving awards such as *Silk* neither bestowing such an honour upon himself.

If Senior Martineau reads this, I do hope he will forgive me for prodding on into the topic. That being said, like a judge concurring with the majority judgment, it may be appropriate for me to say at this juncture – *I have nothing further to add.*

Chapter 13

Jamaica, Jamaica

"Welcome to Jamrock, camp where de thugs dem camp at,
Two pound ah weed inna van back.
It inna ya hand bag, ya knapsack, it inna ya back pack
The smell ah give yah girlfriend contact..."

Damian "Jr. Gong" Marley, son of reggae legend Bob Marley.

Sound systems and Dub Plates

Ever since my father received news of his appointment as Principal he would explain sarcastically to family and friends that he was moving to a safer country. It is true that crime in Jamaica was bad. However he knew the irony in his statement, which was, that crime in Trinidad and Tobago was not that far behind. The truth was that my father was excited about the move to Kingston. The feeling was mutual for my mother who thought that it provided a welcome escape for my father from national politics. Yet the move to Jamaica, quite naturally, brought to life some family changes. If it were up to my father alone, the entire family would have moved at the same time. My mother however had an opposite opinion. She preferred not to uproot Darien and myself from St. Mary's College. Darien at the time was in Form 5 and was to sit Caribbean Examinations Council (CXC) examinations the following year. I was in Form 6 in my final year of A Level studies and was recently selected Head Prefect. My father's response to this was curt – "Are there no good schools in Jamaica?" In the end my mother's viewpoint prevailed. Jules would commence studies at the University of the West Indies, Mona campus and thereby travel to Jamaica with my father. My mother, Darien and I would join them the following year.

And so it happened, my father and Jules left for Kingston in August 1996. My mother cried at the airport and seeing her cry, for some strange reason, made me cry too. After fifteen years of being together as a family unit, we were separated. Waters divided us but not our hearts. My eyes filled with water as I saw my father and Jules slowly slip away through the departure gate.

In Kingston, my father settled down as Principal of the Norman Manley Law School quite easily. For Jules it was different as he found it difficult to adapt to his new student life at Mona. My brother missed the entertainment scene in Trinidad and his friends from *Players Inc.* and *Radioactive*. Despite this nostalgia, Jules found companionship in our cousin Reisan Alexis who also moved to Jamaica to study Environmental Sciences at Mona.

Like any move, things seemed a bit unsettled at first. For starters, my father's residence in Jamaica was not immediately ready upon their arrival. In fact, for about two months, my father and Jules lived in the Jamaica Pegasus Hotel on Knutsford Boulevard. They lived there for so long that Jules became familiar with the pool man, the chef and the hotel's porters on a first name basis. Slowly my brother grew homesick and he struggled to find a way out. But his friend Hopkinson from *Radioactive* had other plans. He urged him to stay, as Jules was now a direct link for *Dub Plates* in Jamaica. In plain terms, a *Dub Plate* is a voiced over version of a popular song, whereby the singer endorses a *disc jockey (selector)* or *sound system (group of disc jockeys)* with witty adapted lyrics. In the heights of the 90s, the *Dub Plate* reigned as King in the grassroots culture of reggae and dancehall music, just in the time of Jules' arrival. Selectors were playing *Dub Plates* in the dark corners of clubs and in open-air yards in Kingston. There would be 'clashes', acts of musical war, perpetuated by one sound system against another. In the late 90s CDs were relatively new so we keenly listened to sound systems like *Stone Love, Ricky Trooper from Killamanjaro, Bass Odyssey, King Addies* and *Mighty Crown* on cassette.

Dub Plates therefore became an asset and the more a sound system possessed, the more their ratings would shoot through the roof. As the *Dub Plate* culture and musical clashes spread overseas to Trinidad it was in *Radioactive's* interest that Jules remain in Jamaica. For Jules, it was equally a worthwhile business because he became the supplier and intermediary between the dancehall artistes and *Radioactive*. But *Dub Plates* were not inexpensive. Four *Dub Plate* songs pressed on a Vinyl record could cost a sound system a minimum of $1,000 USD. The cost triggered a somewhat triangular business chain, where my father would invest in *Radioactive Dub Plates,* my brother would connect with the artiste to press the Vinyl, then ship to Trinidad for *Radioactive* to play in a club. From the proceeds of the parties, *Radioactive* would then transmit the funds back to Jamaica for my father. For the first time in Jamaica my brother became motivated. Arrows Studio on Windward Road would be Jules' home away from home where he would seek and engage artistes to make *Dub Plates* in favour of *Radioactive*.

The first *Dub Plate* that Jules pressed for *Radioactive* was the late Tenor Saw's 1985 hit *Ring the Alarm* on the *Stalag riddim* – sang over by Tenor Saw's brother. The party scene back in Trinidad loved it so much that Hopkinson requested more musical ammunition. Subsequently, my brother managed to secure other *Dub Plates* from artistes and *deejays* (singers) such as Bounty Killer, Beenie Man, Merciless, Buju Banton, Sizzla, Capleton, Everton Blender and Morgan Heritage. In the later years, we made a *Dub Plate* for *Radioactive* with Mr Vegas and Sean Paul singing their hit *'Hot Gal Today'* live at Arrows Studio.

As enterprising as it sounded, everyone in this triangular business chain benefitted except my father. The truth is that my father was operating at a horrible financial loss, in some instances not even recuperating his principal investment. What my father got out of this shoddy business plan back then was not plain for the eye to see. When however one looks a bit closer it was an investment in my brother Jules as a young entrepreneur. Such an investment turned out to be the best investment he ever made in his life.

Trying to settle in (Kingston 1996 – 1998)

In December 1996, Jules returned to Trinidad for a couple weeks for the Christmas holidays. Well so my father thought. I knew something was brewing that evening when we picked up his suitcase outside the Piarco airport to load it in the boot of the car. His suitcase was heavy like a tonne of bricks. I asked Jules why his suitcase was so heavy. He replied with a smile so broad that it reached the Queen's Park Savannah – *"Because I'm not going back"*.

When it came to my father's knowledge that Jules never planned to return he was taken aback by disappointment. He could not believe that his son had abandoned him in Kingston without saying a word. Slowly, he pondered where he went wrong. By this time he had already moved out from the *Jamaica Pegasus Hotel* and took up residence in the Law School's townhouse, *The Pines of Millsborough* just off Babican Road in Kingston.

Jules was no longer there, and it bothered me knowing that my father was now alone in Kingston. That state of affairs did not however last long. In early 1997, my father persuaded my younger brother and myself to visit him for the Easter holidays. I use the word *'persuaded'* quite loosely because who would refuse an all-inclusive trip to Jamaica? Darien and I landed in Kingston, for the very first time, in March 1997. My father, who had a customs pass, was already inside the immigration area of the airport, ready to greet us. After collecting our baggage off the carousel, we proceeded to exit the arrival hall. Damian Marley's signature tune "Welcome to Jamrock" was not even penned yet but back then we already appreciated his words. My brother would often say it and on reflection it was true. Upon exiting the arrival hall at the Norman Manley International airport two things hit us – the sweltering heat and the pungent smell of marijuana. While we got a whiff of the ganja we did not see anyone with a *spliff* (or chalice) in their hand. Maybe the person was behind the tree hiding from both the sun and the police officer nearby directing the airport traffic. Legend has it that the marijuana scent still lingers on since Emperor Haile Selassie landed in the Palisadoes airport in 1966. As we say in Trinidad – Jamaica sun different. Another thing hits you when you leave the Norman Manley airport and head in the direction of Kingston. You are really driving on a narrow strip of land, a peninsular, south of which is the Caribbean Sea. If you exit the second roundabout on your right, you would end up in Port Royal, the former meeting place of pirates and now the home of *Gloria's,* for us, the best fried fish and bammy in town. As soon as my father whisked us away in his navy blue Volvo sedan, we were overlooking the Kingston harbour. With our windows down, the slow rhythm of reggae music outside penetrated our ears. We climbed up Mountain View Avenue, took a right on Old Hope Road, straight through Barbican Road and then up Millsborough Avenue. Voilà, we finally arrived at our home away from home – *The Pines of Millsborough* affectionately known as *The Pines.*

You could see it in my father's eyes that he was happy to have Darien and myself for the Easter weekend. *The Pines* was a very scenic compound. It was a gated community, with a pool and each townhouse had a rectangular shaped patio, covered by cobalt blue awnings. A well-kept garden with tropical flowers surrounded each patio. The environment seemed secluded and private and was without a doubt handpicked by my father. As night fell, I looked out of our bedroom window. Lord Creator's composition *Kingston Town* played from a distance signalling that there was a reggae party somewhere among the twinkling of the lights. *Kingston Town* echoed in my ears like a lullaby which made me fall asleep. My father fell asleep with us that night in the same room. At the break of dawn I realised that my father was a lonely man.

For the Easter weekend my father took us to the north coast to an all-inclusive hotel resort in Ocho Rios. I noticed that he had an extra zeal in his step, perhaps for two reasons. Firstly he wanted us to feel comfortable in our new environment, which in the next few months would be our home. Secondly, he thought that Jules poisoned our minds about his own experience in Jamaica. The fact was that Jules did not dislike Jamaica. It was more that he grew homesick and found it difficult to adjust to the new phase of his life without us. Soon our Easter vacation was over and we flew back to Trinidad. We were eager to return in the next few months to take up permanent residence in *The Pines*.

During the second half of 1997 we were swept with a fury of familial changes. Jules moved to Ohio to commence his studies in Business Administration at *Malone University* while Darien and I returned to the land of Reggae. Realising that Jules missed the Jamaican *Dub Plate* scene, my brother and I sent him by post a cassette with Beenie Man's dancehall hit *Who am I (Sim Simma)*. Upon receiving the cassette Jules replied that this was *"the craziest dancehall riddim"* (rhythm) he had ever heard. Around this same time Princess Diana died in a car crash and my father was deeply saddened by her death as he watched the news live at home on the BBC. A little later in the year, the mood changed when *the Reggae Boys* qualified, for the very first time, for the 1998 FIFA World Cup Finals in France. Driving on Barbican Road immediately after, we witnessed the euphoria of the Jamaican people waving their national flag, some which bore the face of Bob Marley or words of the new craze that hit Jamaica *"More Fire"*. It was indeed a landmark achievement. Jamaica was the first English speaking Caribbean country to make it to the World Cup!

My mother was the last of the family members to join us in Jamaica in October 1997. My father was quite happy to have the majority of the family unit in Kingston. I admit that he was a tad bit disappointed that Jules decided to pursue higher education in the United States. As a true regionalist, my father firmly held the view that an education at UWI was just as equal

221

or even better than an American degree. He would often ask rhetorically – *Why go to America when you can get a cheaper and better education in the West Indies?* Despite this belief, he supported Jules through college and, together with my mother, settled him in to his dormitory in Ohio.

The next couple of weeks we spent organising our registration at school. Darien joined Form 6 classes at Wolmer's Boys School. The Vice Principal, Deanne Robb, was from Trinidad and this facilitated a familiar bond between herself and both my parents. I commenced studies at the Faculty of Law at the UWI, Mona campus. My entering into Mona to undergo my first-year law studies was a bit of an anomaly. Being a national from Trinidad and Tobago I was automatically zoned to commence my first year at UWI in Trinidad. My father stepped in and had a word with Andrew Burgess, the Dean of the Law Faculty in Barbados.[105] After my father explained that I was a Trinidadian, now residing with him in Jamaica, I was accepted to enrol at the Mona campus. From that day on, thanks to my father and Dean Burgess, I became an honorary 'Jamaican' during the first year of my law studies.

Not only did I spend a lot of time at the Faculty of Law but I also spent a significant number of hours at the Norman Manley Law School – which was on the same campus grounds. As my father was Principal I was able to have privileged access to the Law School's library facilities. This proved to be worthwhile because the legal literature there was more updated than that of the UWI general library. During my first year on campus, and on the encouragement of my father, I did an internship at the Law School's library where I assisted the staff with the

---

[105] Andrew Burgess became a Judge of the Caribbean Court of Justice in 2019.

retrieval and re-stacking of law reports and journals. This internship enabled me to become familiar with law reports, library staff and its internal operations. On reflection, I spent more time learning about how a law library operates as opposed to studying substantial law. Nevertheless, I believe that this was my father's subtle way of making me acquainted with legal education from the bottom up.

There are other memories on Mona campus which have stood the test of time. Picking up patties and plantain tarts for our lunch at the Senior Common Room and collecting books at the UWI bookstore at a stroke of a pen – thanks to a University grant allocated to my father; are just some of them worth mentioning.

Another memory, which stands out, occurred after a class. My father trotted over to the Law Faculty where he met a group of us hanging out outside the classroom. I remember he was neatly dressed with his shirt and tie and had this charming smile on his face. He introduced himself and then asked each of us why we decided to pursue a career in law. I remember the answer of one of my classmates, Keisha Hyde, a young girl from Jamaica. She said, *"Well Mr Sobion, I always was interested in law and justice."* *"Are you sure?"* my father replied. Keisha answered to the affirmative. Keith smiled. He smiled that day because he sensed that this was a young student who was to be taken seriously, one who appeared not to be besmirched by material gain, as so often is the case, but had a genuine interest in the welfare of others.

Outside of lectures and tutorials I became a rebel. At first, my mother plaited my hair in neat canerows. Shortly after I opted to grow dreadlocks. Jamaica did just that – it brought out the fire in me. While I spent a lot of time absorbing this alien concept called the law, my mind was adjusting to another dispensation. I wanted to become a Reggae singer, and what better place to launch your musical career than the land of reggae, wood and water? It was however the Reggae and the water which balanced itself out to quench this fire. It was in Jamaica that I went through a self-reconciliation process. I tried to decipher whether I wanted to conform as a lawyer in the strict sense of the word or whether I should be unorthodox. A year earlier, when I was seventeen years old, I remember telling my father that I wanted to become an entertainment lawyer. Maybe this sounded clownish because his reply was that the notion of an 'entertainment lawyer' did not exist. He swiftly explained that I could be a lawyer who specialises in entertainment law. So this was how I was going to jump-start my career in entertainment law − by becoming a musician.

By late 1997, I hooked up with a local producer, known as "Gaddafi" (not to be confused with the Colonel in Libya), attached to the Mixing Lab Studio on Dumbarton Ave, Kingston. He introduced me to a popular rhythm which was made by the sensational duo Sly and Robbie. The cost of producing my tune *"It only comes down to you"* was approximately $30,000 JD (Jamaican dollars). In 1997, $1 USD was about $36 JD and if one does the maths back then, Gaddafi got a good deal. The studio was an experience. Every musician had a *spliff* in his mouth, as ganja smoke serenely floated through the closed studio room. One night my father and my mother came down to the studio to speak with Gaddafi and the owner of the studio about my song and the contractual arrangements. In typical lawyer style, my father asked Gaddafi and the owner the same question, in ten different ways to ascertain whether or not the guys were trying to make a mint out of me − or him.

One thing I learned about some Jamaicans is that they are full of hype. Gaddafi impressed my father with his smooth words when he said – *this ya yute have so much potential tah Raas, we gwan tek him pon tour cause 'im song ah gwan wicked.* In the end my father liked Gaddafi. Maybe he reminded him of a youth, one who may be rough around the edges but was working hard to make an honest living. He never had an air of suspicion about him after that conversation. In the end, I never went on tour despite my musical pursuits. I am however the proud owner of a 45-inch record produced by Sly and Robbie which rightly bears my father's name as the Executive Producer.

The following year I collaborated with a producer named Bobby (also not to be confused with Bobby Digital) who lived close to Half Way Tree. Bobby invited me to his studio in Mona where, for a fair price, we recorded a single entitled *Don't Cry.* Bobby was a fatherly figure and when he played the keyboards he jumped on the chair with so much zeal as if the music was literally speaking to him. At the studio, my father 'loaned' me a member of his administrative staff called Mustafa Ajab, to help me sing the harmony line. Mustafa, a Jamaican and a devout Muslim who always wore a skullcap over his balding head, was also an underground reggae singer who produced a handful of CDs. While recording, it dawned on me that reggae music was not only for the Rastafarians but a world music which knew no borders or religion. On another thought, my time in Jamaica made me realise that besides Mustafa many of the administrative staff at the Law School looked up to my Dad as a father figure. These included Georgette Johnson, Delroy Pinto and Andrew Walker.

For my father, his love and appreciation for reggae music intensified as soon as he arrived in Kingston. Of course he knew reggae many years prior to his arrival. Campus life in the 70s was rife with the music of the likes of Bob Marley and Peter Tosh. He loved Marley's music and once described *I shot the Sheriff* as the ultimate display of the singer's defiance. But living in Jamaica was refreshing as he was exposed to a new generation of the genre. This music also made him skank like he did to Bob in the 70s. Without a doubt his favourite reggae artiste of the new generation was *Buju Banton*. He listened keenly to Buju's *Inna Heights Album* and knew word for word the spiritual songs from Buju's throaty opening *Our Father,* to *Hills and Valleys* and then *Destiny.* Last but not least, I cannot forget his cherished song *Love Sponge.* He would sing along as the track blasted through his stereo just outside the patio. I could hear him now – *I don't wanna let you go, with you I'm in no 'urrrrrrrrrrryyyyyy….*

From this, my father had a master plan of fusing the music and cultures by organising a concert in Trinidad with the calypso artiste David Rudder and the iconic Buju Banton being the top acts. He often spoke about this collaboration with a passion. The concert never materialised as he got caught up with his daily life at the Law School. Another calypsonian my father listened keenly to was Leroy Calliste also known as *The Black Stalin.* The philosophy and wit behind *The Black Stalin*'s songs such as *The Caribbean Man* and *Black Man Feeling to Party* appealed to my father. Besides absorbing himself into the music, Keith tried to integrate himself into every single aspect of the Jamaican fabric. Indeed in August 1997, he had already purchased and read the book "How to Speak Jamaican" by Ken Maxwell. In less than a year he picked up some Jamaican patois and knew the roads of Kingston by rote. Within months he did a road test and acquired his Jamaican driver's permit. He was informed that after five years of being a resident he would be entitled to vote, a franchise that he never exercised. He listened attentively to

Motty Perkins, a well-known radio personality and would call in when Perkins was debating a matter on local politics. The relationship that my father and Motty had was strictly over the airwaves and Motty even knew his voice as soon as he called in. Keith would also listen to IRIE FM on radio on his leisurely drive to work in the morning. IRIE FM broadcasted a station identification about a man speaking to his friend about his broken radio. The man complained to his friend, in Jamaican Patois – *My radio stuck on IRIE FM but yuh know wha?....me nuh bodda fix it.* Keith would give a hearty laugh every time he heard that broadcast.

It was my father who taught me the roads of Jamaica. In a world without GPS and Google Maps my father used a map which he purchased from the *Texaco* gas station at the bottom of Jacks Hill Road. He would put this map on a table, raise his glasses to just over his eyebrows and use his index finger, like it was an invisible pen, tracing which road I should follow. That was how I learned to drive from Mona campus to Wolmer's Boys' School by National Heroes Circle. My routine every day was to leave campus, pick up my brother after school at Wolmer's, head up Slipe Road and return to campus where I would then meet my father after work. All this thanks to my father who taught me the roads on a worn *Texaco* map. When my mother came to Jamaica two months later, I then had to show her my daily route around Kingston. Up to this day, my mother would say that it was I who taught her the roads when in all fairness I learned them from my father.

But learning to navigate the roads of Kingston had its disadvantage. My beloved father would use his benevolent teachings to make me his personal 'gofer', someone who would run his errands, drop off his work documents, buy his lunch, pick up people at the airport while he was resting comfortably at home or at the office. So I had to find a way to level the playing field. By so doing, I risked the chance of getting into big trouble.

One weekend my Trinidadian friend Ronaldo Rollocks asked me to take home a girl he was 'checking' in Portmore a coastal town just outside Kingston. I had never been to Portmore before and the 'gofer' Volvo was at my disposal. Plus, to make my choice easier, Keith was out of town for the weekend. So, I happily obliged. The revered *Texaco* map was rendered useless. The girl was from Portmore so she would show us the way. And she did. She directed us through all the main roads and back roads that in a half an hour we were in front her *Yard* (in Jamaica your home is your *Yard*). We stayed a couple of hours at the girl's yard chatting and after a while I started to feel like a 'third-wheel'. It was close to midnight when Ronaldo gave me the signal for us to leave. We jumped into the car and drove off into the dark night. On the way back is when I thought we needed the *Texaco* map. We tried to remember the girl's directions back to Kingston, but how many back roads could one take before one realises that they are lost? No Portmore co-pilot, No cell phones, No *Texaco* map, No Google maps invented yet. We were so lost in a labyrinth that we could not even remember how to return to the girl's yard for further guidance.

I didn't get scared until Ronaldo muttered under his breath – *I think we in downtown Kingston because this looks like Trench Town.* From the time Ronaldo said *Trench* I became petrified. I tried to keep my cool. At least we were in Kingston but mind you, the supposedly bad part. Then I heard *psssshhhhhhh* like the sound of gushing air being released. I felt the tyre wobble. Ronaldo once again took the occasion to speak, like a biblical prophet – *my yute I think we have a flat.*

Ronaldo warned me that night: whatever you do, do not stop in the middle of the ghetto to change the tyre; *this is a Volvo.* So I kept driving straight along this road, still not so sure where we were going. The tyre was so flat that I heard the rim scraping on the road. No more rubber left. Then I heard *Woop Woop Woooooooop!* I didn't know which part exactly we were but Ronaldo swore we were making circles in *Trench Town.* Maybe he was right because we passed the same man at the corner three times. I knew. I was driving. We reached him a fourth time. The man at the side of the street signalled for us to stop. *Maybe he can help.* Ronaldo warned me again – *We are in the middle of Trench Town don't stop!* I refrained from pressing my brakes. This time it was close to two in the morning.

Somehow, beyond my faintest imagination, we made it to Heroes Circle, a landmark that I knew very well since it was close to Wolmer's Boys' School. We arrived home maybe around three in the morning. As soon as businesses were opened, Ronaldo and I scrapped together some money. We proceeded straight to the tyre shop on Barbican Road. I remember the man at the shop curiously looking at the tyre. He looked more distressed than us when he exclaimed– *Unno ah drive dis cyar down to di rim Star!* We just chuckled nervously. Fortunately the old tyre was replaced with a new one before my father arrived home. He never knew a thing. Or at least so we thought.

Having said this, even if he knew and got angry, the feeling would have lasted a very short duration. My father was not one to be attached to material things. In Jamaica, we had full access to his bank cards and would never hesitate to use them. He would only reproach us if he recognised that we abused the financial privilege that he reposed in us. When our lifestyle became too extravagant for his liking, he would utter wise phrases such as: *Money does not grow on trees.* If we tried to refute our lavish spending, he would add – *You think I was born yesterday* or *remember, I was once your age and the only one you are fooling is yourself.*

Barbados (1998-2000)

Every time, again and again, I cry out against soul destruction

In the early part of 1998, my father travelled with Darien and I to Barbados. The purpose of that visit was to locate, in advance, suitable accommodation for me for my final two years of my law degree. Just like Kingston one year earlier, this was my first visit to *Little England*. I understood that they call Barbados *Little England* because the Brits love to holiday there. Nowadays, there is a more fashionable name for Barbados which is simply – *Bim*.

After landing at the Grantley Adams International Airport and on exiting the terminal by car, I could not believe the amount of sugar cane I saw along the road. That was my first memory of Barbados, the green fields of sugar cane we passed minutes after our arrival. Within a couple days, my father found a two-bedroom apartment in *Wanstead Gardens* that I occupied in my first year of study at Cave Hill. My roommate to be was Duane Allen, a Jamaican and avid cricket fan who would later spend many evenings talking to my Dad about West Indies cricket and Brian Lara.

While we were in Barbados my father could not stop reminiscing about the time when he was a student in Cave Hill in the early 1970s. So much so, he drove us up to *Black Rock* to see the block of apartments on Stanmore Crescent which he, Jawara, Saga and Rajkumar shared. Exiting the car, he handed us his camera and posed in front the apartment, cross-legged, the same way as he did in 1972. Even in 1998, he noted the fresh coat of cobalt blue paint on the wall outside the apartment. We still have the 1972 black and white photo which was originally sent from Bridgetown to Trinidad to his family. Behind the photo Keith wrote a personal note to one of his sisters:

"Every time – again and again I cry out against soul-destruction. Be Peaceful Sis, Love Keith."

More reminiscing took place on that trip. Keith said that while he was a law student in Barbados from 1971 to 1973, he recalled there being only one traffic light. Twenty-five years later there were many more – evidence to him that the economy and the automobile industry were booming. The trip to Barbados ended with a visit to St. Lawrence Gap, where my father introduced us to one of his friends who owned a restaurant and to Oistins – the best place on the island for fried fish.

Back in Jamaica I had roughly three months to prepare for my first-year examinations. Reading law was a totally new concept to me. I grappled to fully comprehend the basic tenets of Constitutional Law and Law and Legal Systems. As a result, even though I passed all my subjects, I was disappointed with my final grades. My father tried to pacify me by reminding me that it was a difficult transition from secondary school to the Law Faculty. He also recalled the Faculty's rules that first year grades did not count. It was the two years in Barbados that mattered the most. In August 1998, I flew from Kingston to Bridgetown with all intentions of doing better.

The Barbados Cave Hill campus was the quintessential melting pot of Caribbean students and culture. I say this without any hesitation whatsoever – to understand the Caribbean and to appreciate the potential of our people, one must be a part of the Cave Hill experience. Many of our regional politicians, entrepreneurs, judges and lawyers for example, passed through the Cave Hill system. As my father used to say, because of Cave Hill, he could travel anywhere in the Caribbean and have a friend who he could contact. Cave Hill therefore became the epitome of Caribbean unity. The island weeks, performing at concerts, and playing football in our CARICOM (Caribbean Community) football league, all brought about social cohesion and solidarity with our brothers and sisters from the region.

At Cave Hill, it was easy to get caught up in the University politics. During my first year, I got involved with the International Affairs Committee in the Guild of Students which was chaired by Mary Krow from Ghana. One instance the University had received a special invitation from Colonel Gaddafi for the student body to be represented at a Pan-African conference in Libya. Krow and another Committee Member named Yvonne Fiadjoe immediately put arrangements in place for me to represent the International Affairs Committee. When I mentioned this opportunity to my father he was quite ecstatic, due to Gaddafi's socialist ideology and Pan-African stance, and encouraged me to follow through with the offer. Unfortunately, the trip never occurred for me due to insufficient funding.

Cave Hill was also a continuation of my inner spiritual journey which first commenced while in Jamaica. I was eighteen years old, and my short dreadlocks started to bloom. I became more militant and Afro-conscious. In the evening after class I would beat drums with a group headed by Ean Maura, my Bahamian friend who later became the President of Guild of Students. I read more about Rasta, Emperor Haile Selassie and Marcus Garvey. Spiritually, in March 1999 I was baptised in the Ethiopian Orthodox Church in Bim where I was given the name *Wolde Amanuel* (meaning *"son of God" in Amharic*) by an Ethiopian priest named Abba Tsige Genet. My father, mother, and brothers flew to Barbados to witness the ceremony. My friend Maura was also present. My baptism was also a turning point for my father as after that he always wore an Ethiopian cross, which hung on a piece of black cord, around his neck. With all that was going on in my life, both spiritually and socially, I had no choice but to be extra diligent in my studies. The story about my father flying to Barbados to save me prior to my Family Law exam is a difficult memory to erase. During my two years at Cave Hill my grades progressively improved. My mission was accomplished and half my journey completed. On 1st July 2000 I graduated with an LLB degree with Honours.

Throughout my sojourn in Barbados, Jamaica was still my home. After graduation, I had a critical decision to make regarding where I should complete my Law School. I already was accepted to undergo two years of compulsory legal training at Norman Manley Law School where my father was Principal. The dilemma I faced was that if I did exceptionally well persons would form the impression that there was an underlying bias because my father was the Principal. On the other hand, if my performance was average, persons would think less of me as a young lawyer and compare me with my father. I raised this quandary with my father and he listened to my arguments carefully. He agreed. There would be mounting pressure on me as a student if I remained in Jamaica. My father however thought of another argument which had not even occurred to me. He indicated that if I wished to practise law in Trinidad and Tobago, attending Law School at home would be ideal as it would introduce me to members of the legal profession and the Judiciary. Indeed some local judges and lawyers served part-time as Associate Tutors at the Law School in Trinidad. Within twenty-four hours of that conversation, he reverted to me with these words: *The Principal at Hugh Wooding Law School has accepted your transfer. We will make the necessary arrangements for you to return to Trinidad.* The Principal at that time was the retired Judge, Madame Justice Annestine Sealey.

Principal Sealey recalled very well that conversation with my father. She expressed to him that students should have a right to express how they feel about the administration. She intimated that with my father at the helm of the Law School in Jamaica, I would waver between his sentiments and that of the students. I later understood that Kathleen Rochford, the then Registrar, also spoke to my father and approved of my transfer to Trinidad. Putting the puzzle together I realised, long after the fact, that my transfer was a well-orchestrated plan among three persons – a Registrar and two Principals. From Jamaica, I then moved to Trinidad to complete my two years practical legal training at the Hugh Wooding Law School. Once again I was caught up in two worlds, studying in Trinidad but regularly returning in between to Jamaica to be with my family.

In between Trinidad and Jamaica (2000 – 2007)

Bring back the Queen

Prior to starting Law School in Trinidad, my father carried us to Montego Bay where he was invited to speak on the implementation of the Caribbean Court of Justice (CCJ) within the region. I would refer to this experience as the *Montego Bay affair*. It was my first time in MoBay, as it is affectionately called, and I was particularly enthusiastic to hear my father talk on a subject which he was most passionate. The scene, a large school hall, was set for the debate, which, to my recollection, was organised by the non-profit organisation Jamaicans for Justice. Besides my father, there were about three other panellists. As the debate commenced it was easy to detect that my father was in the minority as all the other panellists held opposing views towards the CCJ. Judging from the crowd's response it became even more evident that the audience was also against the CCJ. It appeared that most, excluding my father, agreed that Jamaica should retain the Privy Council as the country's final court of appeal. The speakers against the CCJ relied on arguments such as the astronomical costs of establishing a regional court, as opposed to the Privy Council where access to justice was 'free of cost', and the fear that judges of the CCJ could not be insulated from political interference or manipulation. The mood was very emotional and tense. Soon it was my father's turn to take the podium to make his opening remarks. Once introduced by the moderator, the crowd became uncharacteristically quiet. The audience, including myself, listened intently to what he had to say. My father counteracted the views in relation to the partiality of judges by explaining that the region had many well-respected and distinguished jurists who not only argued before the Privy Council but were also members of Her Majesty's

Court. With respect to the financing of the Court he explained, very articulately, that the CCJ was to be financed by a Trust Fund which was financially independent from governments and administered by a Board of Trustees drawn from regional entities. He even quoted an editorial article in the Jamaica *Daily Gleaner* newspaper written in the year 1901 which expressed the view that the UK based Privy Council was *'out of joint'* with the realities of time.

Then came the question and answer segment. It was like a volcano waiting to erupt. The *Montego Bay affair* was in full effect. The audience threw questions left, right and centre to my father about the CCJ. On the podium he was like Muhammad Ali bobbing and weaving to avoid all the jabs of contention. The audience kept on pounding and pounding at him, question after question. It was like the other panellists did not even exist. I remember telling myself: *"Oh God like these people want to kill him!"*

Yet he held his corner. His gesticulations told it all. It was like a political platform once again. He wove his finger in the air while gently bouncing up and down in a 'dance like' manner while responding to questions on the podium. He was forthright, diplomatic and circumspect as he answered each question on the CCJ which the "mob" hurled at him. When the crowd did not appreciate an answer, the room went up in a jeer. In one instance I recalled the audience booing him. Others cried "No, No, No!" in strong disapproval of what he said. Once I heard a single clap of endorsement – or was it from us, one of his family members? The moderator tried a few times, with little or no success to calm the rowdy crowd. But the more the crowd grew rowdy the more passionate he became. At one point I really felt sorry for him and I wanted to cry. I wondered how long he would have to endure this pressure which was building up within the four corners of the school hall.

He however did last the period of tension. In fact at the end of the day I think he made a good showing at *the Montego Bay affair* as he single-handedly took on a strong and opposing audience. Despite the odds, afterwards some members of the audience came over to shake his hand and to offer him words of encouragement. This solidified in my mind that he gained the respect of a few members of the audience. In spite of being in the minority, he was to us a winner. That was a day I will never forget.

Yet this was not the only time in Jamaica that my father was having a difficulty in persuading an audience that the CCJ was a move in the right direction. At another panel discussion in Kingston my father got upset with the feedback from the crowd that he blurted out, quite sarcastically, – *"Well if you want to retain the Privy Council, then Jamaica might as well give up its independence and bring back the Queen."* To this remark, he received the unexpected reply from a member of the audience – *"Yes bring back the Queen that would be better."* My father was in complete shock! He realised that he was facing a daunting task ahead and that there was an immediate need to re-evaluate his strategy.

A few years ago, I read the book *The Life of Captain Cipriani* written by CLR James.[106] In true CLR James' literary style, he posed the following question to the reader:[107]

---

[106] The book included James' pamphlet on *The Case for West Indian Self Government.*

[107] CLR James *The Life of Captain Cipriani,* at pg. 50.

"What sort of people are these who live in the West Indies and claim their place as citizens and not as subjects of the British Empire?"

This question was posed way back in 1932, when independence from Britain was a fleeting dream or, for some, inconceivable. But the question James was posing was quite grave and required clarity of thought and reflection. Today many would claim that CLR James was way before his time. What makes matters even worse is that more than eighty years later we still cannot come to grips with who we are as West Indian people. We still, for example, doubt ourselves and our capabilities. The lack of complete regional endorsement and signing on to the CCJ, at the time of writing, is just one testimony of this. In hindsight at the *Montego Bay affair* what my father was attempting to do, intuitively, was to answer CLR James' question. He was trying to get across to his audience that we the citizens of the West Indies are independent and more than capable of governing our own judicial affairs.

Two years after the *Montego Bay affair*, my father was appointed by CARICOM as a consultant for the Court. During this consultancy, which lasted from 2002 to 2005, he travelled to every single country in the region promoting the CCJ. His public education programmes on the CCJ continued long after the Court was inaugurated in 2005. Michael de la Bastide, the first President of the CCJ, remembers the anxiety Keith had in his quest to lobby the average person, lawyers and politicians to support the Court and its role as the final Court of Appeal for CARICOM States. Whenever Keith visited Trinidad, he would make it a priority to contact President de la Bastide to discuss matters that would always seem to centre around a common theme – how to take the CCJ forward. "He was a great unifying force in Jamaica and a strong integrationist" – de la Bastide would say.

From the Maracas police station to the Bahamas Straw Market

It was Father's Day June 2001 and the place to be was under the scorching heat at a beach. My father was in town and we decided to celebrate the day with him at Maracas Bay. There were six of us in total, this I remember based on how the story eventually unfolds. At the end of our outing at the beach, I mounted the driver's seat and my father sat at the front passenger seat. As I proceeded to exit the Maracas car park, a marked police jeep coming from the opposite direction advanced through the exit. As the exit was a narrow one, the result was that both vehicles came to a halt with our vehicle facing head-on with the police jeep making it impossible to exit the car park. Realising that the police jeep would not budge, I placed my car into reverse gear. My father stopped me. He thought the police should set an example and not come *in* a one-way exit. While in the stationary car, he told the officers that this was an exit and not an entrance. Still the police jeep would not move. After what seemed like an eternity and some cross talk between both vehicles, I reverted to my original plan and reversed my vehicle thereby yielding to the police jeep. These were my radical days and when the police jeep passed by my vehicle I shouted *"Babylon."* For those who may not know, *Babylon* can be found in the Rastafarian lexicon and it is used to refer to someone or something which oppresses another. It is also commonly used to refer to the police. The police know the word *Babylon* and the fact that they are sometimes referred to as such. They may not like this fact, but they know it. After we exited the car park, I looked in my rear view mirror and noticed that the same police jeep was following us. When I mentioned it to Dad he said that I should just remain calm and keep on driving at the same pace. I followed his advice. As we mounted the steep incline (where the old Maracas police station was situated) there was a roadblock set up by the police. There the police in the jeep overtook our vehicle and signalled to their colleagues conducting the roadblock to stop our vehicle. Dad was infuriated. He hastily exited the vehicle and shouted out to the officers in the police jeep who were pursuing us: *"You know, the only reason why you signalled to stop us is because of what transpired in the car park!"*

The police ignored him. On their demand I gave them my licence and insurance papers. They searched the vehicle and each and every one of us. After finding nothing illegal, they searched again. My father warned us – *let the police do their job and do not use any obscene language.* But we were all frustrated especially Darien who, while eating a 'bake and shark' sitting on the bumper of the car trunk, was suddenly choked by one of the officers on duty. The policeman said he used foul language.

Darien was locked up in a holding cell after being charged for using obscene language and resisting police arrest. The very thing that my father predicted came to pass. It was like his worst nightmare. To add salt to the wound, one of the officers reprimanded my father with the following words – *"You feel you big, you are no longer the Attorney General!"* If my father's blood was not boiling then, it surely erupted when he heard that remark. *"Orrrrrrrr so that's what this is all about. I now understand"* – was my father's reply. My father demanded the names of each of the officers involved, a process which took close to an hour for eventual receipt.

Darien eventually got his own bail and was due to appear in Court on Monday. It was nightfall when we eventually left Maracas. What started off as a fun-filled family day turned out to be one full of gloom and despair. As the moon assisted the headlights of the vehicle in illuminating the narrow pathway of the lonely North Coast Road, Dad visibly upset grumbled – *they could have at least charged us for having more than five passengers in the car.*

The matter came up before the Port of Spain Magistrates' Court and my father selected Gilbert Peterson S.C. and Ayanna McGowan as Counsel to represent Darien. Being a witness in the matter, I was not allowed to enter the courtroom when the trial commenced. And the trial did not even last half an hour. I heard that Peterson was deft in his cross-examination of the police officers. One of the famous lines of questioning went like this:

Gilbert Peterson – so why did you arrest my client?

Police officer – because he called me Babylon.

Gilbert Peterson – who, what, where and when is Babylon?

Police officer – ....

It was at that point the prosecutor's case collapsed. I was told the police officer only stuttered and he never really answered the question. But the initial answer was inconsistent with the facts because Darien never called the officer *Babylon* (it was me). My father, quite amused by the said line of questioning, told Peterson afterwards that the latter question put to the witness was unfair as it was asking the officer four questions in one. The important thing was that the Magistrate upheld Peterson's no case submission. Darien was free!

Due to the amicable relationship Peterson had with my father, he never charged a fee for his court appearance. About a year later I referred a client to Peterson and upon asking him his estimated fee, his reply was – 'only *the Sobions* I charge for free'. This was a testament as to how much he respected and believed in my father. After the *Maracas* case, my father immediately instructed his friend Reggie Armour to file a malicious prosecution and false imprisonment case against the State and the police officers. However, as my father returned to Jamaica and time elapsed, he either was too busy or he had a change of heart. The matter was never filed.

This matter involving the Maracas police officers would plague my father's mind for the rest of his life. I arrived at this conclusion because seven years later, after he passed on, neatly tucked away inside his wallet I found a folded piece of paper. On that paper was his handwritten note that contained the date of the incident, the names of all the police officers involved and their identification numbers. My father would tell us that a good lawyer always walks with a pen…even when he goes to the beach.

A couple of months after the *Maracas* incident I had the pleasure of travelling to Nassau, Bahamas with my father. In Nassau, my father attended a meeting of the Council of Legal Education (also referred to as "the Council"), and I used this opportunity to tag along with him as his guest. This was my first time to the Bahamas and through the vehicle's window I saw the white sand beaches, a cyan blue sky and colourful houses with no gates or fences. This trip provided me with the chance to meet up once again with Ean Maura, my friend from Cave Hill campus. Ean, who met my father before at Barbados, took us to his grandmother's shop in the Straw Market on Bay Street close to the wharf. Hours before our appointed departure from Nassau, the Straw Market burned down and Ean was very heartbroken. The respect between Ean and my father was mutual. In his own words:

"When I close my eyes and envision him (Keith) I can see him now in short pants, slippers, his little black pouch around his waist, his glasses and his smile."

The time and experience in Bahamas and other islands instilled in me a love for the Caribbean. In time I realised that I was a reflection of my own father.

A few days later, we returned to Kingston to witness an even bigger fire this time broadcasted over television on CNN. It was the 11th September 2001 and Keith called us to his bedroom to observe the great calamity when two airplanes crashed into the World Trade Centre in New York. Upon seeing the tragedy my father exclaimed – *the world is coming to an end!* Three years later, the Indian Ocean earthquake and tsunami left hundreds of thousands of people dead in Indonesia, Sri Lanka, India and Thailand. Again my father repeated the same refrain. Now, years later, the world still exists – but for how long? Although the world is much different than it was twenty years ago, we continue to face the same wars, natural disasters and human-induced climate change. We owe it to our children and our grandchildren to make the world a better place in which they can live.

A friend in Gordon Draper

Gordon Draper, my father's good friend and former political colleague moved to Kingston in 2001 after being appointed a Fellow at the Mona School of Business; located just across the *Ring Road* from the Norman Manley Law School. My father was eager for his arrival and even more so when Draper and his family moved into the same compound in which we lived in Kingston. Oh how my father loved that man! Part of the reason was that Draper was bright like a bulb. In Kingston, he and my father would have long intellectual conversations. For the most part, these conversations were focused on shaping a new Trinidad and Tobago and fostering good governance within the country. I was surprised that years after both men bowed out of politics, these conversations would continue. Being around them, I formed the impression that both gentlemen still wished that they were sitting in the Parliament.

Draper and Keith enjoyed the Jamaican outdoors and mingling with the grassroots folk in the countryside. One weekend both families drove to the north coast where we visited Nine Mile in Saint Ann, the birth and final resting place of Bob Marley. That trip was a memorable one. To reach our destination we had to drive up a very long and narrow winding road through the mountains. More than once my father stopped the vehicle and asked one of the villagers – *Is this the way to Nine Mile?* The villagers would all reply in the affirmative and would add that Nine Mile was *"ah few chains up the hill"*. Well *a few chains up the hill* turned out to be longer than it sounded. After about two or three hours we finally made it to Nine Mile. Once in Nine Mile my father and Draper sat among the locals (some who claimed they were cousins of Marley; although we were not quite certain) and listened with enthusiasm about the stories of Marley. Shortly after the tour commenced, and we visited the humble home where Marley was born and then his mausoleum. Part of the tour included a visit to the singer's "favourite herb garden". There my father and Draper exchanged awkward grins because they knew that if that experience were made public, it would have created headlines back home.

Sadly, like my father, Draper, died at a fairly young age in London from an aneurysm in 2004 on his way from a business trip in South Africa. My father and I attended Draper's funeral at the Holy Trinity Cathedral in Port of Spain. Quite uncharacteristically Keith did not feel like socialising. He ascended the stairs up to the balcony of the church. I followed. We were both alone at the top of the church overlooking the funeral service beneath. I carefully observed my father. He did not say a word. It was an eerie feeling as despite the singing below, upstairs was quiet as a church mouse. During the service he sniffled. Then water welled up in his eyes. Suddenly I realised why he decided to isolate himself in the seclusion of the balcony. The reality had hit him. His friend, who perhaps reminded him of his own self, was no more. My mother always said that the first time she saw my father cry was when his mother had died. Well, the first time I saw my father weep was for his friend Gordon Draper. I would personally describe Draper as very down to earth, simple and a fine gentleman. He was far from arrogant and was a stranger to being aloof. I would always remember the day when he returned from Ethiopia with a special souvenir for me, an Ethiopian Birr (dollar bill). I also would never forget Gordon Draper.

Settling domestic disputes

Back at *The Pines* we had a neighbour called Fred, a Jamaican man of Japanese descent, who lived with his family, mere metres away from our own townhouse.[108] I remember Fred because he sported these long dreadlocks which were often neatly tucked away under his woollen hat. One afternoon, Jules parked his car at the side of the compound in order to clean the windscreen. Seconds later, Fred's son approached us in a moving vehicle that swerved dangerously just missing the legs of my brother. My brother did not take it lightly and immediately went to speak to the driver and Fred's son. As quick as the discussion started a physical fight ensued. All of a sudden, from the corner of my eye, I saw Fred's son approaching Jules swinging, quite deftly, a nunchucks. I froze, thinking that these are the kind of things that one would see in a '*kickup*' film at a local cinema. Finally someone came to the rescue. It was Jones the security guard at *The Pines* who stopped Fred's son in his tracks by palming down his nunchucks. An Ethiopian lady, a friend of Fred, also arrived at the scene. She placed her right hand on her heart and repeated – *my brothers we are all Ethiopians; we only deal with peace*. Maybe she saw our dreadlocks and wanted to re-emphasise to us the teachings of His Majesty Emperor Haile Selassie. I was just there thinking *it was your friend's son who pulled the nunchucks, not us*.

Fred's son did not want the impasse to end there. He started to threaten us by saying that his friends from *Standpipe* would come to look for Jules. *Standpipe Lane* was said to be a 'bad man area' in the vicinity of Barbican at the back of Old Hope Road. Jones immediately comforted Jules by reassuring him that *Standpipe* men were not really so bad. Then again Jones came from *Tivoli*. With all the commotion taking place, Fred then ran towards us, his dreadlocks flying in the air.

---

[108] "Fred" is a pseudonym and his real identity is withheld to ensure confidentiality.

When my father heard about the incident, he immediately summoned everyone to his patio to explain his side of the story. My father was truly an impartial mediator. He permitted all sides to speak freely without showing any form of favouritism towards his sons. The Ethiopian lady was there, still preaching about peace to which Fred nodded in agreement. Fred's son and his friend explained in their own words what transpired. My father reminded us that we were all neighbours and that we should look out for each other. If for some reason we could not abide by that code of conduct, then we should move out of *The Pines* and live elsewhere. Keith was stern. Fred agreed and even added that his home was open for any of the *Sobion* children to visit. Keith then encouraged both sides to shake hands. A peace truce was settled. There would be no invasion into *The Pines* by men from *Standpipe*. Today I have lost contact with our former neighbours. I am certain that just like me, they would never have forgotten how a peace accord was struck right there on my father's patio.

Besides being a place to settle civil disputes, the patio was my father's sanctuary. It was there he spent most of his time working and reading. Before he went to work, he would read the *Observer* and the *Gleaner* on the patio while drinking his morning cup of coffee. During this morning ritual, he would complete the daily newspaper's crossword puzzle and read his favourite comic, namely *Calvin and Hobbes* which complemented his quirky sense of humour. In terms of novels, my father favoured books authored by Stephen King and other detective stories. The thing is that Keith read so widely and quickly. His cousin Kenny noted, that while in Atlanta visiting, Keith would finish a novel in a matter of hours. There was a joke among the family that Keith would read anything you had to offer him – even if it was your palm. Not surprisingly, when my father passed away, he had hundreds of novels stacked neatly away on bookshelves in the basement. We did not know what to do with all of them so Ms Lindo and my mother decided to give some away to his sisters with the rest being donated to a charitable cause.

Outside of reading, my father started to spend more time watching the television. He stayed up late at night in bed watching movies on a new flat screen TV that my mother purchased (even though before the purchase he claimed it was a waste of money as it was too expensive). For international news his preference was to watch BBC world news channel, especially Stephen Sackur's HARDtalk. Some nights, he would descend the stairs leading to the basement and watch these sci-fi short films with us. These movies were so old that they were transmitted over cable TV in black and white. I detested watching these movies because they always ended when you least expected it and it was always a matter for conjecture as to what was the moral behind the story. My father would happily explain to us his own interpretation of the story line, which in most instances was something that we never even considered.

Tammy and Ethan

Tammy Bryan, a Barbadian lawyer who was our next-door neighbour at *The Pines*, remembered Keith as living on the patio. To appreciate this reasoning one would have to share the following anecdote. To get to the pool or the office on the compound, one would have to walk along a cobbled pathway. My father's patio would be the last landmark just before the pool and office area, and as the neighbours and gardeners shuffled up and down the pathway they would always call out *'Good Day Mr Sobion.'* Due to the cobalt blue awnings hanging around the fringes of the patio together with the ferns outside in the garden it was sometimes difficult to spot my father sitting on his chair. It was like he was sitting in the middle of a pristine forest. Yet everyone still greeted him as they passed by the patio because they believed that he was there, even if in some instances he was not.

Then there was three-year old Ethan, the son of Tammy. He was so accustomed to seeing Keith sitting on the patio that he developed a very amusing habit. Whenever he came home in the afternoon with his parents, he would look out towards the patio and curiously call *"Keith Keith Keith!"* to which Tammy would heartily reply *"Ethan.... that is Uncle Keith for you!"* Over the three years in *The Pines*, Ethan grew close to my father. There was a period where every Thursday afternoon, when Tammy and her husband worked late, my father would look after Ethan for about an hour and a half. When his parents arrived home, they would then fetch Ethan from Keith by the patio. Keith accepted this responsibility with pleasure. Tammy admitted, quite amusingly, "I turned him (Keith) into a babysitter".

Little did he know it, Ethan has the record of being my father's youngest client. One evening Ethan was crying loudly and Tammy could not understand the reason for his crankiness. Keith immediately ventured over to Tammy's home with a book containing *the UN Convention on the Rights of the Child.* Placing the book in the sobbing toddler's hands, my father said to him *"Listen Ethan, I want you to read this book to understand your rights. If anytime you need help, I am your lawyer."*

Tammy also recalled occasions when on her way home from work she would, instead of going directly to her home, walk into the garden and climb up the few spiral steps leading to Keith's patio. Keith as usual was there, dragging on a cigarette or reading a newspaper. When she entered, he would stop whatever he was doing and they would immediately have an *armchair discussion*. In most cases, this discussion would be about Caribbean politics. Tammy was impressed by the breadth of knowledge that my father had on this subject, as he appeared to be on top of all the political developments in the region. She fondly remembers the last few conversations she had with Keith which was on the upcoming Barbados general elections which took place in January 2008.

Sometime in 2006, Tammy noticed that Keith began to look frail. She inquired of him and his health and all he would say is that he went to the doctor and *"well you know it's the liver."* Tammy left it like that. She never appreciated how serious the condition of his health was until after he passed away. Nevertheless, Tammy remembered Keith as someone with a sharp brain and one who was compassionate towards his law students.

But it was not only Tammy who held Keith in high regard but other members of *The Pines* community. One year my father was elected as Chairman of the Residents Association, a position, which I understood, had its ups and downs. You see, my father was a man of little patience and could not stand nonsense. If someone in the Committee was being irrational he would read the riot act and utter – *listen I have better things to do than to be here. I have a Law School to run.* Once some residents strongly opposed a decision to establish a cell tower site in close proximity to the neighbourhood due to the possible radioactive emissions. To this suggestion my father replied – *the same ones who are opposing this site would make noise when a call drops on their mobile phones.* After serving as Chairman for one year my father decided not to seek a second term. In his own words – he had a Law School to run.

Besides being a mediator of disputes inside and outside the home, my father was a control freak. If you were going out, he wanted to know where you were going and exactly what time you would return. If we did not return at the time appointed, he would call us at that very minute demanding where we were and why we were late. It was strongly perceived within the household that he purchased my mother's first mobile phone just to monitor her movements. If this was the objective, he failed miserably because my mother was more inclined to keep her mobile phone off, especially when she was at her work place. To this, my father would utter a witty remark: *"Massy, a mobile phone is only useful if you have it on."*

This same measure of control applied to large windfalls. There was one instance when my mother left her vehicle in the care of our neighbours while she was out of town for a few days. During her absence, the car was involved in a collision and although no-one was seriously injured the vehicle had to be written off. Luckily for her, a gentleman was interested in buying the wreck of the vehicle. The gentleman, who appeared to be quite eager, brought the money in cash, folded up in a paper bag at my mother's work place. Being a bit suspicious about the transaction and probably feeling that a male presence was needed, she informed the gentleman to telephone her husband to complete the transaction. Upon her arrival home from work later that day, Keith confirmed that the transaction was complete and that the money was now safe and secure in his bank account. Thinking that my father was going to arrange the transfer of the money to her at some point, my mother left the matter as is. Days passed and my father made no mention of the money. One day my mother decided to break the silence. She asked for the money from the purchase of the wreck. In reply my father stated that the money was used to pay off the credit card for transactions that "she had made". Despite the long argument that ensued, my mother never saw one 'red cent' for her wrecked vehicle.

At the household, my father always wanted my mother around the home. During the week, he would not hide his disappointment when my mother returned from work late in the evenings. Matters got worse when my mother decided to pursue a Master's degree in International Business by distance learning through the University of New Orleans. My father became overly jealous. Jealous to the extent that my mother's time was focused elsewhere and was no longer centred around him. He would make rash comments like *– your mother would have more degrees than a circle.* Whether he made these comments in jest or not, it did not take away from the hurt felt by my mother. By pursuing her higher learning, my father realised that he lost not only the time spent with my mother but also that firm grip of control. This was something that he was not used to during the entire life of their marriage.

Those weekly meetings

One of my father's favourite pastimes was to sit down privately with his three sons and discuss the philosophy about life. Whether it was on the patio in Jamaica or in our living room in Trinidad, he always engaged us on the assessment of our present life situation. I would like to compare it to a weekly meeting with a professional counsellor. In all honesty, there were times when we tried to avoid such meetings, as he would unilaterally convene them at short notice; like late in the evening when we just arrived home from work. Nevertheless, the meetings were just an opportunity for him to spend some meaningful time with his sons. *Oh how we miss these meetings today!* One important quote he would inevitably use during these philosophical discussions is what I would call *the ladder dialogue*. *"Life is a ladder"* he would muse at his own words. He continued - *"we as parents can only climb to a certain point, but there is a time when you must be able to continue climbing where your parents have left off"*. We understood this to mean that our parents are our role models and that we should always strive to do better than them after they are no longer with us. Another subject he often discussed with us was what he famously called: *where-do-you-see-yourself-in-the-next-five-years*. While at University my father always posed this question to us to assess our mid-term strategic plan. The first time he asked me this particular question, I was in my early twenties. My response then was that in the next five years I would work for the United Nations. Upon hearing this, my father looked perplexed. I was not so sure if he doubted my plan or the timing of it. Maybe it was the latter, because although I represented my country as a diplomat at the UN years after, it actually took me fifteen years to work with the United Nations.

On one occasion we had one of these philosophical discussions in the presence of our family friend Anton Marcial, who was also at the time trying to sell us life insurance. At some point in the conversation, Keith took over and tried to explain to us the transaction in which we were about to embark upon. How he came up with these ideas in his head still amazes me. He explained that with life insurance, the insurance company is taking a bet that you would die. This is a bet that the insurance company wins and that you undoubtedly lose.

Crabs in a pot

It was in Jamaica that my father enhanced his culinary skills. For breakfast, his specialty was what he called a *"pizza egg"* – a rather exotic name for an omelette in the shape of a pizza. At mealtimes, he would never warm up his food using a microwave as he believed that the rays being emitted from it were bad for a person's health. So whenever he had to warm up his food he would re-heat by using the electric stove. In terms of eating habits, my father never ate pork as he claimed he was allergic to it. He would shy away from red meat with his preference being fish, chicken and sometimes lamb. At *The Pines*, French bread, *Crix* crackers, *Edam* cheese and *Mott's* apple juice was our staple breakfast during our first year in Jamaica (when mom was absent). For dinner my father's favourite was escovitched fish with bell peppers, carrots and onions, which we fetched for him at a small restaurant on Barbican Road called *Chasers*. It should however be noted that my father ate very sparingly and this played a role in the deterioration of his health. Besides his stint at the gym in the 1980s and the bit of cricket he played, Keith did not have an exercise regime. He was addicted to TUMS tablets, which he claimed eased his digestive pains, and often sipped tubes of Ginseng Royal Jelly as a dietary supplement which was prescribed to him by his Chinese friend Mr Wong from Charlotte Street in Trinidad.

My father rarely ate crab, but with his Mayaro background he surely must have seen how his grandmother cooked it. While driving on Windward Road, Kingston, my father watched with curiosity, the method used by a gentleman cooking crab at the side of a road. The crabs, fully alive, were placed in a pot of boiling water over a fire. As the crabs tried to climb out of the pot using their claws and *gundy*, the man frantically used his big spoon to push them back inside the bubbling water. To him, this was surely a unique way of cooking crab; a way that was unfamiliar to him and his grandmother.

Admitted to the Bar – Port of Spain, Trinidad, 2002

Back in Trinidad, my academic life at Hugh Wooding moseyed along quite normally; even when I was back and forth between there and Jamaica. The two years passed by quickly and on the 6th September 2002 I graduated from the Hugh Wooding Law School. At the graduation ceremony at St. Augustine, my father was present at the head table along with Principal Sealey, other dignitaries and specially invited guests. Dennis Morrison, who was Chairman of the Council of Legal Education at the time, spearheaded the task of presenting the *Legal Education Certificate* to each student when his or her name was called. When my name was called to receive my certificate, I approached the podium. Before I could even think, my father got up from the head table and slid behind Morrison. Morrison gave me a sturdy handshake but my certificate was not in his hand but rather in my father's. I did not know if they planned it hours before or at that very moment but it was my father who exchanged the certificate with me and then gave me a warm hug. There was a hearty applause from those in the audience. I still have a picture of this – my father and I both donned in dark suits, caught up in a mid-hug, my certificate in my right hand resting comfortably behind my father's back. Morrison is looking on in the corner of his eyes, smiling. After the ceremony a picture was taken of my father, Dennis Morrison, Jawara Mobota and Endell Thomas. This group picture, which he insisted on taking, represented four of the first West Indian law graduates in 1975.

Then came the formal admission before the Court five weeks later. Of course, without any deliberation, my father was chosen to formally present my petition before a special sitting of the Supreme Court. My admission to the Bar of Trinidad and Tobago was however not free from any setbacks. About a week before, my father realised that his name was taken off the roll of Attorneys. *Why?* He had been living in Jamaica for six years and had inadvertently forgotten to pay his annual dues to practise before the Court. My father went into a panic and immediately called up his friend Marcelle Ferdinand at *Sellier* for advice. All hope was not lost as Ferdinand advised that an application could be made before a Judge in Chambers for a waiver and reinstallation of my father's name on the list of Attorneys once special circumstances could be proved. I remember going to the Chamber Court to observe the proceedings with Ferdinand. When the matter came before the Court, after a few questions from the presiding Judge (and if my memory doesn't fail me it was before Justice Peter Jamadar), the application was granted. All this transpired about three days prior to my admission. My father's name was reinstalled on the Roll of Attorneys. What a relief it was for him. He could now formally admit me to practise.

It was Friday 25th October 2002 and some ninety new lawyers, all impeccably dressed in black and white, were ready to be formally presented before the Court in the Convocation Hall. As it was done by surname in alphabetical order, I was number eighty-two on the Registrar's list. Everyone was talking and fidgeting until one heard the voice of the usher echo.

Courrrrrrrrrrrrt!

The newly installed Chief Justice Satnarine Sharma and Madame Justice Maureen Rajnauth-Lee entered the room and took their seats at the front of the Hall. Then the Chief Justice requested for the Petitioner's names to be called. The Registrar obliged.

I felt like I was waiting in vain for number eighty-two and my anxiety set in. Finally when the Registrar called my name, my father, fully robed with bands, brief in hand, briskly stood up. He looked tall and prominent – *"I beg to present the petition of Justin Wolde Amanuel Sekou Sobion."*

As brisk as he stood up, he sat back down. There was a snicker emanating from the courtroom, not that my father pronounced my names incorrectly. It was because my name was the longest one in the batch. After some closing remarks and words of advice by the Chief Justice, the ceremony came to an end. That afternoon we were about ninety lawyers being formally called to practise law at the Bar of Trinidad and Tobago. I remember my father making the remark that every year the Law School produces so many new lawyers and that being out of private practise for so long he felt somewhat alienated. The fact that he was living in Jamaica also played a role in shaping his feelings. My father often lamented that he did not have the opportunity to know the new generation of young lawyers in his own country.

After being admitted, my father gave me his *blue bag* which was traditionally used by junior Counsel to carry their robes outside court. On that bag was inscribed his initials 'K.S'. My father was indeed a very proud man. Come to think about it, it was the first time in a long while that Keith appeared as an Advocate before open Court. To celebrate my initiation at the Bar, later that evening my parents invited friends and family to our home in Flagstaff to share a meal and drink. As if the evening was not already filled with excitement, my father, together with one of his friends, tried to persuade me to enter into an arranged marriage with a girl from Moruga. Though the young lady was charming and well educated, I declined given the fact that I was at the time already committed in another relationship.

People often ask me, why did you become a lawyer? The truth is that I decided to study law because I grew up around my father at *Sellier* and wanted to be like him. It just came naturally. There was no *if*, *but* or *maybe*. I wanted to be a lawyer and that was it. Thanks to my father, there was no turning back. Once I decided to take up this career path it was my father who first taught me how to knot a tie (in fact he taught all three of us). For some reason it was difficult for him to knot the tie directly on our necks. So he would then knot the tie on his own neck, leaving enough room in between to pull it over his head, then gingerly place the loose tie over our head and adjust it at the neck. That is how I learned to knot a tie. *How could I not forget my father?* Every time I put on my suit or my tie I cannot resist thinking of him.

In the end, I do not regret making this decision to become a lawyer because of my love for the law. The words of Emile Ferdinand Q.C. are pertinent here: *law is an opportunity to use one's intellect to impact innumerable real and human issues.* Even my father and I spoke about this during our many *"ladder dialogues"*. During one of these discussions he said: *"you will make a good lawyer, but please stay away from politics. Do not be like me and become a politician."*

In the midst of graduation and being admitted to practise law, I had to decide where I would enter the working world. Luckily for me I had options. One option was to work as a research assistant for the Judges of the Supreme Court. My father and Master Christie-Anne Morris-Alleyne encouraged me to apply. At first I was doubtful. The burning desire of most young lawyers is the glamour of cross-examining a witness in the box while gently pulling back one's robes. The idea of a research assistant perusing through law reports in a corner of a library paled in comparison to being a full-fledged lawyer. In any event, was it not research that I had done throughout my five years as a law student? I also had another more glorious opportunity, which was as a litigator at *Sellier*. My father left a good impression with the firm and, because of this, I believed *Sellier's* door was open.

All these thoughts, I repeated in words to my father and I am certain he discussed them with Master Morris-Alleyne. He returned to the similar reasoning we had which initially brought me to Law School at Trinidad. He felt that being a research assistant would provide me with the perfect opportunity to equip my mind as to how Judges think. This would be an indispensable tool especially if I had to appear before that particular Judge in the future. Furthermore, the contract for the research assistant position was just for a one-year period. One year was just enough time for a Judge to assess your ability, and your work ethic would also be remembered when you appear before them. *Judges never forget,* my father told me.

But my father was always a background negotiator. In his usual wily approach to things, without me knowing at the time, Keith got Master Morris-Alleyne to talk to me separately. In the end, I yielded to his advice and I applied. A few weeks passed and I was called for the interview, was successful and appointed on a one-year contract. Being a Judges' research assistant, even for such a short period, complemented every aspect of my professional path. Had it not been for that one year, my appreciation of Judges and their thought processes would have been lacking. As it panned out, the very next year I was employed in *Sellier's* Litigation department and finally got the opportunity to don my bands and robes before open Court.

On being admitted to practise law, my father continued to offer me professional advice especially as it related to the courtroom. One piece of advice was – *if your Senior is on his or her feet arguing a case wrongly, be bold enough to pull at his or her robe to correct their errors.* Another bit of advice, was – *when cross-examining a witness, never ask a question if you do not know the answer.*

Bracing for Ivan, Keith's inner child

Whenever a hurricane was heading on its path to Jamaica, it would bring out the inner child in Keith. Despite the level of havoc caused by a hurricane, he enjoyed the excitement and the anticipation which came with it. Before hurricane *Ivan* was about to make landfall in September 2004, the media in Trinidad telephoned him for an interview to describe the situation on the ground and the precautions he was taking. In one interview, the interviewer informed that a BWIA plane was being sent to Jamaica to bring home students to Trinidad and Tobago. Keith was then asked if he would consider getting on the flight. My father replied, half-jokingly: '*Well they would hardly take me for a student. No, I'll be here.*' [109] One could glean from the interview that Keith was facing the natural disaster not with any trepidation but rather with calmness and curiosity. I use the words *calmness* and *curiosity* in the truest sense because while *Ivan* was battering Jamaica – according to my mother – "Keith never left the patio". He just sat there in awe watching the heavy winds and rain wreak havoc upon the awnings, the lone obstacle between him and *Ivan*. Hours later, my father and Darien ventured outside and hopped into his parked vehicle. On seeing this, our neighbour Tammy thought that my father and brother had lost their minds. Upon their return, my father told Tammy that he took a drive around Kingston to "assess the situation in the neighbouring surroundings". Tammy was a bit concerned then, but up to today she still laughs at the sight of my father, followed by my brother, running to the vehicle under heavy rainfall, and driving off in the middle of the hurricane.

This was not the only time when Keith's inner child was brought out. While living in Jamaica, he had to travel to Port of Spain on a few occasions to give evidence at the Magistrates' Court in the *Piarco Airport case*. Years before this case commenced, Keith, as a sole arbitrator, made an award in a separate dispute involving an insurance company and a contractor of the airport. His evidence at the Magistrates' Court was focused on how he arrived at that particular award. The nights before giving evidence Keith barely slept as he continuously browsed through his statement. He did all this not because he was nervous, but more because he was fascinated with the idea that he was now acting as a witness in a matter as opposed to a lawyer. I saw

---

[109] *Former AG to ride out Ivan in Jamaica*, Trinidad and Tobago Newsday, 10 September 2004.

him as a kid again as he got dressed in the morning to go to Court. As Principal and an administrator he surely missed the courtroom setting. This was his opportunity to shine and relive his past life.

Tammy works for the Law School

One day Tammy enquired of my father whether there were any vacancies at the Law School. Keith pondered about it. He returned a few weeks later to Tammy with news about a short-term temporary position and advised that she should send him her CV as soon as possible. Within a few days, Tammy was called for an interview. At the interview, my father was one of a panel of four. Keith declared his hand up front saying that he knew Tammy and that she was his friend and neighbour. As a result, he did not wish to participate in the interview. The other three members of the panel understood and the interview proceeded on that basis. Tammy was later selected and appointed as a temporary lecturer. As an afterthought, Tammy believed that due to Keith's position his word may have carried some weight in the decision for her to be recruited. Nevertheless, Tammy equally felt that Keith displayed his professionalism by withdrawing himself from the interview process regarding her candidacy.

Tammy enjoyed my father as her boss. She recalled a situation where evidence came to her attention that suggested that two students breached the Law School's code of ethics. The penalty for such a breach required disciplinary action. My father listened attentively to her as she presented the evidence before him. When she was finished, my father bowed his head and looked up at her over his glasses and said: *"So what do you think is the best course of action we should take?"* Tammy paused to reflect.

She then gave my father her opinion. He agreed. At the end of the day, the students were not expelled and this perhaps was what my father really wanted. You see when Keith was making a decision regarding his students such a decision would often be guided by his own humanity. Tammy remembered incidents where my father allowed students to write exams even when they were not up to date with their school fees. His rationale was that these students came from impoverished backgrounds and the law was an opportunity for them to rise from their dire circumstances. Keith also spoke about his admiration and concern for students who came from a distance just to attend Law School in Kingston. Tammy would never forget what my father wrote in her farewell card once her services with the Law School were completed. His comment was concise but to the point: "You met and exceeded all my expectations."

Dorcas White, a Senior Tutor at the Norman Manley Law School once mentioned to me that my father had a genuine respect for women. These words were perhaps spoken from experience as Keith admired White's personality, including her trademark hat. Besides White, I could recall at least two other women who my father held in high esteem. One was Tammy and the other was his former secretary Maureen Lindo.

Who is this Principal they call Sobion?

In 1996, when my father assumed duties as Principal of the Law School in Jamaica, he was able to re-unite with his long-time classmate and scholar of a friend, Dennis Morrison. In 1998, when Morrison was appointed Chairman of the Council of Legal Education, he worked very closely with my father in the administration of regional legal education. These fine gentlemen shared similar qualities – bright, cool, smooth, down to earth, unassuming and quick witted. And just like my father, Morrison could not be outwitted. One afternoon my father tried to outmanoeuvre the equally shrewd Morrison, who had just completed presiding over a judicial matter of national interest. Morrison was due to deliver his decision the following day when my father called him. Over the telephone, my father asked him to divulge a synopsis of his decision. Not easily persuaded to yield to this request, a steadfast Morrison politely suggested that my father wait until the next day when the decision would be made public. At the end of the conversation, my father smiled awkwardly, suggesting a sign of defeat. He said that his friend Morrison was such a principled man that he could not be flexible. But if one were to put the shoe on the other foot, I am certain that my father would also have withheld the information. In the end, Morrison did the proper thing and the ironic thing was that my father knew this too.

Out of all the persons I know, no one could define my father's role as Principal better than his secretary, Maureen Lindo. Lindo was my father's 'right-hand woman' at the Law School. She was his confidant, loyal staff member and even best friend. When my father came home early from work, Lindo would personally drive her car to *The Pines*, climb up steps to the patio and present a pile of papers to my father for him to sign. At lunchtime she would also see to it that my father ate properly and that he got the necessary pause before he resumed duties. I can say it no other way, never before have I seen any such devotion, such admiration, between an assistant and a superior. It was as if she loved my father like an older brother.

When Lindo first met my father she was assigned to the Registrar of the Law School. Shortly afterwards, she was assigned to my father and the bond was unbreakable. Lindo, thought my father was like a *walking dictionary* because he would often rattle off words that she never even knew existed. Lindo also remembers my father's selflessness. For instance, if a student needed some flexibility regarding their fees, he would step in and approve a generous payment plan. On the other hand, Lindo recalls there were occasions when my father singlehandedly, and discreetly, paid out of his own pocket, fees owing by less fortunate students.

On this point, I noted a couple other 'student related concerns' of my father. The first was his drive to enhance the accessibility of legal education at the Law School. This in itself was a herculean task due to the extraordinarily high demand for student placement within the institution. The second was his commitment to expand the physical space of the Law School thereby creating an enabling environment for students to study and to interact with each other. In this connection, he oversaw the construction of the William Roper wing at the Law School, which opened in 1998.

I also witnessed first-hand Keith's flexibility when it came to making administrative decisions at the Law School. While I was studying law at Cave Hill, Barbados, I came across a fellow Trinidadian student named Lisa. Lisa was one year ahead of me at the Faculty and was in a bit of a dilemma. She met the man of her dreams, a young striking Jamaican student from the Mona Campus who came to Cave Hill for one week to play basketball at the Inter-Campus Games. After a one-week connection, she was confident that she had met her soulmate and wanted to spend the rest of her life with him. Lisa's dilemma was that as a law student from Trinidad, she was zoned to commence her studies at the Hugh Wooding

Law School in Trinidad upon the completion of her bachelor's degree at Cave Hill. But love makes you dream at times. Lisa wanted to break with tradition and attend the Norman Manley Law School in Jamaica to be closer to her gentleman. It was only the Principal who could break with this tradition, if exceptional circumstances prevailed. I confided in Lisa that I would speak to my father as the Principal of Norman Manley. Genuinely not knowing how my father would react, I did not want to hold out any high expectations that things would work out in her favour. When I passed on the information, my father told me to let Lisa contact him.

What Lisa recounted to me years later was astonishing. It was the epitome of what one would call – *Proust's madeleine moment*. Lisa felt like an immature girl telephoning the Principal because of what she called *"the compulsion of youthful passion"*. Her nervousness actually came to the surface when she admitted to my father that she felt utterly foolish making the request for the transfer over the telephone. Despite this, my father patiently listened to her every word. When she finally laid out her case, he asked her the sobering question – *Do you think the relationship will last?* To this, Lisa could not give an honest answer. Her truthful response was that the relationship was definitely worth pursuing. There was a brief pause on the line. My father broke the silence. He told Lisa to put exactly what she had said in writing and that he would approve her transfer request immediately to Norman Manley Law School. My father added that the UWI campuses are a melting pot of Caribbean people and that when UWI brings young people together, there is an expectation that alliances would form. He hoped that in most cases these alliances would become permanent. He concluded that the UWI model is regional integration at its best. In Lisa's case, the alliance did last.

Lisa graduated from Norman Manley Law School in 2001. She has since relocated to Trinidad with her husband and their children. Her Jamaican husband works in Trinidad, thanks to the freedom of movement established under the Caribbean Single Market and Economy (CSME). Lisa now sits as a Judge in the Supreme Court of Trinidad and Tobago. As Keith would have said – *This is regional integration at its best.*

My father always used to say that your ability to regurgitate what a legal textbook says on an exam paper does not make you a good lawyer. Rather, what makes you a good lawyer is your competence and analytical ability. Added to that, a Law School graduate must work for the common benefit of humankind. For him, the social interaction and community service were equally important. Having all these attributes tipped you over the edge from being an average lawyer to one who excels. This was one of his visions which he passed on to his fellow staff and students.

One of the first major projects my father was involved in as Principal was the establishment of the third Law School in the Caribbean – the Eugene Dupuch Law School (EDLS) in Bahamas. For him, the opening of the EDLS was a grand occasion, one that would broaden the access of legal education for students within the region. In fact, Keith was involved in the Bahamas Law School project long before he was Principal. He was a member of the Council's Review Committee, chaired by Dr Lloyd Barnett, which made the original recommendation for the establishment of the EDLS in its 1995 report. Keith was present in Nassau when the EDLS opened its doors in September 1998 and he continued afterwards to offer valuable assistance to the Chairman of Council (then Dennis Morrison) and the staff of the new institution.[110]

This reference to the EDLS brought back memories about a gentleman named Dion Hanna. In March 2002, I travelled to Jamaica to take part in a regional client-interview competition at the Norman Manley Law School. While there, my father indicated that he wanted to introduce me to an "interesting person". That person of interest turned out to be Dion Hanna, a lawyer from the Bahamas. And interesting, this person was. Hanna was one of those persons who, from first sight, assured me that despite my own physical appearance with dreadlocks, I could find a place within the legal profession. That was perhaps the reason my father was so eager to introduce him to me. Hanna had these matted greyish-soon-turned-white dreadlocks hanging down from the side of his head. He also sported a thick grey dreadlocked beard. At the time of the introduction, Hanna was serving as the Director of the Legal Aid Clinic at the EDLS in the Bahamas. It turned out that my father was a member of a five-panel team that interviewed Hanna for the Director role a few years earlier. Having spent a protracted period of time practising law in cold, grey England, when he entered the interview room, Hanna's heart was sun-warmed to see a coloured man as Principal among the panel of interviewers.

Hanna and Keith also shared a bit of Cave Hill history as they lived in the same Stanmore block of apartments in Barbados in the 1970s. He vividly recalled the community structures and national *"Posses"* which existed in Cave Hill such as the *Stanmore Posse* which included both the Trinidad Posse and the Jamaican

---

[110] The new school was established in Nassau in September 1998. It so happened that Dennis Morrison was elected Chairman of the Council of Legal Education at the same place and time.

Posse. Hanna, a Bahamian, gravitated towards the contingent of the Jamaican Posse which included another Jamaican lawyer Derrick McKoy.[111] Hanna found that despite being Trinidadian, my father had a natural attraction towards the Jamaican Posse. Notwithstanding this, Keith and his classmate McKenzie were noted as the informal leaders of the *Trinidad Stanmore Posse*. Another fact, which I never heard of before in my entire life, was that Hanna remembered Keith as being a good drummer at Cave Hill. The image of a drummer was in stark contrast to his Principal days where Hanna saw my father as being laid back, with a swift mind and always ready to challenge him mentally. Yet in both worlds, Hanna affirmatively declared that Keith was Rasta (his constant listening of Count Ossie's Mystic Revelation of Rastafari Groundation CD sealed this for me), or at least Rasta-influenced, with a Pan-African mindset.

Another of my father's pet projects was the co-founding of the American Caribbean Law Initiative (ACLI). The other founders were Professor John Knechtle of the Florida Coastal School of Law (FCSL) and Henry Ramsey Jr. a former Dean at Howard University School of Law. In the late 1990s, Professor Knechtle recognised that there was a need for cultural diversity and deepened mutual relationships between American and Caribbean Law Schools. Ramsey had the key that would open the door to the Caribbean. That door was P.J. Patterson, the then Prime Minister of Jamaica. In June 2000, an American team comprising Knechtle, Ramsey and Don Lively, the Dean of the FCSL, flew to Jamaica to meet Patterson. The Prime Minister was thrilled with the proposed Caribbean initiative and, as protocol would dictate, he fixed another meeting for

---

[111] Derrick McKoy taught me Constitutional Law and Law and Legal Systems at UWI, Mona, Jamaica in 1997.

269

the Americans to meet his Attorney General, A.J. Nicholson. Like Patterson, Nicholson was also quite receptive of the idea. However, the idea needed to be filtered down even further. Nicholson recommended that the Americans meet with another person – my father, the Principal of the Norman Manley Law School.

Years later, while sitting down at a hotel bar in Grenada, Knechtle described this meeting with me. My father was facing them from his side of the desk while the three Americans spoke. He listened attentively to all that they had to say. He never interrupted the speakers and his eyes remained fixed upon them. While listening my father would at times lean forward with his fingers in both hands interlocked and his shoulders squared in towards the speakers. Knechtle said that within seconds he recognised that my father was a keen listener. Furthermore, by his body language, Knechtle knew that Keith was hooked onto their proposal way before the meeting even ended.

Knechtle was forthright – The ACLI project could not have gotten off the ground without Keith's input. Seeing the vision of the project from the outset, Keith immediately took to the task of tapping into his contacts within the region about facilitating the collaborative relationships with American Law Schools. From the inception, my father wanted the project to be called the American and Caribbean Law *Institute* – instead of *Initiative*. In retrospect, Knechtle thought that *Institute* would have been more accurate, as the word gave the entity a sense of being an academic think tank.

After a series of meetings, the ACLI was formally inaugurated on the 29th August 2000 at the Florida Coastal School of

Law in Jacksonville. At the Convocation, A.J. Nicholson was the featured speaker, addressing an audience of some two hundred persons. A Memorandum of Understanding (MoU) was then signed by Heads of the participating Law Schools: the Norman Manley Law School, the FCSL, the Nova Southern University and the Thurgood Marshall School of Law.

Although the ACLI was to initially operate with Law Schools in the United States and Jamaica it became clearer, as the discussions progressed, that the initiative needed to broaden its horizons within the Caribbean region. By the following year, the Council of Legal Education approved the MoU – paving the way for the Trinidad and Bahamas Law Schools to be part of the ACLI family. That same year the ACLI also became affiliated with CARICOM and commenced its flagship project; the Caribbean Law Clinic.

For close to eight years, my father and Knechtle worked closely together to promote legal education between Caribbean and American Law Schools. Knechtle served as the President of the ACLI's Board of Directors from the year 2000 to 2009 while my father served as Vice President from 2000 until his passing in 2008. As Vice President, Keith served as adjunct professor at the FCSL at Jacksonville where he taught Caribbean Law and Legal Systems and Comparative Constitutional Law (as it relates to the Caribbean and the United States). This mix blended well with my father's domestic teaching duties at NMLS where he also taught Constitutional Law and second marked papers. This eight-year period was an instrumental period of my father's academic life. It was a period where, from my perspective, he became steeped in Constitutional Law.

Under the ACLI, Caribbean students visited Florida and vice versa, as part of an exchange programme. Compared to our earlier years, my father's thinking was beginning to broaden. In the late 1990s, Keith was not convinced that UK or North American educational institutions were superior to those in the Caribbean. With globalisation however, he realised that the sharing of experiences and cultures within an educational framework could only benefit both sides of the divide. In other words, Caribbean institutions, or any other institution for that matter, could not stand on their own. In order for education to thrive and benefit a student it needs to be shared across borders. And this is something that my father always taught – *grades alone do not create an individual.* What matters are the experiences, the social interaction and using the law in a creative manner to help others. His philosophy was that a lawyer who graduated in the region should be able to have a legal colleague or friend on every island north of Trinidad. The inclusion of colleagues in North America was seen as an expansion of that philosophy. That in essence was the vision of my father concerning the ACLI.[112]

Apart from the Bahamas Law School and the ACLI my father was an adviser to many. He had a close relationship with Jamaica's Attorney General A.J. Nicholson who, as Lindo recalls, would visit my father at his office to "bounce off" ideas. Then, as with any other organisation, there were the internal politics and my father would often be called to step in as the mediator. During the twelve years of working with him as his assistant, Lindo felt that after a while my father reached the stage where he outgrew the Law School. She saw that the politics of the institution began to place a burden upon him

---

[112] In 2009, the ACLI held its third law conference entitled *"Dispute Resolution and Restorative Justice"* at the Hilton Hotel in Port of Spain, Trinidad. At that conference a reception was held in honour my father.

and that he needed a change in his environment. The fact that he outgrew the Law School to me was a stark reality. For a little while he stopped going to work, choosing to work from home – either by reading or marking papers. My mother would reprimand and remind him that to be a leader, one must be in the office. At least two years before he passed away, the clear indication was that my father had lost his vim and verve towards the Law School. I recall two instances during the twelve years when my father took a sabbatical and it may have been for that very reason – he needed a short pause from the institution. Carol Aina would act as Principal in my father's absence (it was said that Keith identified Aina as his successor). While on sabbatical, he would read and continue his regional travels promoting the CCJ. He made a promise to himself, and to us, to write on a topic of interest while on sabbatical. I deeply regret that he never found time to fulfil this promise. To this day, I do sincerely believe that my father had so much on his mind to offer intellectually.

In between these sabbaticals I could sense that he wanted a change. Around the year 2007, we had a private discussion where he indicated to me his interest in applying for a Judge position in the Cayman Islands. Later in that year his interest shifted further south to St. Lucia where he applied for a Judge position in the Eastern Caribbean Court. I remember often asking him this question – "if you want to apply for a Judgeship position why don't you apply to be a Judge of the CCJ?" His reply would always be the same. "How can I apply to be a Judge at the CCJ when I have been promoting the CCJ for all these years?"

In like manner, he also did not want to apply for a judge position in Trinidad and Tobago because he felt tarnished by politics.

So, in his thrust to become a Judge, the Eastern Caribbean was his preferred and practical option. And there was a reason behind his thoughts. He practised law at the private bar, he was an Attorney General and then later an academic. The next natural step was therefore to become a Judge. Added to this, he looked on with great admiration when his youngest sister Patricia became a Master of the Supreme Court back home in 2002. Lindo even also reconfirmed these words with me when she said – "He wanted to be a Judge."

He mulled over the judgeship position in the Eastern Caribbean for a long while searching every possible consequence of his action. I saw him in his pensive mood many times and it would mostly take place during the dusk, when night started to fall. He would sit on his chair in the patio and take a long drag from his cigarette. And as the smoke floated away he would stare blankly into space, looking at nothing else but complete nothingness. The patio was his special place for this, his place of sanctuary and of deep meditation. In making this decision he did not only think about himself. He thought about my mother and if she would join him in St. Lucia, if he were successful in his application. He considered the words of advice from his close colleagues and mentors. He even asked me my own opinion to which I advised affirmatively – *put in your application.*

After months of deliberation he did apply. He was shortlisted for an interview, did the interview and was not selected (in an unusual move, he never told me that he went to the interview. I found out about it maybe a few weeks later). What a disappointment that was for him! I could see it in his face and hear it in his voice. I knew he was hurt on the inside. Here it is, a well-qualified man, giving his all for Caribbean integration, being turned down for an opportunity to sit on the bench in the

Eastern Caribbean. That certainly must have damaged his ego. Even greater than that, it was his own peers who encouraged him to apply. From that day onward, he stopped talking about becoming a Judge.

Yet I thought – *what could have caused this result which seemed so overwhelmingly in his favour?* Was it simply that his interviewers did not think that he possessed the qualities of being an exemplary Judge? Or was it that, somehow, he managed to bungle the interview? An eminent jurist in the Eastern Caribbean confirmed with me that my father's application was unsuccessful. Surprisingly, the reason given was that there were not sufficient positions at the relevant time to accommodate him. Nevertheless, the jurist did suggest that Keith possessed a scholarship and the temperament to be a good Judge.

Dennis Morrison, described my father as unconventional; in the sense that he did not always do things the way people would normally do. Morrison added that one of the real strengths of my father was that he was a 'people person' who was always in touch with the people's needs. Morrison concurred that Keith would have been a good Judge because he would have understood the 'people aspect' of a case. For him, this individual quality was undervalued and in some instances lacking.

There is an old legal axiom which recognises that being a good lawyer does not necessarily mean that one would be a good Judge. The fact is that both roles are unique and in some instances the qualities and the attributes of the person holding each office would differ. It was my former Principal, Madame Justice Sealey who brought this point home for me. For her, Keith had a fantastic brain which worked over 100 kilometres per hour. Working directly with him at the Law

School, the retired Judge acknowledged that his brain worked on a different plane. Her logic was that if his brain worked so fast, she wondered whether he would have the patience to sit on the Bench. The argument being that patience was one of the key virtues of being a good Judge. Supplementing this, my mother was swift to point out that in the latter part of his life, my father was no longer keen on becoming a Judge. She noted that Keith no longer wanted to be bogged down by a rigid schedule. As he got older, he wanted more freedom to manage his own affairs. Hence, assuming the duties of a Judge would have inhibited such freedom which he so cherished.

The oxymoron is that my father was a simple, but yet complex human being. To get to fully understand him, one would have had to unveil his three personalities. Most people knew my father as having a relaxed, laid-back and good-humoured disposition. Some may have experienced his introverted side when he withdrew himself from the world and did not wish to talk to anyone or to be disturbed; like when he was reading a book or watching the evening news. Others, be it a very few, would have witnessed his no-nonsense side. Patience was definitely not his virtue and if we had to pick him up at the airport, to avoid a tongue-lashing, it was in our interest to arrive before the plane landed. An incident which best reflects his no-nonsense personality was when I permitted my brother Darien to enter the Law School with a 'wife-beater' vest, short pants and slippers while I waited outside in the parked vehicle. When my father saw Darien, he was so infuriated that he gave us marching orders to immediately leave the Law School compound. To Darien he scolded - *How can you dress like that? I am the Principal!* Then it was my turn to feel the wrath of his anger – *How could you allow your little brother to enter the Law School underdressed, you of all persons should know better!* My father detested foolishness. As he once advised one of his students, *don't make foolish people make you do foolish things.*

On this point, Beverley Phillips, Assistant Registrar of the Norman Manley Law School was spot on. Keith "was a fast thinker and did not suffer fools gladly, nor did he like to have long explanations on anything" – she would say. And as if she was speaking from experience, Phillips added that his favourite line was – *"Get to the point!"*

Then something came along which relit any imagination that Keith had left in him. There was a proposal before the Council of Legal Education to create an Executive Secretariat which purpose was to be the implementation arm of the Council. The Head of the Executive Secretariat would be the Executive Director (ED) who would oversee the three Law Schools in the region. Keith seemed to be the obvious choice for ED as by that time he was the most senior Principal of the three Law Schools. With a bit of persuasion, the Council established the Executive Secretariat as a pilot project with Keith as its ED. As it was a pilot project, my father was on secondment from the Norman Manley Law School.

Lindo knew that Keith wanted to be the ED from the outset. As an outsider observing, I also knew that the Executive Secretariat was my father's brainchild. Not only was my father a natural leader, he was also crafty. He strong-armed Margaret Adams-Stowe and a Senior lecturer Michael Theodore at the Hugh Wooding Law School into applying for the positions of Registrar and Researcher respectively. Even his very own confidant Maureen Lindo was appointed the Administrative officer. That was how the Executive Secretariat was born – with my father literally creating the principal organ and handpicking his own team. Once the team was installed, meetings were held at our Flagstaff townhouse in Trinidad. There, many serious, innovative and exciting ideas relating to Council reform were born. An assortment of papers were prepared, formatted, re-formatted and printed over many long hours. It was not a slavish type of work. Rather, his team felt a sense of excitement, a coming of a new age of Council, a feeling of pride in that they contributed in a more tangible manner to the development of the three Law Schools. Adams-Stowe recalled that Keith epitomised a leadership style, which was collaborative and solutions-oriented. He had full confidence in his staff – this confidence in turn inspired and motivated the team members.

Back in 2007, when the pilot project came off the ground, my father spoke about the Executive Secretariat with great conviction. As he manoeuvred for the Secretariat to be based in Trinidad, he saw it as a springboard to return home. But little did he know that time was also against him. Using Lindo's terminology – the Executive Secretariat and the ED position died a "natural death" after my father's passing.

Down in the ghetto

May 2001 my father took all of us to *Trench Town Culture Yard* at 6 and 8 Lower First Street, where Bob Marley sought refuge after returning from living in the United States. We were told that this was the place where Marley was taught to play the guitar by his mentor, community elder Vincent "Tata" Ford, who co-wrote *No Woman, No Cry* with Marley.[113] At the gate of the yard waiting to greet us was a short and stumpy dreadlocked guy in an olive-green jersey. His name was *Stone Man* and he was our guide that afternoon. He took the whole family around the *Yard* and gave us all the historical anecdotes. Like all these Bob Marley related tours, every guide either knew the Reggae King of the World personally or was related to him. For *Stone Man* it was the former. This was a special moment for my father, as he loved to interact with persons from grassroots communities such as Trench Town.

Another ghetto story. It was a Wednesday afternoon when my father and Jones the security guard at *The Pines* decided to watch a football game at the Edward Seaga Sports Complex, downtown Kingston. Jones, a clean shaved gentleman who looked twenty years younger than his real age, came from Tivoli Gardens, a political garrison in West Kingston. Jones jumped in the passenger side of father's BMW and shortly after they drove in the direction of Tivoli. When they arrived at the match venue, it so happened that Jones' Uncle was manning the ticket gate. Upon noticing this, Jones informed my father that they would be able to enter the venue free of charge. As my father was about to enter the gate he handed over to Jones' Uncle a paper note saying – *nah man, let me sponsor the thing.*

At the venue, Keith met with Edward Seaga, the former Prime Minister and the ground's namesake. Keith also spoke to Jones about meeting with *Dudus* the then don of the area. My father was advised that *Dudus* was "unavailable". Sometimes I wonder why would my father want to meet with a don. I then had to go back to a previous question – why would he want to meet with

---

[113] It is argued by some that Bob Marley was the sole author of 'No Woman no Cry.'

Abu Bakr during the attempted coup? I think it all boiled down to Keith wanting to engage and reason with the grassroots. He wanted to find out what motivated them and how in any way he could proffer a solution. Jones speaks about this memory with profound compassion; the Principal, who he called his father, who accompanied him to his own hometown to watch a football match in Seaga's Complex.

Politics still in his blood

In a perfect world for my mother, my father would have moved to Jamaica and never again ponder about the politics in Trinidad and Tobago. Such a perfect world is illusory and according to Haile Selassie *a fleeting illusion to be pursued but never attained.*[114] Even though he was now living in Jamaica, Keith always kept abreast of the domestic politics back in Trinidad and Tobago. The press and politicians would consistently call him for his opinions on what was brewing politically in Port of Spain. In most cases it was an issue relating to the Constitution. I believe that it was these calls and follow up action that also contributed to my father becoming a specialist in constitutional law matters. The next anecdote illustrates how much my father believed in the Constitution. On one occasion while visiting us at home in Trinidad, he was in the middle of his preparations for a legal opinion when he asked me for a copy of the Constitution. When he found out that I did not have one immediately available, he questioned my fitness of being a proper lawyer. From that day

---

[114] Lyrics of Bob Marley's 'War' which encapsulates a speech written by His Imperial Majesty, Emperor Haile Selassie I of Ethiopia that was delivered at the United Nations General Assembly in October 1963.

on, I always ensured that a hard copy of the Constitution was always available at the household.

In the 2001 general elections, the country faced a hung Parliament with the then ruling UNC party and the Opposition PNM party each holding 18 seats in the 36 seat Parliamentary Chamber. Since no party commanded the majority, President A.N.R. Robinson was faced with a grave constitutional duty in appointing a Prime Minister who in his judgment was "most likely to command the support of the majority of members of that House."[115] Leading up to the President's decision, my father was one of a few attorneys whose opinion the President considered. This opinion was written in Kingston and was immediately dispatched under confidential cover to the President's House in Port of Spain. How this written opinion was produced ought to be outlined here. My father wrote by hand, and in between orated, his opinion to Darien and myself. There we were like his personal secretaries, delegated with the task of typing out his words on his computer. From the perspective of a final year law student, I found such an exercise to be enlightening. Given the confidentiality surrounding such a sensitive issue and the person whom he was writing, this action displayed a sense of trust which my father placed in us.

---

[115] Section 76. (1) Where there is occasion for the appointment of a Prime Minister, the President shall appoint as Prime Minister—
(a) a member of the House of Representatives who is the Leader in that House of the party which commands the support of the majority of members of that House; or
(b) where it appears to him that that party does not have an undisputed leader in that House or that no party commands the support of such a majority, the member of the House of Representatives who, in his judgment, is most likely to command the support of the majority of members of that House, and who is willing to accept the office of Prime Minister.

When the President delivered his statement live on television, he prefaced his decision by mentioning that he considered the advice of many legal minds, one of who was *"the Principal of the Norman Washington Manley Law School"*. My father noted, with delight, that the President did not refer to him personally by name but rather carefully elected to mention the full name of Norman Manley. This he thought was a mark of respect for the person whom the Law School was named after. It was minute details like this one which pleased my father.

History reveals that President Robinson, in that same speech, appointed Patrick Manning as Prime Minister. Half of the population was infuriated since the UNC, which was the incumbent in Government, had the popular vote. Due to the 18/18 deadlock, between December 2001 and October 2002, Trinidad and Tobago experienced a hung Parliament. With the seats split evenly between the Government and the Opposition members, it became extremely difficult for the Parliament to pass legislation, especially legislation that needed a special majority. Due to these peculiar circumstances there was a general frustration brewing within the society as most felt that the country was at a standstill. As a youth, I too was feeling that sense of frustration creeping in. I then hatched a plan where myself together with some of my friends would march to the President's House and demand that something be done to remedy the situation. I already strategised with my friends the date of the march and the fact that we needed to source a bullhorn. I was quite excited about my plan and before I placed it into action, I ran it by my father. After listening keenly, what he said next made me stop dead in my tracks. His words were curt yet effective. *So after you get all your people to march to President House, what happens next?*

I could not even answer. To be honest, I never even thought about that question. What appeared to me to be a bright idea ended right there and then. Shortly afterwards Prime Minister Manning, recognising that the situation was ungovernable, called an early election and won. Following that election, the borders were revisited and the total number of electoral districts increased from 36 to 41. It was intentional to have an odd number to prevent another stalemate at the polls. A perhaps fruitless march to the President's House was averted. Thanks to my father, I learnt an invaluable lesson; you must think through your plan of action from the beginning to the end.

Then there was a gentleman called Dr Lenny Saith who had a very cordial relationship with my father. During the 1991-1995 Cabinet, Saith was the Minister of Planning and Development and Leader of Government Business in the Senate. It was speculated by many that Saith wielded heavy political clout as he was the right-hand man of Prime Minister Manning. After my father exited politics, Saith would often contact him in Jamaica via telephone. There they would talk about a wide variety of issues, the national politics certainly being one of them. On one occasion, Keith gave a telephone interview with the media in Trinidad which was critical of the governing PNM party. Shortly after this interview was circulated, Saith telephoned my father in Jamaica stating that persons within the party were concerned that he went public with his views. However my father was a very neutral man and never yielded to political considerations. I would always remember my father's reply, because he often repeated it to us:

"Lenny, I said so many good things publicly in the past about the Government and no one from the party calls me. The day I criticise the Government, the party is concerned and wants to reach out to me."

It was because of this neutrality, the tendency to stand up for what was right and to speak up for what was wrong, that may have caused some of my father's former political colleagues to distance themselves from him while he was in Jamaica.

Lee Kuan Yew, the founding father and former Prime Minister of Singapore once said that he was more interested in being correct than being politically correct.[116] This was the same for my father. He would look at the facts, analyse them and then arrive at an objective conclusion. My father felt shunned whenever he found out that a former political colleague or PNM Minister was in Kingston and they failed to contact him. *"Everyone knows I live in Kingston"* – he would argue aloud with himself. He would always point out that the only person who would pick up the phone and call him while in Jamaica on official business was his political nemesis; Basdeo Panday.

By that time, Panday was the Prime Minister and my father was always pleased to receive his call. In general terms, even though they stood on the opposite sides of the political fence, Keith found Panday to be a clever and witty politician. The only real issue that my father had with Panday was that as Prime Minister, Panday signed the Agreement to establish the Caribbean Court of Justice but when he later came into Opposition, he failed to support the Court. My father thought it unfathomable that the Caribbean Court of Justice was headquartered in Port of Spain, yet Trinidad and Tobago was not a member of the Court's appellate jurisdiction. In fact had he been alive today, he would

---

[116] Shashi Jayakumar and Rahul Sagar *The Big ideas of Lee Kuan Yew* (2014) at pg. 168.

have been extremely disappointed that Trinidad and Tobago and the majority of CARICOM States have still retained the Privy Council as their final Court of Appeal.

Nevertheless, both Panday and Keith had an amiable relationship which was forged out of mutual respect. This relationship blossomed even more when my father left the Parliament and moved to Jamaica. *The Silver Fox*, as he is affectionately known, used phrases such as "learned in law", "soft-spoken", "a very kind gentleman" and "someone who never raised his voice or got angry in the Parliament" to describe my father.

When I asked the former Prime Minister back in November 2012 why they called him the Silver Fox he quipped – *"I guess it's because of my grey hair and the fact that I'm a wily politician."* It suddenly dawned on me that my friend once said that he never saw Panday's hair black. My mind quickly switched back to the conversation as Panday summed up: *"I can't remember who it was who gave me that name. It must have been either my political colleagues or perhaps one of my foes".*[117]

Meeting P.J.

Even though my father was living abroad and was interested in the politics back home, the same level of enthusiasm applied equally to the politics in Jamaica. His constant calling in to Motty Perkins' radio programme to argue about the local politics was evidence of this. Furthermore, his friendly relations and exchanges with Jamaica's Attorney General, A.J. Nicholson also stirred up his *'political appetite'*. In fact, even though he

---

[117] I interviewed Basdeo Panday on the telephone, while I was living in Geneva, in November 2012.

never voted in Jamaica, my father's political philosophy was more aligned to that of the People's National Party (PNP) in Jamaica. One of the reasons for such an alignment was that the PNP were more supportive towards the CCJ. Yet in true Keith fashion, he had more political friends than foes. When he passed away, one of the first condolatory calls my mother received was from Bruce Golding, the then Prime Minister of Jamaica and a member of the Jamaican Labour Party (JLP).

It was New Year's Day, 2014 and my mission was to meet Percival Noel James Patterson (more popularly known as P.J. Patterson) the former Prime Minister of Jamaica under the PNP. Upon arriving at P.J.'s home, I noticed that there were a tent, chairs and tables stacked orderly upon each other and confetti on the ground; a clear indication of the festivities the night before to ring in the new year. I followed P.J. inside his home and we soon descended some steps into a room filled with local art. This room reminded me of a Jamaican art gallery, with bookshelves and books serving as props. In reality the room turned out to be his study and a place where the former Prime Minister kept his prized awards. This was the first time that I actually met P.J. Patterson and he looked just like I envisioned him on the television. He was a towering, medium built, dark skinned gentleman who sported thin black-rimmed glasses. I definitely felt his presence inside the study area. His grey beard was neatly shaved and his hair was low and looked white and soft like cotton. He wore a red short-sleeved shirt with bright orange stripes, brown slacks and leather slippers. P.J. then offered me a seat on a comfortable wooden chair. He sat on a similar chair to my right where a coffee table separated us. A lady, probably in her forties, dressed in a domestic uniform approached inviting us to have a drink. I settled for a glass of water. P.J. settled for a more traditional drink; a *Red Stripe* beer.

The interview began shortly before the drinks were served. As we sat down, I handed over to P.J. a list of six questions about my father which I proposed to ask him. He took his time while he read them. After a short moment, he commenced in his deep baritone voice:

"Young Sobion, I have read your questions, let's put this aside and let's talk about how I met your father and the Caribbean Court of Justice. This, I believe are the most important..."

P.J.'s first and most meaningful connection with my father was when he was Attorney General and Minister of Legal Affairs. Subsequently, he had the opportunity to meet my father again as Principal of the Norman Manley Law School. P.J. described the connection between him and Keith as *"tangential"*. As a Prime Minister and a lawyer, P.J. acknowledged that he had an interest in the development of the Norman Manley Law School. However, it was mostly in relation to the CCJ that he and my father made contact. The exchanges on the CCJ were not planned. They would be done perhaps on a plane between Trinidad and Tobago and Jamaica or while on their way to another regional meeting.

When P.J. served as Prime Minister of Jamaica, my father was the Attorney General of Trinidad and Tobago. P.J. remembered this period quite well. It was a period where the Caribbean Community was formulating the Revised Treaty of Chaguaramas and that my father was the Government's lead adviser regarding this project.[118] During this process, Keith was invited to attend Prime Ministerial meetings and at such

---

[118] The Revised Treaty of Chaguaramas established the Caribbean Community including the CARICOM Single Market & Economy. It was signed by Heads of Government of CARICOM on 5 July 2001 at their twenty-second meeting of the Conference in Nassau, The Bahamas.

gatherings, there was a profound respect for the legal opinions that he rendered even though in some instances they were not in favour of a particular country's political directorate.

Many years after the Revised Treaty of Chaguaramas, the Council of Legal Education was working assiduously to find someone with the highest intellectual calibre to fill the vacancy of Principal of the Law School in Jamaica. P.J. noted that my father was particularly enthused about his appointment as Principal. According to P.J. my father was a regionalist and by appointing him Principal in a Law School in Jamaica was an acknowledgment of his regional commitment. This in return gave my father the possibility of serving in another country, outside of his own, and to serve students who came from other parts of the Caribbean. This statement struck a chord with my own soul. I never thought about it that way until I heard it from the former Prime Minister.

What P.J. said made utmost sense. Sometimes when I sit down and listen to all these stories I cannot help but say to myself that my father was truly a Caribbean man. Keith was not only interested in the betterment of his own country, Trinidad and Tobago. He was interested in the betterment of every single citizen within the CARICOM region. It did not matter which part of the region you came from. If you had a problem with the functioning of politics, the judiciary or education, Keith would eagerly listen to you. All this is not surprising for a man who writes a message to me on the inner cover of a copy of the Revised Treaty of Chaguaramas – *The future development of the Caribbean is written within this treaty.*

I still feel nostalgic about the conversations we had from when I was young up until now. It seemed as if every effort, every sinew he had in his body was forged towards the path of regional integration. His life was for Caribbean people. The Caribbean people were his life. It was like he had a map of the West Indies drawn up in his head. Geographically, he could tell you where each island was situated and their own individual idiosyncrasies. He knew about the island politics; he had his own views as to the intellect and capability of a country's Prime Minister, Attorney General or even a Judge. He knew about the latest case or legal challenge that was brewing up in any West Indian island and the lawyers who were involved. He travelled the region widely for meetings. So much so, that often he would relate to us stories like *"I woke up in Trinidad thinking that I was in St. Vincent"* or *"I admire how Haiti's public signs are written in French and in Créole."* He would even correct you on your pronunciation of *Antigua*, which he claimed was pronounced as: *An-tea-gwa*.

Once, while Principal, he sent me an email pointing out that he was elated with the new appointments of Chief Justice, Attorney General, Minister of Tertiary Education and Minister of Finance on a particular island as these offices had a direct impact on Caribbean Legal Education. That was the level of his thinking. He wasn't concerned about the politics but more concerned that the right people were appointed. His mind was always focussed on one thing; how could this course of action benefit the Caribbean region? Not any individual island…but the region.

At the Law School, his travels were not only limited to North America and the Caribbean. For work, he had the opportunity to travel to the United Kingdom and other Commonwealth countries such as Mauritius, Malaysia and to Australia. He claimed that his flight from Jamaica to Australia was the longest he ever experienced. He entertainingly noted that on the flight from Perth to Sydney, he was able to eat breakfast, then lunch, then sleep while still flying over this vast continent. Keith also once told me that he never visited Canada and that he vowed one day to make a trip there. Having said this, I found this quotation from the *Trinidad and Tobago Newsday* to be on point:

"When one considers that Sobion's legal practice encompassed company law, commercial contracts, banking, shipping and admiralty, investment financing and joint ventures, arbitration and dispute resolution, it becomes even more significant that he chose to be in education rather than active practice. This is because he was a man more interested in ideas and civic duty than in making money. The Caribbean could use more people like him."[119]

---

[119] Excerpt from the Trinidad and Tobago Newsday (archives), Saturday 16 February 2008.

Chapter 14

London and South Africa

The Commonwealth Law Conference

September 2005 was a defining moment in my professional legal career. That month, I joined my father at the 50th Commonwealth Law Conference (CLC) which was held at the *Queen Elizabeth II Conference* centre in London. My father attended in his capacity as Principal of the Law School while I found myself, once again, as his specially paid for guest. It had been a long while since I last visited the British capital. The city looked unexpectedly the same after many years, with its sleek black taxicabs, red double decker buses and phone booths. The only subtle difference then, perhaps hastened with the advent of mobile phones, were that the red phone booths appeared more to be an attraction for photo ops rather than for their original use.

Besides interacting with lawyers from all across the Commonwealth, one of the objectives of this visit was to meet up with a colleague of my father, a South African lawyer and professor named David McQuoid-Mason who taught at the University of KwaZulu-Natal. As I had intentions to pursue a Master's degree in law in South Africa, my father thought that the Professor would have been the ideal person to have an initial discussion with.

I received an advanced briefing from my father on Professor McQuoid. He was a white man, with long hair and often wore a dashiki. I was not surprised. My father fancied the company of those who I would call — *intellectual radicals* or persons who did not conform to what society would deem the norm. Professor McQuoid certainly fell within that category. My father's briefing was on point. When I was introduced to him, I immediately noticed the professor's medium length hair touched his dashiki at the shoulders. The professor was a kind and gracious gentleman, and after an enlightening conversation about South Africa and its universities, we vowed to keep in touch. Much later I learned that professor McQuoid was the President of the Commonwealth Legal Education Association (CLEA). My father also served on the CLEA with McQuoid as a Vice-President. Despite these back and forth communications, both men never disclosed to me these intricate details.

Also present in London for the conference from Trinidad and Tobago included Principal Annestine Sealey, Geoffrey Henderson (the then DPP) and Michael de la Bastide (the then President of the Caribbean Court of Justice). At the conference, de la Bastide delivered a timely paper entitled *"Caseflow Management in a Unified Family Court. A Caribbean Experiment."* I also attended a breakout session entitled *"The Death Penalty — Can it survive?"* which was chaired by Karl Hudson Phillips Q.C. There, a middle-aged British Queen's Counsel made a passionate plea for the moratorium of the death penalty. It was clear from the outset that the purpose of his delivery was to persuade the former colonies, which still retained the death penalty inherited by the coloniser, to revisit and revise these *"barbarous laws."* The British Q.C. was articulate and his arguments managed to persuade me at the time. Unfortunately, my father missed this particularly thought-provoking session and I wondered if the Q.C.'s lecture would have softened his position on reserving the death penalty only for a premeditated and cold-blooded murderer.

This however was not the only breakout session that he missed. As the days passed by, my father became visibly absent. The fact was that Keith looked fatigued. He became introverted and preferred to stay in his hotel room and sleep in late. When he woke up, most of his day was spent drinking coffee and reading novels. The position of Principal demanded a heavy travelling schedule and his lack of an appetite did not ameliorate the situation. At the Law conference, I would not hesitate to say that my father looked rather drawn and lethargic. This was also a time when my father was starting to peak at his career at the Law School and the law of diminishing returns, started to hit him. It was September 2005 and my father had roughly two and a half more years to live. Despite being engulfed in his introversion in England, Keith was still in the mood for jokes. One morning as I was in the hotel room getting dressed for the conference, he looked at my suit and he put on that old silly grin of his. When I asked him what the problem was, he replied that he found my suit pants to be too tight. I told him, quite truthfully, that I borrowed Jules' suit. Knowing my elder brother's style in wearing tight clothing, we both had a hearty laugh.

Sometime towards the end of the conference, my father and I took the afternoon off to walk the streets of London. On the way Keith was particularly enthused in passing by *10 Downing Street*. From there we strolled passed *New Square, Lincoln's Inn* and shopped at *Ede & Ravenscroft*, which specialises in the making of robes for the legal profession and handmade wigs. It was at this part of the trip that my father became more animated. For someone who was pro-West Indian, he was now eagerly inspired by British politics, wigs and legal tradition.[120] Another day of walking and bonding, found us passing through the thoroughfare of Chinatown and then the art shop *Green & Stone* in Chelsea. At *Green & Stone* we browsed the vibrant colours of acrylics and khadi papers on display which brought back memories of our days of shopping for art materials at Deltex on Pembroke Street, Trinidad.

Before we left London, we visited the Hackney home of Carl and Barbara Julian, two longstanding family friends. The Julians, who originally are from Trinidad, first met my father in the 1980s while he was on a trip to London attending to a land matter before the Privy Council. Upon their invitation, my father stayed at their home in Hackney for about one week, taking the public transport every morning to Court in central London. Later when Carl received the news about my father and his team's victory at the Privy Council, he spoke to Keith in Trinidad on the telephone to congratulate him. Upon asking what he would like from London to celebrate this legal milestone, my father's request was for *"a pack of four Guinness."*

To get from central London to Hackney that September afternoon was a bit tricky. My father being adventurous as he is, tried to retrace every step of a journey he made almost two decades before (I was impressed because my father even remembered the number of one of the buses which he took years ago). However, along the way we got lost and we had

---

[120] I could not say the same about British sports – cricket to be exact. While we were in London, the English defeated the Australians 2-1 in the Ashes series. Getting caught up in the jubilation, I purchased a t-shirt glorifying the English victory. My father flatly told me that evening, that he would never wear the t-shirt as it would not be "politically correct". His defiance was because he was West Indian and that he would not support any other team, even if the West Indians were not playing.

to hop off a double decker bus a couple of times for my father to assess our location and to recall certain landmarks. My father was determined. He refused to telephone the Julians for directions, preferring instead to rely on his own memory. It was as if that was his challenge for the afternoon. Finally, after descending a bus my father looked around curiously and said – *"Ah! this is the street."* That was how we arrived at the Julians' home that afternoon, operating on a bit of trial, error and most importantly memory. At Hackney we were greeted with a warm welcome. It did not take long for my father to scuttle away with Carl to the latter's private room for a drink of whiskey and to reminisce on old memories. Although they had not seen Keith much during his political years, the Julians remembered him as being someone entertaining and generous with his friends.

The September 2005 London trip, together with my father's own perspective on the development of the law, changed the course of my professional life forever. His perspective was that the law was evolving from the traditional sense and that a lawyer of today had to swim with the tide in order to become the lawyer of tomorrow. A lawyer could no longer be straitjacketed, and globalisation provided ample room to manoeuvre. All of a sudden specialised niches started to bloom, as if out of the blue, in areas such as environmental law, international trade, arbitration and intellectual property. The game was changing and lawyers needed to keep up with the pace or else face the inescapable chance of slowly becoming outmoded. With this lesson, I came face to face with this glaring reality. I wanted to be unique and unorthodox at the same time, not following the same beaten track, but exploring my own. By the time we took off from the Heathrow tarmac I was determined to become an international jurist.

Upon my return to Trinidad, I intensified my searches over the internet and solicited further opinions on which University to pursue a Master of Laws. Studying in a Commonwealth country, like my own, was a mandatory condition. I spoke to my father and we shortlisted two countries, Australia and South Africa. I always wanted to visit the African continent, so the latter was chosen. Having arrived at a decision on the country, another critical decision had to be made – Which University? Two universities were then recommended, The University of Witwatersrand in Johannesburg and the University of Cape Town. After final discussions, with my parents, it was agreed that Cape Town would be the better option. In February 2007, a little more than one year after the London Conference, I travelled from Port of Spain to Cape Town with my father.

Cape Town – the Mother City

To this day, I do not know who was more excited to travel to Cape Town, whether it was my father or myself. His excitement was only natural as just like me, this was his first time travelling to the African continent. Prior to our departure, my father confided in his sisters that the only reason he was travelling to South Africa was to settle me down by purchasing "pots and pans" for my apartment thereby downplaying the fact that I was mature enough to handle my own affairs. The reality was that my father just wanted to be there. Besides this, the novelty of my pursuing a postgraduate degree in law in South Africa enthused my father. I was told that he spoke proudly to his colleagues at the Law School about my pursuits at Cape Town.

On our way to South Africa we spent a couple of days in London. One evening we went for dinner at a restaurant in

Chinatown. Midway through the meal my father was repulsed by a conversation that two English men were having. These men were sitting at a table beside us and were uttering some distasteful words which I ought not repeat here. My father immediately interjected asking them to discontinue their conversation as he was in the company of his young son. The men hesitated, looked stunned for a short while, and then eventually obliged. Although they did not say, I could see it in their eyes that they were wondering who was this man who calmly, yet boldly, interrupted their conversation.

The next day we boarded our 'eleven-and-a-half-hour' British Airways flight to Cape Town (also fondly referred to as *the Mother City*). When the wheels of the plane touched down on the tarmac of the Cape Town International Airport, the first view that I had was Table Mountain in all its splendour. A bit jet-lagged, we quickly installed ourselves at the cosy *Protea Hotel* which was walking distance from the famous V&A Waterfront. We stayed at the *Protea* for about a week and there are a few memories which stood out during that period. Firstly, due to a mix-up in the dates with the tour operators, we missed our guided tour to Robben Island where Nelson Mandela was imprisoned for some eighteen years. As there were no other dates available for a tour before my father's departure date, he became visibly disappointed. For him, one of the reasons he made the journey to South Africa was to see first-hand the prison where Mandela was detained.

Walking through Cape Town city, Keith was also searching for a chain to replace his worn black cord which suspended his Ethiopian cross pendant below his neck. Ever since I was baptised in the Ethiopian Orthodox Church, Keith had displayed an interest in Ethiopia and the religion. We were four that day, Keith, my South African friend Haneem, her mother and myself, who strolled through Greenmarket Square looking for a cord. Remembering that day, Haneem shared with me her moving narrative of my father, whom she met only once:

"On a windy day on the streets of Greenpoint, I met Justin and Keith Sobion. I thought he was just another doting father who wanted to ensure that his dreamer son knew what he was getting into by coming all the way to Africa. I had no clue that the same figure that greeted my mother like a queen and told us to call him Keith, was the honourable former Attorney General. Accepting that we did not own a car, Keith climbed into the minibus taxi so that we could go and take a look around downtown Cape Town. I was nervous that my visitors wouldn't like the experience but Keith and his son with their extra-long limbs squashed into the taxi and they were game for anything. I still remember Keith's powerful but calming voice compared to his son's easy-going singsong voice. Keith became the most emotive when he spoke of his family. It is easy to see that he would have crossed even more miles and gone to more continents to ensure that his sons were happy."

Apart from the "pots and pans" we also had to search for an appropriate student residence. The first residence we visited was in the Mowbray suburb, and my father was not too keen on its facilities. The second one was in Rondebosch, the *Rondeberg flats*, right opposite the Baxter Theatre. There we were shown a more modern studio apartment, fully furnished with a bathroom and kitchen. Upon viewing the apartment, we quickly hurried ourselves to the warden's office to confirm my place. When the lady in charge saw us, she was pleasantly surprised. She expressed to us, that in all her years this was the first time she was seeing a father accompanying a son to secure his residence at the University. My father smiled his trademark smirk and he in turn flattered the lady with some of his own kind words. The lady then asked us if we came from Ethiopia. My father blushed again. It was quite funny in hindsight. About a year later, my father had a similar interaction with a porter in a hotel in the Cayman Islands. The porter, upon bringing his luggage to his room, asked my father if he was a relative of Haile Selassie. My father used this experience to suggest that he was more Rasta than us, as even strangers believed that he was of direct lineage *to the Conquering Lion of Judah.* My father always felt somewhat complimented when persons asked him if he was Ethiopian. And looking back at it now, he could probably pass as one too.

With the pots, pans and housing sorted out we then needed to finalise the registration of my courses at the University. In the registration area on 'Middle Campus' we sat down to confirm the details of my studies. It was agreed that I pursue a specialisation in International Law. The core courses we selected were *International Trade Law, International Law of the Sea, Marine Pollution Law* and *Environmental Law.* The latter course came highly recommended by my father. He did not tell me then, but later I realised that he was awarded a consultancy to draft environmental laws for two countries in the Caribbean region. I was to assist him in the research after my Masters was completed. I also discussed with him about the possibility of pursuing a course entitled *Use of Force.* His reply was classic Keith – *"Why do you want to do such a course? You plan to work in a country where there is an armed conflict?"*

No one could predict the future. To date I have never worked in a conflict zone but I have worked close enough in the periphery that an understanding of the 'use of force' would have been appreciative. Needless to say the possibility of registering for such a subject was immediately dropped. Thinking of it, if this conversation took place at the time of writing, my father's opinion on the Use of Force course *may* have changed.

The next step was to settle my school fees. At the cashier I paid the total amount of $5,000 USD, in cash, which then represented my entire life savings. I was short of a few hundred dollars in fees and I asked my father on the spot to assist me with the balance. My father openly paid the balance but he did not hide his displeasure. When we left the cashier, he revealed to me that he detested disorganisation and that I should have known beforehand the full cost of my school fees. Keith was really a stickler when it came to financial affairs. If you wanted to borrow money from my father, you could not simply make a vague request. One had to explain in exact detail the amount (down to every penny), the purpose of the loan and the timeframe in which the monies were to be repaid. By dint of this, borrowing money from my father was like borrowing money from a commercial bank. Your application had to be rigorous and intentions proper. This course of conduct undoubtedly was embedded in his genes and came from his mother.

With no money to my name after I paid my fees, my father left me in South Africa with $400 USD. Later, he would send me money but only if I made a demand for it. The truth is that I was fearful of asking him for money. On each occasion I had to explain to him, in painful detail, what the money was to be used for. If my explanation did not pass his stringent *'commercial bank'* test, the amount originally requested would be diminished thus resulting in my dissatisfaction. My father requested that I keep count of his generosity because when I returned to Trinidad from South Africa I had to repay him every cent. Although he sounded serious, I knew deep down in my heart, that he was a kind father who would forgive me all my debts.

After a couple of months passed my financial situation worsened. I was forced to call Lucina, my maternal grandmother, to explain to her my dilemma. God bless her soul because after she heard of my plight, every month she would deposit $500 TT dollars (approximately $85 USD at the time) into my bank account. I never told my parents about this because my grandmother preferred to keep it between the both of us. In any event, if I truly was in need of any extra financial assistance I knew that I could have also relied on my parents. All this ended up being a blessing in disguise because that year in Cape Town made me appreciate the valuable lesson of managing my scarce financial resources. Like when two of my classmates planned a road trip from Namibia to Zimbabwe, I had to opt out because I knew that I could not afford it financially. I still feel a mix of sadness and guilt that I never repaid my father the money he loaned me in Cape Town. But money cannot buy life. By the time I returned to the Caribbean a year later he fell sick.

By no means was my father a miser. In fact, he was the opposite. Money and assets meant little to him. It was more the lesson, a lesson which he was committed to teaching his children. He was teaching me about priorities; how to make do with the little that you have. For instance, my father would prefer to spend money on a university textbook than on a pair of fancy sneakers (to prove this, for my studies he shipped from Jamaica to South Africa the textbook, *Law of the Sea 3rd ed. by Churchill & Lowe*). Things like books and education were important to him. In reality I could get whatever I wanted from him, I just had to ask for the right things.

On the morning of 14th February 2007, just before the sun came up, my father left South Africa for London. From the *Protea Hotel*, he hired a taxi to the airport and then to my studio apartment in Rondebosch. In the taxi, my father was preparing for an argument with the British Airways ground staff. Apparently, when he travelled to South Africa he checked in two bags free of charge. The day before, British Airways issued a new policy, with immediate effect, whereby passengers were only allowed to check in one single luggage free of charge. My father's argument was that he was not entitled to pay to check in his second luggage because when he bought his return ticket that new policy did not form part of the contract. It was a clever yet straightforward argument. I never found out if he managed to persuade the BA authorities on the ground.

When we arrived at the airport, it was still dark. Kissing me he whispered *"Be good Kiddo, I'll call you when I arrive in London"*. And just like that he made it into the airport's terminal. It happened so quickly. I do not remember telling him – *I love you* or *Thank You Daddy for bailing me out with the university fees.* He just left me like that and my heart sank. I looked at him go through the airport door and he never looked back. At that moment, I never knew that my father now had exactly one year to live. I crawled back into the taxi. *"Ronderberg flats"* the taxi driver half asked, half told. Yes, I replied. We returned on the highway where the sun and the township on our left were now waking up. It suddenly dawned on me; I was alone in Africa.

It was difficult to settle down in South Africa knowing that you were all alone. It's only natural to feel homesick. The saving grace was that after a few days I commenced my University classes and met new friends from all over the world. I could sense that doing a Master's in Law in South Africa was something which made my father proud. Perhaps it reminded him of something which he would also have liked to do when he was my age. For the next ten months we would exchange email and *Skype* video calls. I remember I would send him drafts of my assignments and he would respond. (On this note, he joked that the title of my thesis was longer than the thesis itself). In times when I was down, Keith reminded me about the reasons I was there, which was to learn and to meet new people. At the University one of my tutors was a PhD candidate from Cameroon who was interested in undergoing research in the Caribbean. I immediately gave him my father's contact in Jamaica. This was the type of relationship that my father expected me to cultivate while I was living in South Africa. And as the days passed by, I grew less and less homesick.

In November 2007, I decided to return home for Christmas and to finish my thesis paper in Trinidad. To this, my father was taken aback. I suspected he thought that I went back to my roots in Africa and would never return to the Caribbean. However, in the Christmas spirit he probably understood. I remember writing him, together with other family members, an email about my time spent in South Africa, my exploits in Ethiopia and my imminent return to Trinidad for Christmas. The subject of my email was – *NEW CHAPTER*. His email in response is inspiring. I still read it over, from time to time, searching on each occasion for a hidden meaning between each line. Today, his response encourages me to be a better person both now and in the future.

Dear Sekou,

I can only say that whilst the time appears to have passed quickly in terms of the passage of measurable time, it was immeasurable for all of us who care and have great love for you. So, another chapter in your life has ended and I know that the experiences you have had would make you a better person, not for yourself only, but for all who expect much more from you.

All you are experiencing only puts more demands on you from the point of view of service to your people, the country and the region; it also requires your continuing humility and dedication to the higher purpose of life.

I am anxious for your return just to have you in my arms again and hear the stories of C/Town (Cape Town), the kids with whom you interacted, the time in Ethiopia and of course the fine work you have done at the University so far.... I will be here when you get here.

Yes a chapter has ended but, my son, the book is far from being completed.

Selah and Blessings,

The Prophet...Le Papa Skeef [121]

There were other times, when his email was more humorous and light-hearted. Like the 50th birthday greeting which he sent by email to his cousin Kenny Frontin on the 25th January 2008:

Dear Kenny,

I believe I am a little older than you so here is something I have learnt:

'You know you are middle aged when you keep forgetting to pull up your zipper after leaving the bathroom. You know you are getting old when you forget to pull it down when you are in the bathroom'

Do have a great day and welcome to the club 50+.

KSS

---

[121] My father wrote this email to me on Tuesday 11th December 2007.

Chapter 15

I Return to the Caribbean

Keith spent Christmas 2007 with us in Trinidad. As usual, the Christmas Day festivity was with all the family by his sister Teresa at her home in Maracas Valley, St. Joseph. Later in the evening he was present at the annual *Caesar's Army* fete – *Christmas Passion* hosted by my brother Jules. While home for the season, my father also had me busy. I was once again providing "secretarial" duties for him, regarding his next consultancy project. In the latter part of the year, my father was contracted to draft environmental legislation for two Eastern Caribbean States, St. Vincent and the Grenadines and Grenada. He had already established a small team of lawyers to assist namely, John Knechtle, Keith Friday and Sandra Nichols. I was the latest addition to his team and at first was a bit reluctant given my arduous task of completing my own project; my Cape Town dissertation.[122]

Keith flew back to Jamaica for the New Year. On the 6th January 2008 he travelled to the Cayman Islands for a Law School meeting. It was on that trip that the porter at the hotel asked him if he was related to Haile Selassie. Throughout this time, I was still receiving emails from my father with respect to the environmental law project in the Eastern Caribbean. My father expected that I read every email and the model legislation contained therein. This, I admit, proved to be challenging given my own academic commitments. Still, I prodded on. My

---

[122] When my father passed away, John Knechtle took over as the team leader for the OECS Consultancy.

father was due to return to Trinidad on the 1st February for the Carnival season.

Early that morning, while exiting the *Beach House* Carnival fete, I received a very troubling telephone call from my mother in Jamaica. On the next line, she explained to me the horrifying situation. She woke up in the middle of the night hearing my father coughing in the bathroom. When she got up to look for him, he was over the bathroom sink spitting out blood. My mother immediately called the hospital and an ambulance arrived at *The Pines* in a few minutes. My father was a stubborn man. Even in a weak physical state, he was unwilling to go to the hospital and it took some coaxing from the medical team and my mother for him to enter the ambulance. For my mother, she could not understand how one person could lose so much blood from his mouth. At some point that morning, my father revealed to my mother that he had gone to the dentist to remove a tooth the day before and that the bleeding would not stop. My father lost so much blood that morning that he had to be placed in intensive care. It was such a bizarre moment because we could not comprehend how my father could have been hospitalised after removing a tooth. As one of the gardeners at *The Pines* retorted after the fact, in his classical Jamaican patois; *"Mista Sobion....'im shoulda neva tek out 'im teeth."* My mother's instructions were clear. We had to pack our bags immediately and take the next flight to Jamaica.

It was Carnival Friday morning, when I first made contact with Kathleen Rochford the Registrar of the Hugh Wooding Law School to make our travel arrangements. The flights being fully booked, Rochford managed to obtain the last two seats on Carnival Sunday on a Caribbean Airlines flight for Darien and myself. Jules would travel the day after, on Carnival Monday.

The stern maternal words of Rochford still echo in my head –
*make sure you get on that plane because flights are full and things do not
look good for your father.* So said so done. Darien and I arrived
in Kingston on Sunday around midday. I would never forget
that Jules arrived at the Norman Manley International airport
on the Monday with fresh paint on his body from the J'ouvert
celebrations.

My mind was not prepared to face the situation before me at
the University Hospital in Mona. My father was in the intensive
care unit (ICU) and was bareback to the hip and looked extra
frail. He had all these 'cords' attached to his skeletal frame and
his beard was scraggly and looking more grey than usual. His
eyes were bulging and bloodshot and they opened even wider
with excitement when he saw us. For a moment he looked
strange without his glasses. But for me the most heart-breaking
part was that he could not speak coherently. When he did try
to speak his words came out like muffled screams. He was
excited to see us but he could not find the words – just these
painful screams. I stroked his hair, which was also more grey
and amazingly soft, and said *"Skeef don't worry it will be ok".* At
that moment I found he aged in just one month from the last
time I saw him. His lips were dry and there was some spittle
suspending between his upper and lower lip. I tried to wipe
it off. Then the muffled screams came again. I would never
forget that. Those dreadful screams! I was not so sure if he was
screaming for help or if he was just excited to see us. Or maybe
he just woke up and was delirious. I reassured him that he
would pull through all of his discomfort and that he just needed
to calm down. From the corner of one of his eyes, water trickled

down. He wept. With his small frame on the bed, unable to speak, my father looked like a child.

After a few minutes we left the room. I tried to hold up but as soon as I exited the main building and was outside on the compound of the hospital, I broke down into tears. Rochford was right. Maybe this was the end of Keith. The next day it was all over the newspapers in Trinidad, Jamaica and I suspect certain parts of the Caribbean that the former Attorney General, turned Principal was seriously ill. That same day, I found out that my father lost a lot of blood. I would be forever grateful for those UWI students who generously came forth and donated blood in order to help save my father. However the doctors advised that my father also needed blood plasma. I remember we had to spend a couple hours in the car park of Andrews Memorial hospital waiting for the delivery of the blood plasma. As soon as we received the package we hurriedly returned to the University Hospital for onward delivery to the doctors. The next problem was his lungs. I remember one of the doctors asking us if my father smoked because one of his lungs suffered an infection. I do not even remember responding to the doctor's question but I am certain that he saw the answer in our eyes.

Despite the odds, brighter days seemed to be on the horizons. Within a few days Keith's health was on the mend. One indication of this was his discharge from the ICU and admission into the general ward of the University Hospital. Another indication was that he was now starting to speak, even though quite gingerly. The doctors conveyed to us that our presence enhanced his morale. My mother concurred and she repeatedly said that when we, his three sons, visited the hospital for the first time Keith's condition took an upward turn. My father also received numerous visits in the ward from friends and colleagues from the Norman Manley Law School. It was like a healing therapy – the cards, the flowers, the letter and the kind words.[123] It goes without saying that Keith loved company. The good news filtered down swiftly from Kingston to Port of Spain; *Principal Sobion was on the road to recovery.*

As the days passed by, Keith grew more and more miserable on the ward. It was as if the more strength he acquired, the more anxious and impatient he became. He was more vocal and demanded to leave the hospital and return home. He complained that he was fit enough to attend a Council meeting which was due to take place in Guyana. He even engaged us in acts of subterfuge claiming that his doctors even gave him a clean bill of health. When we did approach the doctors about this, we found out that my father's statements were false. I could not believe that my father was trying to deceive us, just to come out of the hospital. At that time I did not put it beyond him to secretly discharge himself. Although he possibly thought of that option, he realised that it would have been difficult to execute as his feet were badly swollen due to his illness. His feet were so bloated that he could not have put on his shoes. It would therefore have been quite painful and uncomfortable for him to walk. The only form of mobility Keith had on the ward was his wheelchair. Whenever he became tired of seeing the four walls of the ward, a nurse would carry him outside in his wheelchair.

---

[123] We still have in our possession a letter from Georgette Johnson, an administrative staff member, who in the letter referred to Keith as "her father". Needless to say Keith and Georgette had a very close relationship at the Norman Manley Law School.

There he would breathe in some fresh air into his lungs, have a view of the garden and hear the birds singing. During these times, Keith was his happiest. They were however short-lived because after about half an hour, the nurses would then return my father to his dreadful bed.

There was always a constant movement of patients within the ward. At the beginning, Keith shared an open space with about four other patients. On the ward, Keith tried to develop a relationship with each patient. Midway through his stay, there was a young lady lying down next to him who he often chatted with. Dennis Morrison, while visiting Keith on one occasion, noticed that the young lady, who did not have any visitors at the time, looked dejected. Morrison witnessed Keith turning his head on the bed and whispering towards the young girl – *Hey, you all right?* The girl smiled. Today I have no idea as to what brought the young lady to the hospital. But she did not last long on the ward. Maybe three days. Whatever happened to her, we never knew. I sincerely hope that she is alive today. In the twelve days while my father was in hospital, there was a heavy rotation on the ward. I believe most of the patients did not make it and as a result they passed on. As fast as each patient left, there was a replacement. When one patient left, Keith may have lost another friend – for better or for worse. Keith probably wondered if he would be next. I remember a close relative once saying that it must have been difficult for him to sleep at night because once he closed his eyes he did not know if he would wake up to see the next morning.

Every day we were there at the ward visiting my father. It was like clockwork. As visiting hours were during the day and the evening, my mother would arrange a shift programme among us. That way Keith would have seen us at least twice a day. Because the doctors realised whom he was and that we were his family members, in most cases we were granted the privilege of staying beyond the normal visiting hours. We were always positive that my dear father would have been discharged. While at the hospital ward, he became animated. He checked his email on his hospital bed and smiled at all the mail he received wishing him a speedy recovery. He read the newspapers online. He gave legal advice to one of our friends regarding a lease agreement she was about to enter into. He was even deeply engaged in the US Democratic primary elections between Barack Obama and Hillary Clinton. Keith strongly supported Obama, even though he noted that at times he dressed informally without a tie. As a woman, my mother naturally supported Clinton. While at the hospital, they both put forward arguments as to why the candidate of their choice was better equipped to lead America.

Then there were the little things that, on reflection, we may have overlooked. Like the day when he just sat down on his bed feebly staring at his laptop on the *gmail.com* homepage because he could not remember his email password. The other occasion was when I presented to him a draft chapter of my Master's thesis to read. After a few days he returned the paper to me saying that he found my draft to be *"good"*. Unlike him, there was not one scribble or penned correction on my draft paper. I therefore formed the impression that he never read the draft and that his mind was not as sharp as it was. *Oh how all this must have frustrated him!* Yet his hospitalisation provided ample opportunity to have many intimate discussions. Once I asked him if he was a member of a Lodge. Keith looked at me with his usual side grin. He blinked a few times as if he was shocked by the question I asked. Finally, he replied – *"I used to be, but that was a very long time ago."* Even today I still feel like he was stretching the truth.

I regretted a few things which we did while my father was a patient on the ward. One was giving him my thesis to read when he was not lucid. He deserved to rest and ease his mind and not focus on legalese written on pieces of paper. The second regret was equally painful. One visit, my brother came to the ward drinking a *Red Bull* at my father's bedside. My father desired a taste of the drink and we obliged. While sipping through the straw, my mother suddenly entered into the room. Upon seeing what was taking place, she angrily pulled away the can from my father's hand thereby spilling a blob of the fizzy drink on the hospital floor. My mother gave us a heavy scolding afterwards saying that *Red Bull* was not good for his health and that we should not allow Keith to manipulate us (something which he was very good at doing). Little did my mother know that this was not the first time that we gave in to my father's demands to taste *the drink which gives you wings.*

The last regret is one which, if given another chance, I would never dare repeat. I had a personal problem and my father disagreed on the manner in which I was handling it. Even today, the words of his email still haunt me:

I will say it now...I have been quite distressed over this matter...sometimes I wonder whether it is worth the while...I really care for and love you all.... but at times when I can't sleep I think it is my fault or at least my responsibility.[124]

The day before he passed away we had a long discussion on

---

[124] My father's email to me dated 7 December 2007.

this particular issue and he urged me to follow his advice. From our conversation it was easy to sense that the dilemma pained him. When we returned in the night he reverted to the discussion that we had earlier in the day. He said that I should resolve this problem as soon as possible. My mother was also standing at the bedside looking on. Leaving the room, I gave him a *thumbs-up* sign indicating that the issue would be resolved. He returned the favour by feebly raising his right thumb. On the bed, he adjusted his glasses and closed his eyes. As the lights went out on the ward, my mother and I exited the room. Because of what transpired next, today I still feel that I should never have burdened my father with that conversation over his hospital bed.

It was the morning of Thursday 14th February 2008. I was sitting on the patio at *The Pines* when the telephone rang. I answered the phone, not expecting anything unusual. It was the doctor who was overseeing my father. He expressed that a member of the family should come to the hospital immediately. Fear kicked in. I asked him if my father was fine, to which he replied *yes, but please hurry*. At least he is not dead I thought. But the warning call certainly appeared urgent.

I immediately called my mother who was in a meeting at her work place. She would join us at the hospital after her meeting was finished. I went to the fridge and withdrew some ice cubes for my father, which he preferred to suck rather than drinking water directly from a cup. With that, my brothers and I jumped into the vehicle and headed straight to the University Hospital. There we received the bad news. I knew it was coming when I saw the unusual sight of my father's bed completely surrounded by a curtain. The doctor explained that my father's heart stopped beating earlier in the morning and despite the efforts used to revive him, he was pronounced dead. The three of us stared into nothingness trying to internalise what the doctor was saying. I for myself was in complete denial. I remember asking an unintelligent question at the time; *"are you sure he is dead?"* to which the doctor nodded.

We were then invited to view the body behind the curtains. At that point I made a vow to myself that I did not want to see my father dead. I wanted my last memory of him to be one with the side smirk and infectious laugh. Maybe Darien also felt that way because only Jules mustered up the courage to view the face of my father. Behind the curtain, Jules' last rites were to kiss my father on the forehead. After we exited the hospital, tears swelled up in all our eyes. We mounted the vehicle with me behind the steering wheel. The next question was − *who will tell our mother?* In the end it was our little brother Darien who broke the news over the mobile phone. Darien chose his few words curtly and carefully − *"Mom…Dad just passed".* I could still hear the screams of my mother vibrating from the next line. While all this was happening in Jamaica, there was a meeting of the Council of Legal Education taking place in Georgetown, Guyana. This Georgetown meeting was the very same one which my father was looking forward to attending while he was hospitalised. Emile Ferdinand, the Chairman of the Council at the time delivered a very telling tale. When the news of Keith's passing was communicated to those present in the room, the whole meeting was shut down and everyone went straight to their hotel room in complete shock. There was no further Council business to discuss. In their moment of solitude one thing was surely echoing through their minds; *like a thief in the night, how could Keith, so swiftly, be taken away from us.*

The very next day, in the Trinidad and Tobago Parliament, tributes poured in from colleagues on both sides of the political fence. Colm Imbert expressed condolences on behalf of the PNM and the Government and Kamla Persad-Bissessar on behalf of the Opposition. In her statement, Persad-Bissessar brought back to life her first day in office as Attorney General: [125]

"As a politician, I do recall Mr Sobion as a gentleman of class at all times. We may have had our differences but, most certainly, I do recall the class and maturity he demonstrated when, in 1995, he offered me his chair when I was appointed Attorney General at that time. So I do believe as we pay tribute to Keith Sobion, we will miss him in more ways than one. As I say, to us, he was a colleague in the law; he was a colleague in the politics, but above all, Mr Sobion was also a friend."

Back in Jamaica, around midday, my father's cousin Kenny Frontin flew in to Jamaica from Atlanta. A medical doctor by profession, the reason for Kenny's visit was to check up on his cousin. Unfortunately, he arrived just a few hours too late. When we met up with Kenny that afternoon he cried in my arms, repeating; *"what happened to Keith…"* After all our tears were finally wiped away, we drove to a restaurant on Old Hope Road where the family ordered escovietch fish, fried bammy and rice and peas. Remembering how my father loved the escovietch fish at *Chasers* restaurant, I am convinced that he would have loved to be there, sharing a meal together with his family.

Later that evening, we hosted a wake at *The Pines* where family and friends came over to pay their respects. There in the garden outside of our townhouse, a friend of the Orisha faith performed

---

[125] *Hansard*, Friday 15 February 2008 at pg 515.

a spiritual ceremony. She lit a candle, gingerly placed it in the earth, then sprinkled in a circular manner; some alcohol around the candle making sure that the liquid did not spill on the flame itself. The flame immediately grew bigger and almost out of control while she performed this act. Seconds after she stopped sprinkling, the flame returned to its original state and then it slowly extinguished. Our friend said the alcohol was an offering to the gods of the earth as a thanksgiving for Keith's life. The offering was accepted when the flame grew bigger and brighter. Yet one of the most poignant memories was when my mother asked me for a second opinion as to what suit and tie to bury my father in. Fighting back her tears and while carefully displaying the items of clothing on her matrimonial bed, she expressed to me her choice of suit, shirt and matching tie. I thought to myself that it must have taken a great deal of strength and courage on the part of my mother to undergo this solemn act of dressing her husband for the very last time.

A more pleasant memory, if I may say, occurred the morning after my father's passing. My family and friends are always quick to point out that I resemble my father. This same perception applied to my parent's new domestic assistant, who I never met until that very morning. Coming down the steps I headed to the kitchen to prepare breakfast. There I saw the lady with a bowl in her hand. Before I could introduce myself, the bowl almost crashed to the ground. She started breathing heavily with her hands crossing her chest. Then she exclaimed *Oh my Lord, is how you tek afta yuh fadda. Me ah say is 'im duppy*. The word "*duppy*" meaning that she thought that she had seen my father's ghost.

After a few days passed, it was time for us to take our flight from Kingston to Port of Spain to prepare for the funeral. While departing *The Pines*, there was a strange feeling and confusion in the air. We were running late for our flight and mom screamed out orders in the following manner –

"Jules, Justin and Darien are you ready? Make sure you take off all the lights! Please take all the suitcases downstairs!"

The home was a bit chaotic, littered with flowers, dried leaves and cards from friends and well-wishers spilling over the table. We were all running into each other as we scampered to leave *The Pines*. I sensed that Keith was there in the corner, sitting in the patio watching and smiling at the commotion that we left behind.

Since then, I have heard many stories about death. I have heard that after the body dies the spirit roams for seven nights visiting loved ones. Others have said that if you do not wish for the travelling spirit to revisit your home you should rearrange your furniture so that the spirit will get confused. Or if you wish, then simply leave the furniture as is. On a more spiritual level, birth and death are two normal transitions and birth is not the beginning of life just like death is not the end.[126] Or like my father used to say, *from the day you are born you begin to die.*

Personally, I sense that my father is still around even if not in the flesh. Most nights I dream of him and some dreams are more vivid than the others. The first night he passed away, I dreamt that I was in an unfamiliar room and the telephone rang. As quickly as I put the receiver to my ear, I heard his

---

[126] *Teachings of Amma (Mata Amritanandamayi) – What Amma says to the World,* at pg. 223.

laughter. *Dad is that you?* I asked. He responded, *Yes, and you don't have to worry, everything is alright.*

Six months later I dreamt of him again. It was August 2008 and I had just received a lucrative job offer with a law firm in the British Virgin Islands. That night I had a vivid dream of my father advising me not to take up the offer and to wait for another opportunity. When I woke up, I hastily acted upon "his advice" even though I did not have another job option. I never disclosed this reason to the hiring law firm, or anyone as a matter of fact, as I was too embarrassed to disclose that I believed in the dream of a dead man. I admit that sometimes I do wonder how life would have turned out had I taken up the offer. When this occurs, I train my mind to never regret past decisions. On the positive side, I probably would have never worked alongside my mentor and friend Reggie Armour S.C. or moved to Geneva where I met my wife Aurélie. Life has a way, of directing us unto paths that were originally meant and chosen for us. Other dreams which stand out, include him getting called to the Bar in Canada, a country he never visited in his lifetime, speaking in the Parliament and him being disappointed with the fact that most Caribbean countries do not have the Caribbean Court of Justice as their final Court of Appeal.

I hope one day I'll see my father just as he is when I see him in my dreams.

Chapter 16

The Final Farewell

Our Father,
Who art in Zion,
Hallowed be thy name,
Thy Kingdom come on earth,
Thine will be done on earth,
Hallowed be thy name.

Buju Banton – 'Our Father in Zion'

My father planned his funeral while he was alive. It was as if he knew he was going to die young. While alive, he told us that he did not want any choir to sing gloomy songs at his funeral. Instead he preferred the upbeat voices of Buju Banton or David Rudder to sing at his funeral. His dream of wanting Buju (also known as Gargamel) to perform at his funeral was accurately reported after his funeral by *The Daily Observer* in Jamaica.[127] His other wishes were that he be cremated and that no one was to cry at his funeral. His wishes were fairly easy (in Buju's absence we played the coarse voice of singer's version of *'Our Father'*) and we managed to fulfil all his expectations save and except the crying.

For these reasons, I could not concur more with the words of his friend Tammy: "Keith's funeral was unorthodox and was

---

[127] *Till I'm laid to rest – The Gargamel and the Principal,* The Daily Observer (Jamaica), Monday 25 February 2008.

a perfect reflection of his own humanity. It was as though he planned his own funeral."[128]

Despite all this detail about his funeral, how ironic was it that my father never left a will. At first it shocked all of us. How could someone like Keith, so meticulous, not even leave a copy or a trace of a will? As a lawyer he advised his own clients to draw up their last wishes, yet he never heeded to his own advice. It took me a little while to realise that this was done intentionally. There is a myth, or perhaps a fear by some, that as soon as you draft your will you would die shortly after. My father, in my opinion, would have followed this line of thinking. At the very least, he would have thought that drafting a will was unnecessary as everything he possessed was for his wife and sons. It was implicit. There was no need to put that in writing. According to his wishes, we buried Keith's ashes at the Woodbrook Cemetery on Mucurapo Road, walking distance from his old family home on Panka Street. He rests at the side of his mother Clerine. His father Dad Otto was also present at this solemn ceremony. Sadly, six years later Dad Otto also passed away. He was buried alongside Keith and his wife Clerine. The trio of mother, father and son rest there to this day.

Shortly after the funeral the Norman Manley Law School also hosted a memorial service for Keith at the University Chapel at the Mona campus in Jamaica. This service was well organised and my family was humbled by the kind words extended to my father by his colleagues and former students. The words were so emotional that I could not hold in the feelings that welled up inside of me. At the end of the service I broke down

---

[128] My father's funeral and celebration of his life took place on 23 February 2008 at the Assumption RC Church in Maraval, Trinidad. The presiding Priest was Fr. Clyde Harvey.

in tears. I looked over my shoulder and remembered seeing my mother crying as well. Outside the Chapel we were greeted with smiling faces and a small photo exhibition about my father and the Law School. This managed to temporarily soothe my emotions.

The loss of my father left a void within my life. He left me at a time when I was in the middle of completing my Master's thesis at the University of Cape Town. When my deadline to hand in the thesis was looming I remember emailing my supervisor, Professor Richard Christie, informing him about the sudden passing of my father. Professor Christie was such a compassionate and understanding man. His reply was – "Justin take all the time in the world that you need." Knowing that my father would be most upset if I did not hand in my thesis, I pressed on with my writing and submitted my thesis in April. It was the writing that kept me sane, even though I still had my moments. I flew to Cape Town in June of that year to attend my graduation ceremony.

After graduating, I started searching for a job in Trinidad. It was then that I slowly slipped back down the slope of depression. I felt sad and angry at the same time. The sadness was normal but why was I angry? I was angry with my father because it was his fault that he did not take care of his health while he was alive. I was angry for every time he smoked and every time, when walking together side by side, he would accidently burn my hand with his lit cigarette. He would say *'sorry Kiddo'*. Now I wondered if he really meant it. I was angry because my father did not take his friend Brian des Vignes' advice, that he should at least live until he was seventy-years old. In the midst of all these thoughts, I also was angry with myself. I was angry because I placed an undue burden on him while he was on his deathbed. I was angry because I did not pour more of his vodka, hidden in his secret storage cabinet, into the kitchen sink. I was angry that I did not do enough to help him overcome his vices – smoking and drinking. I was angry that I did not cook for him so that he would eat a proper meal. For many days I convinced myself that my own acts, my own omissions, caused my father, my role model, to die. These sudden spurts of anger overshadowed my sorrow. Putting all things aside – my father did not only die because he failed to take care of himself. Because I struggled with him during his hospitalisation, I sense that my father in the end, died from a broken heart.

Suspecting my unstable state, my godfather Kenny Frontin invited me to visit his home in Atlanta "free of all expenses" and for as long as I wanted. I politely declined his offer. Our friend in art, Peter Kwang, also called me one morning. When he heard my dejected voice he immediately ordered that I drop what I was doing and come over to his frame shop to talk. This offer I also denied. The truth is that I just wanted to deal with my depression on my own. During this dark period, I was advised to go through professional counselling. This advice I also ignored. I chose to battle this *demon* quietly within myself. This *demon* called depression was fiercely attacking me day and night.

After many years, like a flower freeing itself from the pressing thorns, I managed to bloom. One of the things that carried me throughout this dark period was the fact that I could not deny that my father was my role model. There was however a twist to this plot. All the while, when I was thinking that my father was my role model, it suddenly came to me that we, his three children, were his own role models. For instance, he wanted to be like us and sport dreadlocks but his professional duties at the time would not permit it. He wanted to pursue a Master's degree in law abroad, but he did not get the opportunity to do so. He wanted to be a successful event manager like Jules but the *Impact Night Club* went bankrupt. He wanted someone to keep challenging him intellectually like my little brother Darien (when asked by my father about the details of the US Supreme Court judgment of *Roe v Wade* Darien was the only one who could give a meaningful account of the case). Everything that we were, he wanted to be. In a sense, we were his role models. He was proud of the persons we became. I closed my eyes. Like a burden releasing itself from my shoulders, I released myself from the pain. After many years of dying inside, I was finally able to live.

The Hummingbird Gold Medal

Around the month of June 2008 I was flipping through one of Trinidad's daily newspapers when, by mere coincidence, I came across a full-page advertisement inviting applications for individuals or groups to be nominated for a national award. I immediately thought that my father was a deserving candidate since he served not only his beloved nation Trinidad and Tobago but also the wider Caribbean region. Hence, I felt that his work should not go down in history unnoticed. I hastily filled out a nomination paper and submitted it at the designated location at the Stollmeyer's Castle around the Queen's Park Savannah.

Knowing that emotions were still running high, I never told my mother until after the nomination papers were submitted. Sometime during the month of August, I received a telephone call from the Office of the President that my father was nominated to receive the *Hummingbird Gold Medal* for his commitment to Regional Education. The person on the end of the line asked if I would accept. To this question my reply was that I had to defer to my family. At a subsequent family meeting, we agreed to accept the honour bestowed posthumously on my father and this message was immediately conveyed to the Office of the President. A couple days later, the matter became public knowledge as the daily newspapers published a list of all national award recipients. On Independence Day, the 31st August 2008, we accepted the *Hummingbird Gold Medal* on behalf of my father from His Excellency George Maxwell Richards, President of the Republic of Trinidad and Tobago.

On this subject of national medals, around the early part of the twenty-first century there was a debate stirring up across the country as to whether, or not, to replace the *Trinity Cross* as the nation's highest award. It was perceived by some quarters within the society that the *Trinity Cross* was a Christian symbol and it failed to embrace the religious and cultural values within our plural State. After carefully pondering on this argument my father was not entirely convinced. His reasoning was that the word 'Trinidad' found its origins in the word 'Trinity.' After all, Columbus when he first spotted the three hills, called the island *La Trinity* (even the French call Trinidad *"Trinité"*). My father added that if we as a nation decided to change the name of the award based on religious grounds, we should also invariably change the name of our country – as it also had religious connotations.

The constitutionality of the award of the *Trinity Cross* was ventilated and argued at length before the High Court and the

Court of Appeal.[129] The matter was always a complex one to resolve. On one side there was history and conservatism and on the other; religion and the multi-ethnic makeup of Trinidad and Tobago. In the end, the *Trinity Cross* was replaced with the *Order of the Republic of Trinidad and Tobago* in 2008.

A sunset in one land is a sunrise in another

I often ask myself what my father would have done, thought or said about the world in which we are living today. Maybe he would have upgraded his *tech-game* and joined *Facebook* and send us *WhatsApp* messages every day. Regionally, without any doubt or hesitation, he would have been disappointed that after all these years only a handful of Caribbean countries have abolished appeals to the Privy Council thereby paving the way for the CCJ to become their final Court of Appeal. As it stands at the time of writing, only Guyana, Barbados, Belize and Dominica have decided to make the CCJ their final Court of Appeal. Given the status quo, my father would have spared no effort to ensure that more countries within the region, especially his native Trinidad and Tobago, had fully implemented the CCJ as a final recourse to justice.

I also often thought about his reaction to the prevailing scene in international politics such as *Brexit* and President Trump's rhetoric to *"Make America Great Again."* While I strongly gather

---

[129] See *Sanatan Dharma Maha Sabha of Trinidad and Tobago Inc. and Others v The Attorney General of Trinidad and Tobago* (H.C.A. No. Cv. S – 2065/2004) and *Sanatan Dharma Maha Sabha of Trinidad and Tobago Inc. and Others v The Attorney General of Trinidad and Tobago* (Civil Appeal No. 71 of 2006).

what his views may have been on these subjects, I would not be so bold to carelessly immortalise them in his story. Instead I would prefer to preserve this information to myself and not put words into my father's mouth. Out of respect, I would abide by the phrase – *dead men tell no tales,* even though I know my father fully well that I am certain as to what those tales would be.

Not one day passes that I do not think about what my father would have been doing. Many years ago, he spoke about establishing a specialised family law firm in the Caribbean called *Sobion, Sobion & Sobion*; the three Sobions being himself, his youngest sister Patricia and myself. As the vicissitudes of life unfolded, this plan never transpired. After spending twelve years as a Principal in Jamaica, Keith was at the stage of his career where he was ready for another challenge. He appeared to be leaning towards consultancies within the Caribbean region, like the Eastern Caribbean environmental law project which he enthusiastically introduced me to after I returned from Cape Town (the care for the environment through the law seemed to be his emerging passion). He even proposed to us the name of his consultancy firm, which he called by its acronym *POPS.* Unfortunately we do not have an entire recollection of the full name of the firm but as the acronym suggests, he wanted to be a paternal figure behind an organisation that aimed to use the law as a tool to uplift the youth.

I agree that life is uncertain and spontaneous and you never know where it may take you. I respect the way my father lived and what he did during his life, both as a parent and as a professional. But that does not stop me from dreaming about his life continuing here on earth. But who knows, if he was still here with us today he may have been fully retired sitting on his patio reading books or pulling seine on Mayaro beach.

Some days we felt Keith would never leave his patio at *The Pines* in Kingston. It was his place of refuge, solace and reflection.

POSTSCRIPT

I think about the last time I saw you…all the time

Years after it still hits me: my father is dead. Death is like a nightmare which plays with my mind. We miss him and wish he were here to see the men we have become. I sense, however, that he already knows.

The age of fifty-six is relatively young in the general scheme of things. A couple years ago, I was speaking to a complete stranger and somehow the conversation shifted to my father. When I told her my father's age at the time of his passing, she gasped. The stranger expressed to me that fifty-six is the age when you become well established in your calling. It is also an age when you must take care of your spiritual soul. To justify her theory, she added that Saturn makes a full turn around the sun approximately every twenty-eight years. My father, at age fifty-six, was experiencing a second return of the planet. Was it also a coincidence that I was twenty-eight years when he passed on? Not surprisingly, the stranger revealed to me that she studied astrology; a subject that I am aware of, but admittedly one in which I have limited knowledge. Yet we know that time waits for no one.

It is now 11th April in the Year of Our Lord 2015. I am in a room filled with about ninety family and friends in the town hall of *Aubonne* a small quaint Swiss town. My soon to be wife Aurélie enters the town hall with her father in her beautiful white dress and my eyes water. There are no tears. I'm not so sure if it's because I'm entering into a new chapter of my life or because my father is not in the room smiling like the other guests. The scene shifts to the reception, *L'Esplanade* restaurant, walking distance from the town hall. Someone hands me a microphone to say a few words. My bride is smiling. In about five minutes, I talk about all things under the heaven but the last words were important. I wish my father were here. He would love her even though he never met her before.

Life goes on. For us it is August 2015. For him it is perhaps a matter of seconds. We are in Ethiopia. It is my third time and my wife's first. My friend Ademe meets us in Bahir Dar. He looks the same after all these years. Tariku Tsegaye now lives in the United States but we still keep in touch. I remember the poem I wrote *'Like my fadda'* eight years ago in a small room in *Nefas Meewcha*. I breathe in the fresh air which feeds my inner soul.

My mind wanders again to 15th October 2016. We are back in Jamaica but this time for another family wedding. Jules exchanges vows with his bride Candace in Ocho Rios, close to Dunn's River Falls where we have an old picture of my father hugging my mother with a silly grin. The best man is Darien and he looks smart in his white shirt and royal blue bow tie. One year later, Darien launches his business *10 Caribbean*, a Digital Marketing agency that specialises in influencer marketing for Caribbean brands. Just the word 'Caribbean' impresses him. He smiles. My father is proud. The familial bonds still remain. Jamaica, the last place he lived; Jamaica, the country where he died as a legal scholar and academic. Looking at it this way, the "University" Hospital was perhaps the most befitting place to spend the last hours of his life. In memory of his name the Norman Manley Law School describes him as a "dyed-in-the-wool" regionalist. My mind moves again.

The 6th October 2016. I'm running along the *Lac Léman* in Geneva. Autumn is surely here because I suck in the air and it cools my lungs. I think about him. It's not unusual because not a day passes by when I do not. He absorbs my thoughts sometimes. I'm running alone yet I have an uncanny feeling that I have a running mate. *'Kiddo, you're not finished yet...this should be your next step...'* I agree. I smile. Then I want to cry. I keep on running and stop after eight kilometres. I now understand my grandmother's poem and the mystery of life. My father is not from an island but from the entire Caribbean region where the sun always shines. He is no longer sad but happy; and he wants us to be happy as well. So now I am finally free.

ACKNOWLEDGEMENTS

I started to write these *Memoirs* some nine years ago in Switzerland, the 6th December 2010 to be exact. At first, my intention was to write a full-fledged biography on my Dad. However as the time passed by, the storyline took a different course and morphed into my own memoirs and intimate accounts with my father. The latter part of these *Memoirs* was written in the Véranda Café on Rue du Vieux-Collége in Geneva. In this café I spent countless hours writing as it was a sanctuary of reflection and, because of its name, it naturally reminded me of my father's own *veranda/patio* at our home in *The Pines,* at Kingston, Jamaica.

The truth be told, it was always an uphill task to produce an accurate piece of literary work on my Dad. Although his life was a short one, at 56 years he made an indelible contribution to the development of the law and Caribbean legal education. Throughout the period of my writing, I kept wondering aloud to myself: what did Keith really think about this particular issue? Or, why did he take this course of action? Indeed the only person who could have written an impeccable biography on my father, would have been my father himself. In fact, after speaking to various persons, I learnt some interesting facts about my father that I never knew before.

During my research for these *Memoirs,* I had the pleasure to interview more than 80 persons. These included family members, friends, members of Keith's 1975 graduating class (the "locally assembled lawyers!"), colleagues at J.D. Sellier & Co., the Ortoire/Mayaro campaign team, lawyers, judges, politicians, parliamentary staff and colleagues at Hugh Wooding, Eugene Dupuch and Norman Manley Law Schools.

Many days and nights were spent on Skype, the telephone and face-to-face, conducting interviews with these persons as I attempted to zero in to capture every single aspect of my father's life. All the contributions I received over the course of nine years were invaluable and are now immortalised within the pages of this book. I thank all these persons for their patience. Without your contributions, these *Memoirs* would have been incomplete.

Unfortunately, some of these persons who I had interviewed have since transitioned and have never read the complete product. These include my grandparents Otto Sobion and Lucina Connor. Lenny Jacobs, a dear friend of my father, passed away in 2018. I suppose that my father and Lenny no longer need to write each other letters and I hope wherever they may be that they are together in perfect happiness and eternal peace. Patrick Manning, a former Prime Minister, who had unwavering trust in my father as a fairly young lawyer. As well as Peter Kwang, a friend in art, to both my father and myself.

At this juncture, I would just like to make a special mention of my great Uncle Harold Frontin who, at the time of writing this, is 99 years old and the most senior family member alive. He made these *Memoirs* much richer with his sterling memory of Mayaro in the early 20th century. Caribbean author Michael Anthony and my cousin Natasha Richardson also provided me with some intricate details on the history of Mayaro. Many thanks also to Principal Nigel Joseph, and the staff of St. Mary's College for their kind assistance in obtaining my father's academic transcript. To Lynn Buckley at the University of Auckland for her assistance in formatting these pages. To the Controller, Regan Asgarali and his staff at the Trinidad and Tobago Intellectual Property Office for their legal advice relating to this publication. Also a heartfelt thanks to my cousin Jeanelle Frontin for her expert advice relating to publishing my very first book!

To the Permanent Mission of the Republic of Trinidad and Tobago in Geneva, Switzerland, especially staff member Sophie Tournet who, in 2014, brought to my attention international documents published by the United Nations relating to the Glen Ashby case. Also to my 'Uncle' Reginald Armour S.C. for his vivid recollection which assisted me in writing the chapter pertaining to Glen Ashby.

I would like to thank all those who proofread these *Memoirs* in advance. Firstly, I had a stringent team of 'internal' family proofreaders who my aunt Teresa Davidson managed with great care and scrutiny. Outside of my family, persons who assisted with proofreading were Chief Justice Ivor Archie, Justice Humphrey Stollmeyer, Ria Rambally and Silvia Scozia. Many thanks also to my 'Uncle', Justice Dennis Morrison for providing a fitting foreword for these *Memoirs* and for being a dear friend to my father.

I would also like to thank from the bottom of my heart, Principal Carol Aina of the Norman Manley Law School for her kind support throughout. When I first mentioned to Principal Aina that I was searching for a publisher, her exact response was, "I think Mr Sobion would have wanted the Council of Legal Education to publish his book." And voilà, the rest is history. Consequently, I wish to express my gratitude to my publishers; the Council of Legal Education and its Research Publication and Legal Education Unit, managed by Ms Eulalie Greenaway; and also for all those who provided further remarks and advice under the stewardship of the Norman Manley Law School.

I would like to thank my immediate family for their tireless support and encouragement over the years. To my mother, Judith Sobion, who spent a significant time with me to give a detailed account of her intimate relationship with my father. To my brothers Jules and Darien: thank you for your advice, your work "behind the scenes" and for reading my thousands of emails and drafts. Special tribute must be attributed to the creative work and ideas of Caesar's Army, 10 Caribbean and the Keith Stanford Sobion Foundation; all family projects which strive to continue our father's legacy in relation to Caribbean integration. And to my wife Aurélie, who always supported my dream to publish these *Memoirs* and to travel the Caribbean to promote the life of my father. I love all of you, and will never stop doing so.

Last but never least, I give thanks to JAH for the patience and inspiration.

Justin Sobion

18th July 2019

Auckland, New Zealand

APPENDIX

Images 1 to 4: Mayaro history/Early years

Images 5 to 7: A young law student

Images 8 to 11: The Lawyer and Family Man

Images 12 to 26: The Politician

Images 27 to 31: Newspaper articles

Images 32 to 36: Principal Sobion

Images 37 to 44: Family Time

Image 45: Original cover photo

Image 1: Keith's grandparents, Edwin and Emelda Frontin in front of St. Peter RC Church on Church Road, Mayaro on the occasion of their 50th wedding anniversary.

Image 2: The Sobion family in 1970 at the graduation of the Stanford Commercial Institute in Maracaibo, Venezuela. From Left to Right, Stanford Sobion (Keith's grandfather), Clerine Sobion née Frontin (Keith's mother), Otto Sobion (Keith's father) and the wife of Stanford Sobion.

Image 3: Young Keith at his first communion.

Image 4: Emelda Frontin, Keith's grandmother, at 121 Emerald Drive, Diamond Vale, Trinidad (Picture taken by Kenny Frontin circa 1980).

A Young Law Student

Image 5: The West Indian Lawyer, Keith Sobion. Valedictorian and graduate from the Hugh Wooding Law School, Trinidad in 1975.

Image 6: A picture taken after the last exam of the 1975 Hugh Wooding Law School graduates. Keith is the second person on the second row from the left. Other persons in this picture include: H.E. Sandra Mason (third row, third from right, Barbados), Justin Simon Q.C. (first row, first from left, Dominica/Antigua and Barbuda), Mayo Robertson (first row, second from left, Guyana) and Endell Thomas (back row, second from right, Trinidad and Tobago). Photo courtesy the Robertson family.

Trinidad & Tobago Guardian newspaper article in 1975 indicating the first Law School graduates from the Hugh Wooding Law School, Trinidad. Keith "topped the honours list, has indicated his willingness to return to the school as Associate Tutor."

Published with the kind courtesy of the Trinidad & Tobago Guardian Newspaper.

The Lawyer and Family Man

Image 8: Keith and his sister Patricia at her graduation from the Hugh Wooding Law School, Trinidad in 1982.

Image 9: Another generation is admitted to the Bar. Keith, with his son Justin, at the Hall of Justice during the admission ceremony in October 2002, Trinidad.

Image 10: Young Solicitor Keith at work at J.D. Sellier & Co. (old office) on St. Vincent Street, Port of Spain.

Image 11: Love is forever. Judith and Keith during his days as Attorney General and Minister of Legal Affairs.

Image 12: 'My brother's keeper'. Keith speaking at a public political meeting on Upper Bournes Road, St. James, 1996. Sheltering him from the rain is his colleague Fitzgerald Hinds. (Photo courtesy the Office of the Prime Minister of Trinidad and Tobago).

Image 13: In front the home of Martin Luther King Jr. in Atlanta with a gentleman from the United States. This picture was taken while Keith was Attorney General and Minister of Legal Affairs around 1994.

Image 14: Government greets the Opposition. From left to right – Gordon Draper, Camille Robinson-Regis, Keith, Wade Mark, Basdeo Panday. Far right is Ramesh Lawrence Maharaj. (Photo courtesy the Office of the Prime Minister of Trinidad and Tobago).

Image 15: On a visit to Ortoire/Mayaro with Colm Imbert (centre), then Minister of Works and Transport, to plan the construction of a new bridge to provide better access to the area. This picture was taken on or around 1992. (Photo courtesy the Office of the Prime Minister of Trinidad and Tobago).

Image 16: Your problems are my problems and I'm always here to listen to you. (Photo courtesy the Office of the Prime Minister of Trinidad and Tobago).

Image 17: Opening the San Fernando High Court with Chief Justice, The Hon. Clinton Angelo Bernard TC, SC in November 1993. (Photo courtesy the Office of the Prime Minister of Trinidad and Tobago).

Image 18: 'Let us get this straight'. From left to right: The Hon. Prime Minister, Patrick Manning, Dr Lenny Saith and Keith (Photo courtesy the Office of the Prime Minister of Trinidad and Tobago).

Image 19: Opening ceremony (from left to right): Keith, The Hon. Prime Minister Patrick Manning and the H.E. Brian J. Donnelly, the US Ambassador to Trinidad and Tobago, circa 1994. (Photo courtesy the Office of the Prime Minister of Trinidad and Tobago).

Image 20: Press conference with Kenneth Valley (Left) and Keith (Right) (Photo courtesy the Office of the Prime Minister of Trinidad and Tobago).

Image 21: Signing the agreement. From second left – Prime Minister Manning, Keith Sobion, Keith Rowley and Camille Robinson-Regis. (Photo courtesy the Office of the Prime Minister of Trinidad and Tobago).

Image 22: An Official Government photo.
(Photo courtesy the Office of the Prime
Minister of Trinidad and Tobago).

Image 23: Keith congratulating calypsonian Slinger Francisco 'The Mighty Sparrow' on receiving the Chaconia Gold Medal in 1993. (Photo courtesy the Trinidad Express Newspaper).

Image 24: Strategizing with Dr Lenny Saith (left) and Prime Minister Patrick Manning (right). (Photo courtesy the Trinidad Express Newspaper).

Image 25: Keith exchanges a light moment with Russell Huggins (on the left) in the Parliament. (Photo courtesy the Trinidad Express Newspaper).

Image 26: 'This smile can brighten up any Parliament'. Keith in the Red House. (Photo courtesy the Parliament of the Republic of Trinidad and Tobago).

Newspaper Articles (page 354-356)

The articles in this section are published with the kind courtesy of The Trinidad and Tobago Newsday, the Jamaica Observer Limited and the Trinidad & Tobago Guardian.

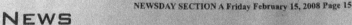

NEWSDAY SECTION A Friday February 15, 2008 Page 15

NEWS

Mayaro mourns Sobion

By RICHARDSON DHALAI

UNC A Mayaro MP Winston 'Gypsy' Peters yesterday expressed sadness over the passing of his cousin, former PNM Attorney General Keith Sobion, who died yesterday at 10 am after being admitted to University Hospital in Jamaica.

Peters, who at the time was attending a party strategy session, admitted that he cried on hearing the news of his cousin's death. "I am really, deeply saddened by his passing and I take this opportunity to extend to his wife Judith my deepest condolences," Peters said, adding that Sobion's death was a "shock and surprise."

Peters said "the whole of Mayaro" was plunged into mourning over Sobion's untimely passing adding that the former AG was very popular in Mayaro and often visited the community whenever he returned home.

Chairman of the PNM Mayaro

KEITH SOBION

constituency Clifford Campbell said Sobion, who represented the constituency (formerly known as Ortoire/Mayaro) from 1991 to 1995, was an extremely popular person who maintained links with

in the rural community. "All of Mayaro is in mourning. He was a popular MP and while he may have had his issues following the 1995 electoral defeat, he was still popular and would always keep in touch," Campbell said.

"I am really shocked and saddened by his death and on behalf of the PNM Mayaro constituency, I offer my condolences to his family," he said.

Former UNC Attorney General Ramesh Lawrence Maharaj also extended condolences to the Sobion family saying Sobion, who was principal of the Norman Manley Law School, made a significant contribution to the Caribbean in the field of legal education.

"I got to know him very well during my tenure as Attorney General and no doubt, he made a significant contribution in legal education to this country. May God bless his soul," Maharaj ended.

Page 4 NEWSDAY, SECTION B Wednesday January 28, 2004

IN THE NEWS

Sobion: Judges must accept criticism

TOBAGO BUREAU

PRINCIPAL of the Norman Manley Law School, Keith Sobion, said local judges must be more open and sensitive to public criticism of their rulings. Sobion, a former Attorney General of Trinidad and Tobago, made the point while fielding questions at a

public consultation on the Caribbean Court of Justice (CCJ) at Works Building, Shaw Park, Tobago.

Sobion said: "I think that our judges have to become a little more open and a little more sensitive to people's response to what they do and the decisions that they make.

They must remove the old wig and gown from their

(make-up), and the whole attitude that you have of courts being some separate and high and mighty body, and they must be able to accept feedback from the general public.

"If the public does it in a constructive way and not to attempt to denigrate the Judiciary, I think that the judges that we have now in

Trinidad are persons who are receptive to that kind of approach; but I think it requires that kind of approach generally."

He said it would not be possible to build a jurisprudence if you cannot talk about what a judge has done. "You can't build a legal

body of learning unless you can criticise decisions that are being made by the judges, so I expect and hope that our judiciary becomes comfortable with that kind of interplay between the public, who deserve to know, and themselves."

Santa Cruz man dies after crash

By SAMUEL MCKNIGHT

ditch on the western side of the hill. He suffered extensive

354

NEWS

FORMER AG TO RIDE OUT IVAN IN JAMAICA

BY JULIE MITCHELL

FORMER attorney general Keith Sobion, principal of the Norman Manley Law School in Mona-Jamaica, yesterday said that while adequate precautions were being taken in Jamaica for Hurricane Ivan, "one could never really prepare for something like this. Things are frantic out here," he said.

"The supermarkets are full. The hardware shops are busy, worse. Most people were preparing for Charley (which changed course and spared Jamaica). But the intensity of Ivan is here, when they heard it was going to be worse than Gilbert. That reinforced in their minds what they were up against, especially when they saw what happened in Grenada where Ivan passed as Category Three," he told Newsday.

Sobion said he, like everyone else, had been stocking up on emergency essentials. Still displaying his Trinidad sense of humour, he said there was one vital supply he was missing. "No cuss in the grocery, I had to settle for another brand of crackers."

Sobion, who said he was tracking the progress of Ivan both on the local and international media, stated that the part of Jamaica where he was located (Mona), which is just outside of Kingston) is expected to be the first area to be hit.

He said while the housing in Jamaica was a real mix, he anticipated that if Ivan hits, some of the inner city communities would suffer serious damage. "There are still a lot of zinc-coated (galvanise) and wooden houses there," he said.

He said the government was doing some evacuation of low-lying areas and was telling people to leave these areas by a pm yesterday afternoon.

He said Port Royal, which is a low strip of land in the middle of the sea, was also due to be evacuated. Sobion, who will be facing the hurricane in Jamaica with his wife Judith and Gae sons, said this is his first real hurricane. He said his last experience of a hurricane was Hurricane Flora, which hit Trinidad in the 1960s.

"I was a little boy and was quite excited at seeing galvanise flying," he recalled. "We are comfortable in the sense until things worry up and then I suppose we will start to panic," he said.

Sobion said he was telling his neighbour, who is a Barbadian, that if this were Trinidad and Tobago they would be organising a hurricane party.

"The Mayor of Kingston, who appeared on television yesterday morning to implore people to take the threat of Ivan seriously, was relating a story a fellow was telling him only some moments earlier. 'why are all keep fooling us. Look the sun shining," Sobion said.

He said the weather was pretty calm. It almost seemed like a normal day, with the sun shining brightly.

However, he said it is expected that by 6 to 7 pm that nights there would be heavier winds – tropical storm winds for the next 24 to 36 hours, which would then intensify into hurricane strength.

Told that the TT Government had sent a BWIA plane to Jamaica to bring home Trinidad and Tobago students, Sobion was then asked if he would consider getting on that flight.

He replied half-jokingly: "Well they would hardly take me for a student. No, I'll be here."

KEITH SOBION

'Til I'm laid to rest — the Gargamel and the Principal

THIS has to qualify as one of the most 'feel good' things to happen during Reggae Month. One of the dying wishes of the late Keith Sobion, Principal of the Norman Manley Law School at the University of the West Indies, was that Jamaican dancehall deejay, Buju Banton perform at his funeral.

Yes ... you heard right. His relatives got in touch with Buju's management to see if it could be arranged, but unfortunately, the artiste was unable to make it. The interesting thing about Buju is that his repertoire is so versatile that there are a number of songs that he could have selected that would not detract from the solemnity of the occasion — from his interpretation of the 23rd Psalm to 'Til Shiloh. Keith Sobion served in the government of Trinidad as attorney general and Minister of Legal Affairs from 1991 to 1995 and since 1996 was Principal of the Norman Manley Law School.

Monday MUSINGS
With Yasmine

One of the dying wishes of the late Keith Sobion (right), Principal of the Norman Manley Law School, was that Buju Banton (left) perform at his funeral.

PM: Nation has lost a great mind

PRIME MINISTER Patrick Manning took the opportunity yesterday, on behalf of the Government, to express his deepest sympathy to the family of the late Keith Sobion.

Manning said Sobion had made important contributions to the legal framework of T&T.

The PM's sentiments were expressed yesterday in a press release from the Office of the Prime Minster.

Manning said said Sobion performed his duties as AG with great distinction and his death would

KEITH SOBION

leave a void in the legal fraternity.

The PM statement added: "Mr Sobion has made important contributions to the legal framework of T&T and to its politics. The nation has lost a great mind, a contributor to our development and a national asset.

"We are grateful for the contribution Mr Sobion has made and wish to assure his family that their grief is shared and that they have the support of the nation at this difficult time."

The release also confirmed that a letter of condolence had been signed by the PM and was dispatched to Sobion's family.

Principal Sobion

Image 32: The ACLI Team at the graduation of the Florida Coastal School of Law in Jacksonville, Florida in 2001. From left to right – Keith, A.J. Nicholson and John Knechtle.

Image 33: Two 1975 Law School graduates and friends – Mayo Robertson (left) and Keith, in Atlanta, Georgia.

Image 34: 1975 law graduates at the 2002 Hugh Wooding Law School graduation ceremony in Trinidad (from left to right): Endell Thomas, Dennis Morrison, Jawara Mobota and Keith.

Image 35: Law School Graduation Day, with Justice Annestine Sealey, then Principal of the Hugh Wooding Law School.

Image 36: Speaking at a Law School graduation ceremony.

Family Time

Image 37: 'Christmas is for family'. Keith with members of the family including: the Sobions, Frontins, Hassanalis, and Davidsons.

Image 38: Family time with the Sobions, Frontins and the Davidsons. Harold Frontin, Keith's Uncle and the eldest family member, is seated on the right.

Image 39: Family together again.
50th wedding anniversary celebration of Harold and Julie Frontin, at San Fernando, Trinidad.
From left to right: Lennox Sobion, Kenny Frontin, Keith, Harold Frontin, Julie Frontin, Russell Frontin and Gerry Frontin.

Image 40: Hanging in between Lucina Connor (mother of Judith Sobion) on the left and Tanty Dora (Keith's grandmother) on the right.

Image 41: Cousins, Kenny Frontin (Left) and Keith together in Port of Spain, Trinidad enjoying the Carnival festivities in the early 1990s.

Image 42: 'I love you baby.' Keith and his nephew/godson, Jabal Hassanali, at 121 Emerald Drive, Diamond Vale.

Image 43: With my three sons on vacation in Florida.
(From left to right): Justin, Jules, Keith and Darien.

Image 44: A family portrait, Kingston, Jamaica (from left to right)
Darien, Judith, Justin, Keith and Jules Sobion.

Image 45: Keith at the opening of Court at Port of Spain, Trinidad. In the background looking on is his security William Mckay. (Photo courtesy the Supreme Court of Trinidad and Tobago).

ANNEX I

POEM TO MY FATHER

6th November 2007, 'Like my fadda'

Gayint, Ethiopia – on the way to Lalibela

7:36 pm

When I grow up;
I want to be like my fadda;
Papa love me like no odda;
My fadda, grow three of we;
There is no odda;
Than my Papa;
Some people say I resemble my fadda;
I am lanky just like my papa;
My fadda is no skylarker;
When I grow up;
I want to be like my fadda;
I wear glasses;
Just like my fadda;
I tun' lawyer;
Like my fadda;
There is no odda;
Than my Papa;
My Papa ain't no skylarker;
My fadda ain't no joker;
He don't skylark;
So dey ain't no odda;
Some say I resemble my fadda;
Only thing I have a Rasta.

ANNEX II

List of Bills moved by Mr Keith Sobion, Former Attorney General and Minister of Legal Affairs from 1991-1995 (courtesy the Parliament of the Republic of Trinidad and Tobago).

HOUSE OF REPRESENTATIVES

NO.	BILLS	BILL NO.	HOR DATES	COMMENTS
1.	Sakina Juman (Pension) Bill	2 of 1992	20.03.92 13.03.92	ACT 3 OF 1992
2.	Customs (Amendment) Bill	4 of 1992	13.03.92	ACT 5 OF 1992
3.	Maxi Taxi Bill	(S) 1 of 1992	29.05.92 30.05.92	ACT 6 OF 1992
4.	Judicial And Legal Services (Amendment) Bill	22 of 1992	04.09.92 11.09.92	ACT 13 OF 1992
5.	Validation of The 5th Report Of The EBC (Tobago Bill)	25 of 1992	09.10.92 06.11.92	ACT 21 OF 1992
6.	Firearms (Amendment) Bill	(S) 6 of 1992	13.11.92	ACT 20 OF 1992
7.	Tax Appeal Board (Amendment) Bill	30 of 1992	30.10.92 13.11.92	ACT 24 OF 1992
8.	Supreme Court Of Judicature (Amendment) Bill	(S) 9 of 1992	04.12.92	ACT 23 OF 1992
9.	Central Tenders Board (Amendment) Bill	2 of 1993	08.01.93 04.01.93 15.01.93	ACT 3 OF 1993
10.	Companies Bill	13 of 1993	14.05.93 21.05.93	LAPSED
11.	Council Of Legal Education (Amendment) Bill	14 of 1993	04.06.93	Incorporated under Finance (No.2) Bill
12.	Companies Bill	16 of 1993	15.09.93 08.10.93	LAPSED
13.	Indictable Offences (Preliminary Enquiry) (Amendment) Bill	17 of 1993	15.09.93 01.10.93	ACT 20 OF 1994
14.	Corporal Punishment (Offenders over Sixteen) (Amendment) Bill	4 of 1994	18.03.94 24.06.94	ACT 9 OF 1994

HOUSE OF REPRESENTATIVES continued

NO.	BILLS	BILL NO.	HOR DATES	COMMENTS
15.	Corporal Punishment (Offenders not over Sixteen) (Amendment) Bill	9 of 1994	13.05.94 24.06.94	ACT 10 OF 1994
16.	Land Acquisition	18 of 1994	10.06.94	ACT 28 OF 1994
17.	Bail Bill	13 of 1994	29.07.94 12.08.94	ACT 18 OF 1994
18.	Supreme Court of Judicature (Amendment) Bill	(S) 12 of 1994	02.11.94	ACT 21 OF 1994
19.	Dangerous Drugs (Amendment) Bill	17 of 1994	04.11.94	ACT 27 OF 1994
20.	Constitution (Amendment) (No.2) Bill	20 of 1994	11.11.94	ACT 30 OF 1994
21.	Companies Bill	12 of 1995	10.03.95	ACT 35 OF 1995
22.	Constitution (Amendment) (No.2) (1995) Bill	(S) 9 of 1995	05.05.95 19.05.95 09.06.95	ACT 10 OF 1995
23.	Regularization of Tenure (State Lands) Bill	18 of 1995	30.06.95	LAPSED
24.	Constitution (Amendment) (No. 3) Bill	(S) 17 of 1995	24.07.95 04.08.95	ACT 17 OF 1995
25.	Secondary Schools Football League (Including Bill)	(S) 10 of 1995	24.07.95	ACT 19 OF 1995

SENATE

NO.	BILLS	BILL NO.	SENATE DATES	COMMENTS
1.	Sakina Juman (Pension) Bill	(H) 2 of 1992	24.03.92	ACT 3 OF 1992
2.	Maxi-Taxi (Amendment) Bill	1 of 1992	26.05.92 28.05.92 02.06.92	PASSED
3.	Judicial and Legal Service (Amendment) Bill	(H) 22 of 1992	15.09.92 29.09.92	PASSED

4.	Supreme Court of Judicature (Amendment) Bill	9 of 1992	20.10.92 17.11.92	ACT 23 OF 1992
5.	Validation of the 5TH Report of the Elections and Boundaries Commission (Tobago) Bill	(H) 25 of 1992	10.11.92 17.11.92	PASSED
6.	Tax Appeal Board (Amendment) Bill	(H) 30 of 1992	17.11.92 08.12.92	PASSED
7.	Transfer of Prisoners Bill	1 of 1993	12.01.93 26.01.93	ACT 12 OF 1993
8.	Central Tenders Board (Amendment) Bill	(H) 2 of 1993	19.01.93 26.01.93	PASSED
9.	Constitution (Amendment) Bill	1 of 1994	08.03.94 15.03.94	COMMITTEE
10.	Bail Bill	(H) 13 of 1994	30.08.94 06.09.94	PASSED
11.	Supreme Court of Judicature (Amendment) Bill	12 of 1994	01.11.94	ACT 21 OF 1994
12.	Indictable Offenses (Preliminary Enquiry) (Amendment) Bill		06.09.94	PASSED
13.	Constitution (Amendment) Bill	5 of 1995	14.03.95	LAPSED
14.	Constitution (Amendment) (No. 2) Bill	9 of 1995	24.04.95 02.05.95	ACT 10 OF 1995
15.	Attachment of Earnings (Maintenance) (Amendment) Bill	14 of 1995	27.06.95	ACT 28 OF 1995
16.	Constitution (Amendment) (No.3) Bill	17 of 1995	20.07.95	ACT 17 OF 1995

ABOUT THE AUTHOR

Justin Sobion was born in Trinidad and is the second son of Keith and Judith Sobion. He is an Attorney at Law by profession having graduated from the University of the West Indies and the Hugh Wooding Law School. He is also the holder of an LLM from the University of Cape Town in South Africa. His other passions include art, music, reading, yoga and caring for the environment. He also serves as a Director of the Keith Stanford Sobion Foundation. Justin is married to Aurélie Sobion and they currently reside in New Zealand. *The West Indian Lawyer* is Justin's first literary work.

Lightning Source UK Ltd.
Milton Keynes UK
UKHW020636151122
412232UK00017B/764